THE

HISTORY

OF THE

REBELLION

In the YEAR 1715.

WITH

ORIGINAL PAPERS,

AND THE

CHARACTERS

Of the PRINCIPAL

NOBLEMEN and GENTLEMEN

Concern'd in it.

By the Reverend
Mr. *ROBERT PATTEN*,
Formerly Chaplain to Mr. FORSTER.

The THIRD EDITION.

LONDON:
Printed for JAMES ROBERTS, in *Warwick-Lane.*

MDCCXLV.

Price 2 *s.* 6 *d.*

TO THE

Lieutenant-Generals

CARPENTER and WILLS,

AND

The reſt of the Commanding Officers
of his Majeſty's Forces at the Attack
at *Preſton.*

GENTLEMEN,

AS you had the Honour to command his
Majeſty's Troops againſt the Rebels at
Preſton, in honour to your Courage and Conduct I thought myſelf engag'd, when I under-
took the writing this ſhort Hiſtory of the Rebellion, to do you that Juſtice which is due
to your Merit, by aſſuring the World that it
was to your prudent Management and unſha-
ken Bravery, animated by the Juſtice of the
Cauſe, the ſignal Defeat of that Day was juſtly owing. There have been ſome indeed, with
a View to leſſen the Characters of brave Men,
in the way of arrogating Praiſe to their own

A 2   Party,

DEDICATION.

Party, who have pretended to affert the contrary (fome of which kept themfelves warm in a Chimney-Corner during the Heat of the Action;) but I, who was an Eye-witnefs to all the great and refolute Attacks made by you under the greateft Difadvantage imaginable, can boldly affirm, that never did Men behave better, efpecially in your Circumftances, being all the time naked, and expos'd to the Fire of the Rebels from Windows, Barriers, and Entrenchments, &c. All which, I prefume, will appear in the following Hiftory, humbly dedicated to you by,

GENTLEMEN,

Your moft obedient Servant,

Robert Patten.

THE
PREFACE
TO THE
READER.

THE *following Sheets are what I may justly call,* An Impartial History of the late Rebellion. *If it seem to you that I treat some of my Brethren the* Clergy *a little too smartly, I protest it is out of no Disrespect to their Persons, much less to the Sacred Function they bear, which I retain the greatest Veneration and Respect for, notwithstanding any Calumnies that may be laid to my Charge.*

Amidst some strange Notions broach'd amongst us, it ought to be Matter of our grateful Returns to Heaven, that we have still a Set of Reverend, Learned, and Pious Divines; who, animated by a true Spirit of Piety, by their Example, Pen, and Preaching, are eminent Ornaments to the Establish'd Government in Church *and* State; *whose serious Admonitions and grave Counsels, if duly regarded, would speedily and effectually redress all our Grievances and Divisions. However the Reflections may seem to others, I must own they have been of singular Use to me; for whilst I continued among those Unfortunate Gentlemen (whose Principles were once my own) I look'd no farther than esteeming what I had done, the least Part of my Guilt. But no sooner was I removed into the Custody of a*

Messenger,

The Preface to the Reader.

Messenger, and there closely confined, where I had Leisure to reflect upon my past Life, (and especially that of engaging in the Rebellion) than a great many Scruples offered themselves to my Consideration. In consequence of which, I made it my Request to Lord Townshend, that he would be pleased to allow a Clergyman to converse with me: which that Noble Lord freely granted, and sent to me the Reverend Dr. Cannon, a Man of singular good Temper and Literature, who applied his best Endeavours to satisfy me in every Point and Query I proposed; in which his Learning and solid Reasoning prevailed upon me: For which good Service, my best Wishes shall always attend him.

From thence I began to think it a Duty incumbent on me, to make all the Reparation I could, for the Injury I had done the Government: And, as the first thing in that way, I became an Evidence for the King; which I am far from being ashamed of, let what Calumnies will follow. In the Interim, I cannot but particularly observe one thing, in opposition to what has been printed and reported by the Enemies of the Government, viz. That the King's Witnesses were brib'd and Brow-beaten, to extort from them the Matters which they gave in Evidence.

As to my own part, and I dare say I may speak it for others, I never knew any thing of this kind: But in Honour to those who were employed to take my Examination, I must affirm, that I was used in the most Gentleman-like manner, far from extorting any thing by such base Arts, which no doubt would e're now have appear'd under the foulest Reflections; seeing the other Party did not stick to bribe all that would take their Money, and by that means too frequently gained their Ends: While on the other hand, it may be said in the Face of Heaven, That fairer Trials were never allow-ed, at least to Men who so little deserv'd it.

I pray God, that the Clemency shewn them may not be a Temptation to them to repeat their Crimes; from which,

which, of his infinite Mercy, I beg he will deliver these Kingdoms.

It is worth Observation, that nothing contributed more to raise the People of this Nation to a Spirit of Rebellion, than the licentious Freedom of some in their publick Discourses, and others in their Addresses, to cry up the old Doctrines of Passive Obedience, and to give Hints and Arguments to prove Hereditary Right; then publick Shews were encouraged with designing Emblems and legible Badges of their Ends; then ill-natured Distinctions and Designations were fomented, and with Malice upbraiding one another. This introduced Mobs; so that the Party in Disgrace with the Court had their own Houses, and those of their Worship, pulled about their Ears, themselves insulted and assaulted by the very Dregs of the People: Like a Flood they carried all before them without Check or Controul. Nay, their ill Nature could not be confined within these Realms; but they found Means to raise the basest of Reflections, and the worst of lying Stories, upon the most Illustrious House in Europe, that had a just Title to the Imperial Diadems of these Kingdoms, with no other Design but to blacken with their foul Breath their Persons and bright Characters. I am ashamed that I, with so many deluded People, upon bare Reports, should be blindly led to give Credit to such incredible Legends and Lies reported by the Fomenters of the late Rebellion; but being prepared with the noisy Notion of the Church's being in danger, easily complied with the Party, Healths and full Bumpers were tossed about with disguis'd Names, Characters, and Wishes, and concluded with Confusion, Damnation, and Destruction to Others whom they durst not name. Did not all these Concurrences spirit up the Populace to be guilty of so many egregious Miscarriages, as they have been of late towards his Sacred Majesty King GEORGE? So by degrees, they abandon'd all Reverence, Respect, nay, Obedience due to him, and listed themselves in open Defiance and Rebel-

lion

The Preface to the Reader.

tion to his *Laws, and against his Person and Family :*
So true is the old Proverb, Nemo repente fuit turpif-
fimus. *Though it had been the Care and indefati-*
gable Pains of some, during some Part of the
Reign of the late Queen; yet if the latter Part was
Tory, the first Part so established the other Party,
well inclined to the Succession in the Illustrious House
of Hanover, *that nothing could have so speedily un-*
done such a cemented and solid Establishment, but
some more Years Countenance under a blinded Patron.
How many have the Disappointments been, which that
aspiring Party have met with since the late Revo-
lution under King William ? *And yet their Managers*
still indulge the Infatuation. The very Disappointments
they met with lately by the Death of a nursing Parent,
and the King of France : *Their many private Plots*
were all made ineffectual, and their declared Force
useless. Yet when the Turk *threatened* Europe, *then*
he was to be the Restorer ; but when so many Turk
Tories were killed by the brave Prince Eugene, *then*
they grew flat. Then the King of Sweden *appeared in*
their Cause : The Purse was opened, and their Minds
declared, by large Encomiums on his Force, his Con-
duct, his Resolution, and invincible Courage ; which
were now levelled against King GEORGE *in behalf of*
their Darling : So true is the old Saying, Quos Jupi-
ter vult perdere prius dementat.

   Yet it is reasonable to imagine that His Majesty's most
gracious Clemency and Mercy shewn to these Gentlemen,
will inspire them with grateful Returns of Thankfulness,
and make them peaceable and passive during the Enjoy-
ment of those Years he has granted them.

   But so ungenerous are some, that they upbraid His
Majesty with Cruelty, for the few Examples made of
those that suffered. May not this Question be put to
these People ; Did not the Blood spilt at Preston *re-*
quire no Satisfaction, considering how it was spilt ? Yet
there have not suffered upon that Account the fourth

Part,

The Preface to the Reader.

Part, in proportion to those that were killed, (*I should have said murthered*). Did not the Blood shed at Sheriffmore, *though not so brutely as that at* Preston, *require some Satisfaction? And yet not one has suffered upon that Account? So variable are our human Passions, that those who have been the Objects of our greatest Indignations, when we consider the Nature of their Guilt, that our greatest Resentments to their Persons for their Crimes, is expressed with the utmost Abhorrence; yet when these Wretches are brought to Judgment, and are going to receive the just Reward of their Crimes, our Bowels commiserate, our Eyes bewail them, when before they were condemned to greater Severities by ourselves, than they receive from their Judges. Thus it fares with the greatest Villains; and thus it has appeared in the Case of the Rebels: Were they not the very Derision and Scorn of the People, when led into this famous City? Did not all the Faces in general that beheld them, speak their Resentment to their Crimes? And yet, when brought to the Place of Execution, none were more pitied by a great many of the unthinking Populace; nay, those that least deserved it, that had formerly professed the establish'd Religion, and now at their Exit professed themselves of another Faith, excluding by their Principles all others from the Hopes of Salvation, that would not follow their Example: But as the former Part of their Lives had been a Contradiction to all Morality, so the latter Part was a direct Opposition to all Honesty. The* Roman-Catholicks *died like Men, never varying from their Principles; but our* Tories *or* High-Churchmen *went into other Extremes. A true Badge of the Men and their Manners, not one of them being touched in the least with Remorse, though they had pleaded guilty. However, that may be lessened, because of the Frailty of the Flesh; yet giving themselves the Lie at their very Departure, and Brink of Eternity, is enough to satisfy any rational Being. I must own, Mr.* Man-caster,

The Preface to the Reader.

faster, that was executed in Lancashire, *in his dying Speech, declared the greatest Detestation to his Guilt, and earnestly begged the Almighty's Pardon for rebelling against his lawful Sovereign. This Man could not be imposed upon to speak contrary to his Conscience, which the Party had persuaded others to do.*

Having premised these Things, I shall detain my Reader no longer, but only to acquaint him, That the Reason why a Second Part or Edition of The History of the Rebellion *came out so soon after the other, was, that when I writ the First, I did it in a very little Time; but finding they sold very well, I was willing to add a great many valuable Pieces, Accidents, and Characters; which I hope will please, seeing I write without Partiality.*

THE

THE
HISTORY
OF THE
REBELLION.

THE several secret Steps which of late have been taken to establish the pretended Son of King *James* II. upon the Imperial Throne of these Realms, and which for many Years have been carried on by Intrigues and Cabals of Parties and Persons against the Establishment of this Nation both in Church and State, have now at last discovered themselves in open Rebellion. Whatever Pretences they have made to cover their secret Practices, whatever different Measures they have taken to carry on their Designs, they have all appeared to center in this one Point, *viz.* to dethrone his Majesty King GEORGE, and to set aside the Protestant Succession in his illustrious Family. There is no question to be made but that they would gladly have brought this to pass by quiet and easy Methods, and that (if possible) they would have brought the Nation into it on the Pretences of *Hereditary Right*, *Legitimacy of Blood*, and the *divine Law of Primogeniture*, which

for

for many Years they had preach'd up as a Principle in the Church, raifing innumerable Inventions of forged Stories and falfe Reprefentations, to prepoffefs the Minds of the People in Favour of a *Popifh* Pretender, and in Prejudice of the Houfe of *Hanover*; but Heaven having difappointed all their clandeftine Meafures by the fudden and unexpected Death of the late Queen, and efpecially of the late King of *France*, on whofe open and avowed Engagements of Support they entirely depended ; and King GEORGE, in Right of the feveral parliamentary Settlements of the Entail, being peaceably poffeffed of and eftablifhed in the Throne, they had then no way left but to fly to the laft Refort of defperate Men, and taking Arms, to break out in open Rebellion.

Being to write of this remarkable Event, as one among the reft deluded to take an unhappy Share in its Progrefs and Confequences, I fhall rather confine myfelf to the Matters of Fact hiftorically to be related, than go back to the fecret Confultations and Refolutions by which the Perfons concern'd ripen'd one another up to a Spirit of Rebellion ; only obferving one thing previous to the Rebellion itfelf, and very aggravating upon thofe concerned in it, *viz.* that not only many of the Gentlemen concerned, but even the Earl of *Mar* himfelf, who was the firft Mover and Head of the Rebellion itfelf, had not only offered their Service to the King, but had taken Oaths to continue faithful to him, and had in particular abjur'd the Intereft of the Pretender. I fay no more of it here, being to mention it again in its Courfe, but this, that it was a fad Token of what Principles either of Honour or Confcience thefe Men proceeded upon ; which, had it been known fooner, would certainly have been an Antidote to have cured not me only, but many

more

more deluded Men, of the moſt favourable Thoughts we had entertain'd for their Perſons and Deſigns.

To look then no farther back, we find the firſt beginning of this Rebellion diſcovered itſelf in the Eaſtern Parts of *Scotland*, in the Provinces of *Merns*, *Perthſhire*, *Angus*, &c. in the following manner.

Several Noblemen, Gentlemen, and others in *Scotland*, being prepared by the Management and Influence of the Earl of *Mar*, began to draw together their Servants and Dependants in all the Places where they had Intereſt, making divers Pretences for ſo doing, but not for ſome Time diſcovering the real Deſign ; till at length Things ripening upon them, and Notice being taken of them, and eſpecially the Earl of *Mar* being arrived among them, they boldly drew together, and openly declared themſelves to have taken up Arms againſt King George, giving Defiance to his Forces, and ſuppreſſing all that were loyally affeċted to his Perſon. This daring Attempt began firſt about the latter End of *Auguſt*, 1715, in the Shire of *Perth*, and in the Highlands of the Shire or County of *Mar*, where they continued ſome Days, gathering their People together till their Number increaſed ; and then barefacedly they advanc'd to other Places, forming themſelves into a Body, and particularly at a ſmall Market-Town nam'd *Kirk-Michael*, where the *Pretender* was firſt proclaim'd, and his Standard ſet up, with a Summons for all People to attend it. This was on the 9th of *September*, where they continued four or five Days, and then made their way to *Moulin*, another ſmall Market-Town in the ſame Shire. Here they likewiſe proclaim'd the *Pretender*, and reſted fourteen Days, gathering Forces, where, by the coming in of others of their Party, they conſiderably increaſed their Number. From hence they marched to another Market-Town call'd *Logarett*, their Number now amounting to 1000 Men well

arm'd ;

arm'd; from *Logareit* they march'd to an ancient City which formerly gave Title to a Bishop, call'd *Dunkeld*. This Place they made their Head-Quarters, and here their Numbers increas'd again confiderably, for here they were join'd by 2000 Men from the Highlands by the Marquis of *Tullibardin*, by the Earl of *Broadalbin*'s Men, and feveral others. Here finding themfelves ftrengthen'd by the Addition of the Highland-Men, as above, they refolved to extend their Quarters; and the Earl of *Mar* having Intelligence that the Earl of *Rothes* and the Gentlemen of *Fife*, who were up in Arms for the King, were advancing to poffefs themfelves of *Perth*, called alfo St. *John's-Town*, the principal City of thefe Parts, and which commands the Paffage over the *Tay*, refolv'd to be beforehand with them; and having Intelligence in the Place, he detached Mr. *John Hay*, Brother to the Earl of *Kinoul*, with a ftrong Party, giving him Orders to poffefs himfelf of that Place, which he performed effectually; which Action, as it was a great Difappointment to the King's Troops, fo it was a very great Advantage to the Earl of *Mar* and his Party:

1. As it gave him the Command of the whole Province of *Fife*, the moft fruitful, rich, and for the Convenience of the Sea-Coaft, the moft commodious to him of any of the Provinces in that Part of *Scotland*, as will foon appear.

2. As it gave a great Reputation as well to his Conduct as to his Party, who upon this Succefs made Preparations in all Parts to draw together and join him. And now indeed they began to have the Face of a ftrong Army, making this City their chief Garifon and Head-Quarters. A great many Lords, Chiefs of Clans, and other Gentlemen from all Quarters flock'd to them, with their Followers, and fome of them in very good Order, and well armed, particularly the Marquis of *Huntley*, the

Earl

Earl of *Seaforth*, the *Macintoſh*'s, the Earl *Mareſ-chall*, and with them ſo many, that their Number were ſaid to be about 12000 Men, very well appointed, as well Horſe as Foot.

From thence extending their Quarters, they performed an Exploit at *Brunt-Iſland*, which ſtill added to their Reputation; where they not only ſurpriſed the Town, being ſtrong by Situation, and a Sea-Port on the *Firth* of *Forth*, in view of the very City of *Edinburgh*; but manning out ſome Boats in the Harbour, they went off, and ſeiz'd a Ship loaden with Arms, Ammunition, and other warlike Stores, which lay in the *Firth*, bound to the North, for the Uſe of the Earl of *Sutherland*.

Subſequent to this, they immediately made themſelves Maſters of all the Towns upon the Coaſt, even to the Mouth of the *Firth*, and, in a word, of the whole Province of *Fife*, the Earl of *Rothes* and the Gentlemen with him being obliged to ſeparate, or retire to *Stirling*, to the King's Army.

The Rebellion being come to this length, the Earl of *Mar* reſolvd, in Concert with his Confederates, who by this time began to appear likewiſe in other Places, to make an Attempt upon the South Parts of *Scotland*; and this by a Method which at that Time was not expected, and indeed ſcarce practicable, *viz.* By ſending a ſtrong Detachment of Men to croſs the *Firth* of *Forth*, to land on *Lothian* ſide, there to be joined by their Friends, who they expected to riſe about *Haddingtoun*, and on the Borders of *England*. On their March to the Sea-Coaſt they were covered by ſome Horſemen under the Command of Sir *John Areſkin* of *Alva*, the Maſter of *Sinclar*, and Sir *James Sharp*, Grandſon to Archbiſhop *Sharp* of St. *Andrews*, who was murder'd in his Coach by the old *Cameronians*. This Body was commanded by the Laird of *Borlam*, better known by the Name of Brigadier *Macintoſh*, and conſiſted of 2500 Men well arm'd.

arm'd. Orders had been given for all the Boats on that Side to be got ready to tranfport them over. His Majefty's Ships then in the *Firth* either efpying them, or having Notice of the Defign, prepar'd to prevent them, and weighing their Anchors upon the Top of the Flood, let fail to intercept them, if they fhould attempt the Paffage ; but the Rebels made feveral Counter-marches to amufe them till Night came on. They drew all down to the Shore on *Wednefday* Night, the 11th of *October*. Several embark'd that Night, and others the next Night, making directly over the South Shore, the Men of War not being able to come time enough ; yet one Boat was taken with forty Men on Board ; others were forced back to the *Fife* Side again ; among whom my Lord *Strathmore* and his Lieutenant-Colonel *Walkinfhaw* of *Barrowfield*, and a great many Men were forced into the Ifle of *May*. Of the 2500 defigned for this Defcent upon the *Lothians*, only 1500 of them landed ; the Men of War being come down, made it impracticable for the other to pafs ; fo they were oblig'd to ftay till the next Night, and then to get back to *Criel* on the Shore of *Fife* : The other getting to the Shore, landed at *North Berwick*, *Aberlady*, and other Places on that Coaft, and quarter'd at *Haddingtoun* and *Trannent* the firft Night. This was a bold, and, to give them their due, a brave Attempt, for Men in open Boats to crofs an Arm of the Sea fixteen or feventeen Miles broad, in fight, and indeed in Defiance of three Men of War, whom they fell in among, but received no Damage from them, but rather an Advantage ; for the Lights of the Ships fhewed them how to row to the Shore. On the other hand, the Government omitted nothing that could be done to prevent this bold Attempt ; no Care was wanting to difappoint them of Veffels for the Undertaking ; the Magiftrates of *Edinburgh* and of the other

Towns

Towns on the *Edith*, having had Notice from the Duke of *Argyle* of this Defign, had ordered all the Boats that could be got to be brought to *Leith*; and befides the Three Ships of War that lay in the Road, ordered the Three Cuftom-houfe Smacks either to burn or bring over from *Fife* all the Boats and Veffels they could find, to prevent the Rebels coming over. But all thefe Precautions proved ineffectual: The Rebels being Mafters of all the Sea-Shore, from *Cromarty* to the *Forth* of *Edinburgh*, they eafily found Means to get Boats for their Purpofe; nor did they fail of all neceffary Policy in the Management of the Defign; for whilft fome of them amufed the King's Ships about *Brunt-Ifland*, as if they would pafs above *Leith*-Road, their main Body embarked on the other fide, under the Conduct, as before, of Brigadier *Mackintofh* of *Borlam*, and quite out of fight of the Ships; and by this Means came fafe afhore, as above.

Whilft this Defign was putting in Execution, the Earl of *Mar* made a feigned March from *Perth* towards *Dumblain*, as if he defigned to attempt to crofs the *Forth* at *Stirling*-Bridge, or there-abouts, with an Intent to divert the Duke of *Argyle* from falling upon thofe that had croffed the *Firth*, as before: Nor was this part of their Defign ineffectual; for it obliged the Duke of *Argyle* to return to *Stirling* in all hafte; which you fhall have related afterwards.

The *Highlanders* having thus croffed the *Firth*, and refrefh'd themfelves but one Night at *Haddington*, march'd directly towards *Edinburgh*, where they caufed greater Fear than there was real Danger; for unlefs their Number had been greater, it was as unlikely they fhould be able to force that City, as it was improbable that City fhould have refifted them, had their Number been greater. It was indeed fuppofed that they expected to be joined by the

B   Rabble,

Rabble, and to have rais'd some Tumult in the City in their Favour: But by the good Conduct of the Magistrates, and the Unanimity of the Citizens, who immediately took Arms, and formed themselves, they were disappointed; and especially by the speedy Approach of the Duke of *Argyle*, who, on Notice of their Approach, came with a swift March from *Stirling* with a Detachment of Dragoons to the Assistance of the Citizens.

The Rebels march'd up within Sight of the City; but finding no Numbers come out to them, and being informed as well of the Posture of the Citizens, as of the Approach of the Duke of *Argyle*, and, which was more than all, being sensible of the Weakness of their own Power, they halted, and calling a short Council, they resolv'd to attack *Leith*; so they turn'd to the Right, and marching to *Leith*, they entred the Town without Resistance.

Here they were entire Masters of the Place; and that they might not be fallen on to their Disadvantage, they marched over the Bridge, and posted themselves in the old demolished Fort there built by *Oliver Cromwell*, and called the Citadel. Here they began to fortify; and first they went on board the Ships in the Harbour, and seized several Pieces of Cannon, with Powder and Ball, and what else was proper for their Defence, together with a good Quantity of Brandy, Meal, Flesh, and other Provisions: And here they continued all *Friday* and *Saturday* the 13th and 14th of *October*. On *Saturday*, the Duke of *Argyle*, who, as above, had come from *Stirling*, upon Notice of their coming over the *Firth*, and had first given the Forces he had brought with him a little Time to refresh themselves after their long and hasty March, I say, on *Saturday* march'd down from *Edinburgh* with the 400 Horse and 200 Foot which he brought with him, and had mounted upon Country Horses for Expedition, to whom he join'd 400 Militia, and the Town-Guard of *Edinburgh*

burgh of 120 Men: With thefe his Grace fet out of
Edinburgh about Ten in the Morning ; but finding
the *Highlanders* fo well intrenched, that it was impracticable to attack them without Cannon, by reafon the Horfe he had with him could do him little or
no Service, he returned to *Edinburgh* about two in
the Afternoon, and gave Orders that neceffary Preparations fhould be made for attacking the Rebels
with Artillery the next Day.

The Forces which his Grace commanded were
part of Lord *Portmore's*, commonly called the *Scots*
Gray, part of Lieutenant-General *Carpenter's*, and
the Earl of *Stair's* Dragoons, part of *Shannon's*, part
of the Lord *Forfar's*, and part of the *Scots* Fuziliers
Foot, befides the Militia above, and feveral Noblemen and Gentlemen Voluntiers.

The Rebels ftill expected that great Numbers
from *Edinburgh* would have come out and joined
them, being encouraged by the good Pofture they
were in ; which, had it happened, they had yet a
ftrong Inclination to attempt to enter the City ; but
feeing there was no longer Expectation of Encouragement, (for there only came fix or feven Gentlemen to them, and gave them an Account that no
Body ftirr'd, and that the Town was in a Pofture
to oppofe any Attempt they fhould make,) and being likewife informed of the Preparations that the
Duke of *Argyle* was making to fall upon them the
next Day, that fame *Saturday* Night, about feven
o'Clock, they prepared to be gone, refolving to make
a Retreat under the Favour of the Darknefs of the
Night. Before they did this, they fent off a Boat
with an Exprefs to the Earl of *Mar*, to acquaint him
with their Proceedings. As foon as the Boat went
off, they difcharged one of their Cannon after her,
to make the Men of War imagine her an Enemy to
the Rebels. Nor did that Stratagem fail, but fully
anfwered the Defign ; the Boat efcap'd unpurfu'd,

and

and returned to them again with Letters from the Earl of *Mar*, and new Orders, about three Hours before they left *Seaton*-House. Night being come, all things were made ready with the greatest Caution and Secrecy imaginable for their Retreat, which they performed in the deepest Silence ; taking the Advantage of the Low Ebb of the Tide, they marched off by the Head of the *Peer* on the Sands, crossing the Mouth of the River no deeper than to the Knees in Water, making Eastward ; so covered their Retreat, and came safe to *Seaton*-House, leaving about Forty behind them that had made too free with the Brandy which they found in the Custom-House, besides some Stragglers, who lagg'd behind in their March. Several little odd Accidents happened to them in that March, occasioned by the Darkness of the Night, and the Mistakes natural to Attempts of this kind : First of all, when they came near *Musleburgh*, some People from the End of that Town fired upon their Front, but did no Harm, yet occasioned a great Disorder among them. At first this made the Highlanders suspect all Horsemen for Enemies ; the Consequence of which was very unhappy to one of their own Number, a Gentleman of no mean Quality, Character, and Fortune, and who had just joined them, whose Name was Mr. *Alexander Maloch*, of *Mutree-Shields* : This Gentleman being on Horseback, was challenged by a Highlander in his Language ; to which the Gentleman being a Stranger, and not able to answer in that Dialect, the Highlander shot him dead on the Spot. The Brigadier took what Money and Gold he had about him, which was about sixty Guineas, and left him ; for they could not stay to bury him. Soon after this, *viz.* about a Mile farther from *Musleburgh*, on the other Side of the Town, they were again alarm'd with the Noise of Guns firing upon the Front : And here the like Mistake occasioned

fioned the like Mifchief; for taking a Party of their
own Men for Enemies, the foremoft of the Body
fired upon them, and killed a Serjeant belonging to
the Earl of *Mar's* Regiment, and a private Soldier.
The Night proved fo very dark, that they could not
diftinguifh Friends from Enemies ; which was their
Happinefs one way, as it prevented their being difcovered and purfued ; but their great Mifchief ano-
nother way, as it made them liable to fuch falfe
Alarms, and made them kill their own Friends inftead of Enemies : At laft they arrived at *Seaton-*
Houfe about two in the Morning, which is an ancient Caftle, very large, encompafs'd with a ftrong,
high Stone-Wall, but no Ditch. Here fome of
their Men join'd them, who croffing the *Firth* farther Eaftward, had not landed fo foon, and had not
been able to come up to them on their March to
Leith ; thefe Men brought them an Account of
Strathmore, and other Gentlemen being forc'd
afhore on the Ifle of *May*, that were obliged to return to the Earl of *Mar*. On *Sunday* the 16th of
October, whilft they were in *Seaton*-Houfe, feveral
of His Majefty's Forces, join'd with the well-affected Gentlemen of the Country, came from *Edinburgh*,
and appeared near *Prefton-Pans*, which gave an
Alarm to the Highlanders ; upon which, a Party
marched out of the Caftle, and formed themfelves
in order to receive thofe that appeared againft them :
But thofe from *Edinburgh* having made a Halt, retir'd ; which the Rebels likewife did into their Garifon at *Seaton*-Houfe. Upon *Monday* the 17th, the
Earl of *Rothes*, with 300 Gentlemen Voluntiers,
and the Lord *Torphichen* with 200 Dragoons which
the Duke of *Argyle* had left, marched to *Seaton-*
Houfe, but found the Rebels fo ftrongly pofted,
that it was impoffible to diflodge or reduce them
without Artillery. This ftill animated the Rebels,
and a good Body advanc'd, as if they would charge

B 3   the

the Gentlemen, and some Shot were exchanged, but at too great Distance to do any Harm on either Side; and the King's Troops seeing no Good to be done, retir'd

On *Sunday* the Duke of *Argyle* having Intelligence from *Stirling* that the Earl of *Mar*, and the Rebels under his Command, were marching from *Perth*, he returned to *Stirling* to observe the Motion of the Rebels, leaving a Party to protect the People of *Edinburgh* from the Insults of the Rabble. This was the Earl of *Mar*'s feigned March, to withdraw the Duke of *Argyle* from attempting any thing upon the Highlanders that had crossed the *Firth:* He gave out, he would pass the *Forth* with all his Army, either at *Stirling* or at the Bridge of *Down*. They began their March in the Night, *October* 17, and advanced in three Bodies; but upon the Notice that the Duke of *Argyle* was returned from pursuing the Enemy, he marched back to *Perth:* All this was a Stratagem and an Amusement, which indeed succeeded; for he got his Design answer'd, and broke the Measures of the Duke of *Argyle*, who resolv'd to attack *Seaton*-House. As to the Earl of *Mar*, he was resolv'd not to cross the *Forth* till he had got all the Clans together, and had reduced the Earl of *Sutherland*, whom if he should leave unvanquished upon his Rear, might prove fatal to his Designs, and expose all he had gained without Opposition, to be regained by that Lord.

The Highlanders continued all this while at *Seaton*-House, and sent out Parties to bring in Provisions, of which they brought in great Plenty, as Cows, Sheep, Meal, &c. and gave out that they resolv'd to fortify there, and make *Seaton*-House a Magazine, while they raised an Army, as they pretended also, as well from the Country round about, and from *Edinburgh*, and from other Friends to their Design in the West part of *Scotland*, who were

pre-

preparing to join them, as from the Borders of *England*, where by this time Numbers were rifen in *Northumberland* by the Lords and others in *England*; of whom I fhall fay farther hereafter.

While they continued here they difcovered a Boat at Sea, making towards the Shore from the *Fife*-fide of the *Firth*: The Men of War fired very hotly at her; but the Boat keeping to the Windward at a Diftance, fhe got fafe to Shore. This was the fame Boat that went off from *Leith*, and brought News concerning their Friends Proceeding at *Perth*, and Orders to march toward *England*, to join the New-rifen Rebels in *Northumberland*. The Boat landed them at a fmall Harbour called *Port-Seaton*, a fmall Town where Ships ufed to take in Coal and Salt. Prefently after thefe Orders, (*viz.*) on *Tuefday* the 18th, two Gentlemen brought them an Account of the Infurrection in *Northumberland* for the *Pretender*, under the Command of Mr. *Forfter*; and of the South-Country *Scots* Gentlemen, under the Command of the Lord Vifcount *Kenmure*. Upon thofe feveral Pieces of Intelligence, they altered their Refolution of continuing at *Seaton*-Houfe; and at the fame time receiving alfo an Exprefs from Mr. *Forfter*, inviting them to meet him at *Kelfo* on the Border, they refolved to march next Day to meet him. This was *Wednefday* the 19th, which they did accordingly, fetting out in the Morning for a fmall Country Town called *Lonformachus*, which is feventeen long *Scots* Miles from *Seaton*-Houfe. During this Day's March, feveral of the Highlanders lagg'd behind and deferted. As foon as Major-General *Wightman* received Intelligence of their Motion, he marched from *Edinburgh* with 80 Dragoons, 50 Militia, and fome Voluntiers, to attack their Rear; but returned in the Evening, *re infecta*, having only taken up fome of the Rebel Deferters, whom he made Prifoners, and left the 50

Foot

Foot in *Seaton*-Houfe, recovering a great deal of
their Spoil which was left there behind. *Mackintofh*
and his Men fet out again from their Night's Quarters at *Lonformachus*, towards another fmall Town
in the *Mers* called *Dunfe*, the Place of Nativity of
the learned and famous *Johannes Dunfe Scotus:* Here
they drew up in Order of Battle whilft the *Pretender*
was proclaimed, retiring afterwards to their Quarters
in that Town. The next Morning, being *Saturday*
the 22d of *October*, they marched towards *Kelfo*,
which Town the *Englifh* and *Scots* Horfe, that is to
fay, the *Northumberland* and *Nithfdale* Rebels, entred the fame Evening. The Highlanders, in Compliment to their Bravery and Conduct fhewn in paffing the *Firth*, and fo often facing their Enemies,
were met by the *Scots* Horfe at *Ednembridge:* It
feems the Cavalry were fo earneft to pay this Refpect to the Foot, that they made no Stop at *Kelfo*,
but went forward to conduct the Foot into the
Town; which they did accordingly about three a
Clock in the Afternoon; fo that at that time all
their Forces were got together. Brigadier *Mackintofh*,
upon all the Marches he had made, and in all the
feveral Towns he came at, had been very careful to
collect all the Money he could get of the Publick
Revenue. His Avarice and Covetoufnefs very much
difcover'd the Man: For it is well known that he
made falfe Mufters of his Men, and gave them in
far more numerous than they were, and fo put the
Old Soldier upon the Young General; which was
difcovered at laft. Befides feveral little fmall-fpi-
rited Actions of taking Bribes: For at *Prefton* he
took a Silver Watch from one Mr. *Wyburgh*, whom
he had made Prifoner, as one of the Officers of the
Militia, with a Promife to get him his Liberty,
which he could not obtain for that Gentleman, but
kept his Watch; though upon Complaint made by
that Prifoner, then at Liberty, to General *Wills*,
the

the Brigadier was, to his Shame, obliged to return it. An Action very much becoming a Tory Captain. In one of his Marches, passing by the House of one Dr. *Sinclair*, he gave Orders to set fire to it; but one Mr. *William Miller*, who had the Title of Major in his Regiment, by his Persuasion prevailed with him to forbear those Reprisals for the present. The Reason why the Brigadier would have done this, is as follows: This Dr. *Sinclair* and the Laird of *Humby* had Intelligence that there were some People got together in the House of Mr. *Hepburne* of *Keith*, near *Haddingtoun*: This *Hepburne* was a Gentleman known to be a Friend of the *Pretender's*, and no Question had a Design to join the Rebels. Upon this Intelligence, Dr. *Sinclair* got some of the Militia and Neigbours together to attack them, and, if possible, prevent their Design. Mr. *Hepburne* and his Sons, with a Relation and some Servants, who were all that were in the House, took the Alarm, and finding they were beset, mounted their Horses, resolving to break through, and make their Escapes: Dr. *Sinclair* and his Troop finding they were better mounted than his Men, and resolute also not to surrender, fired upon them, and killed Mr. *Hepburne's* younger Son, a Youth wonderfully lamented, being singularly beloved by all that knew him. Dr. *Sinclair* was blamed for this, and his too particular Behaviour against Mr. *Hepburne*, who was his next Door Neighbour: And this caused many to press the Brigadier to fire his House; which however, as above, was not done. This was the first Blood spilt in the Rebellion.

Having thus brought all the Rebels into *Kelso* to their Rendezvous, as well from the North and West Parts of *Scotland* as from *England*, I must leave them there a little, while I go back into *Northumberland*, and give some Account of the Rising and Motion of the Rebels on that Side; as also of
some

some of their Measures and Marches, till they came and joined the Highland Foot at *Kelso*, as above.

There had been Measures concerted at *London*, by the *Pretender's* Friends, some time before the Insurrection in *Northumberland* broke out; to which Capt. *John Shaftoe*, a Half-pay Officer, since executed at *Preston*, and Capt. *John Hunter* of *North-Tyne* in the County of *Northumberland*, who had a Commission from Queen *Anne* to raise an independent Company, but did not, assisted: Besides these two, there was one Capt. *Robert Talbot*, an *Irishman* and *Papist*, formerly in the *French* Service, who likewise being acquainted with the Design in *August*, 1715. took Shipping at *London*, and went to *New-castle*. By this Gentleman, the Resolutions taken at *London* were first communicated to their Friends in the North of *England*, and Means us'd to persuade and prepare the Gentlemen they had embark'd with them, to be ready to rise upon Warning given. And here, that I may enter into that Part of the History of the Rebellion, which though most useful to be known, yet none of those who have pretended to write of these Things, have yet been able to give a particular Account of, or indeed so much as to entertain any Notion of; I say, that this needful Part may be laid open, I must observe, That as it is very reasonable to suppose a Design of this Consequence could not be carried on by the Measures concerted, the Parties furnished, prepared, and brought together in a Posture fit to appear in Arms against the Government, without long Debates, frequent Correspondences, carrying and re-carrying of Letters, Orders, &c. and abundance of People employed to concert Measures, and ripen up Things to the height they afterwards were brought to; so it is worth observing, how that Intelligence was managed, and in what manner they went on for some time before they broke out into

open

open Rebellion, And firſt we are to obſerve, that the grand Deſign was laid at *London*, and that there the Meaſures were principally concerted; from whence, as from the Center conveying Life and Vigour to the Parts, a Correſpondence and Intelligence was ſettled with all the Conſpirators in the ſeveral Parts of *Britain*. But as this was a Correſpondence of too much Weight to be carried on by the ordinary Conveyance of Letters, there were ſeveral Gentlemen, from ſundry Parts in the Kingdom, riding from Place to Place as Travellers, pretending a Curioſity to view the Country, and thereby carrying Intelligence, diſcourſing with Perſons, and ſettling and appointing their Buſineſs. The principal Men entruſted with theſe Negociations, were Colonel *Oxburgh*, Mr. *Nicholas Wogan*, Mr. *Charles Wogan*, and Mr. *James Talbot*, all *Iriſh* and *Papiſts*: A ſecond Claſs of Agents conſiſted of Mr. *Clifton* Brother to Sir *Gervaſe Clifton*, and Mr. *Beaumont*, both Gentlemen of *Nottinghamſhire*, and Mr. *Buxton* a Clergyman of *Derbyſhire*. All theſe rid like Gentlemen, with Servants and Attendants, and were armed with Swords and Piſtols. They kept always moving, and travelled from Place to Place, till things ripen'd for Action. The firſt Step towards their appearing in Arms was, when, about the latter end of *September*, the Lord *Derwentwater* had Notice that there was a Warrant out from the Secretary of State to apprehend him, and that the Meſſengers were come to *Durham* that were to take him. This Lord went to the Houſe of one Mr. *B---n*, in his Neighbourhood, a Juſtice of the Peace, who, if zealouſly affected to His Majeſty's Government, or that Lord's Intereſt, might have honourably enough taken him, or at leaſt perſuaded him to ſurrender; which, it is preſumed, would not have been Matter of great Difficulty to have been done. Here it is ſuppoſed he went from thence to the

Houſe

House of one *Richard Lambert*, thought more private, and least suspected. Mr. *Forster* likewise having Notice of the like Warrant against him, went from Place to Place, 'till at last he came to the House of one Mr. *Fenwick* of *Bywell*. The Messenger in pursuit of him was got within half a Mile of that Place; but staying or calling for a Constable to his Aid, whether the other had notice thereof, or not, yet he found time to out-distance the Messenger, so that he never overtook him, 'till they met at *Barnet*, when the Messenger brought Ropes to pinion him that had led him such a Dance. It has been reported (not without good Reason) that Mr. *Fenwick* had given shrewd Demonstrations, if not plain Evidence, of his good Inclinations to join the Rebels. Upon this News they had a full Meeting of the Parties concern'd, in *Northumberland*; where consulting all the Circumstances of their Friends, and of the Interest they were embark'd in, they boldly resolv'd, since there was no Safety any longer in shifting from Place to Place; that in a few Days they should be all secur'd, and clapp'd up in several Prisons, or hurried away to *London*; that as they should be severally confin'd, so they would be severally examined, and none could say what the other should answer: So that for fear of betraying one another, they should be really brought to do it; That now was the time to shew their Loyalty to their King (*Pretender*), and that if this Opportunity was lost, they had no room to hope for another; and that therefore they would immediately appear in Arms. At this time the Lord *Derwentwater's* Horses had been in Custody of one Mr. *Coatforth*, in that Lord's Neighbourhood, a Justice of the Peace for the County, for several Weeks, according to an Order from Council: But when that Lord had need of them, he had them returned. I afterwards asked that Lord, how he came so quietly by

his

his Horfes from the Juftice's Poffeffion, whom the
believing Neighbourhood efteem'd a moft rigid
Whig ? I was anfwered thus, by that Lord's repeat-
ing a Saying of *Oliver Cromwell's*, *That he could
gain his Ends in any Place with an Afs-load of Gold* ;
and left me to make Application. Purfuant to this
Refolution, an Appointment was made, and Notice
of it fent to all their Friends, to meet the next
Morning, which was the 6th of *October*, at a Place
called *Green-rig*, which was done accordingly ; for
Mr. *Forster*, with feveral Gentlemen, in Number
at firft about twenty, met at the Rendezvous ; but
made no ftay here, thinking the Place inconvenient,
but rode immediately to the top of a Hill called the
Waterfalls; from whence they might difcover any
that came either to join them, or to oppofe them.
They had not been long here, before they difcovered
the Earl of *Derwentwater*, who came that Morning from his own Seat at *Dilston*, with fome Friends,
and all his Servants, mounted fome upon his Coach-
Horfes, and all very well arm'd. In coming from
Dilston-Hall, they all drew their Swords as they
marched along *Corbridge*, and thro' that Town. They
halted at the Seat of Mr. *Errington*, where there were
feveral other Gentlemen appointed to meet, who
join'd the Lord *Derwentwater*, and then they came
on all together to the Places appointed, and where
the forenamed Company attended. They were now
near 60 Horfe, moft Gentlemen and their Attendants ; when calling a fhort Council, it was concluded to march towards the River *Coquett*, to a Place
called *Plainfield :* Here they were join'd by others,
who came ftraggling in, and having made fome
Stay here, they refolved to go that Night to *Rothbury*, a fmall Market-Town : Here they ftay'd all
Night ; and next Morning, being the 7th of *October*, their Number ftill increafing, they march'd to
Warkworth, another Market-Town upon the Sea-
Coaft,

Coaſt, and ſtrong by its Situation, famous formerly for a Caſtle, the Body of which ſtill remains, and an ancient Cell cut out of a ſolid Rock. Here they continued till *Monday*, during which time nothing material happened, except that on *Sunday* Morning Mr. *Forſter*, who now ſtiled himſelf General, ſent Mr. *Buxton* their Chaplain to Mr. *Ion* the Parſon of the Pariſh, with Orders for him *to pray for the Pretender as King*; *and in the Litany, for* Mary *Queen-Mother, and all the dutiful Branches of the Royal Family*; and to omit the uſual Names of *King* George, *the Prince and Princeſs*; which Mr. *Ion* wiſely declining, the other, *viz.* Mr. *Buxton*, took Poſſeſſion of the Church, read Prayers, and preach'd. Mean while the Parſon went to *Newcaſtle* to conſult his own Safety, and acquaint the Government with what happened. The next thing they did, was openly to proclaim the *Pretender* as King of *Great Britain, &c.* It was done by Mr. *Forſter* in Diſguiſe, and by the Sound of Trumpet, and all the Formality that the Circumſtances and Place would admit. It may be obſerv'd, that this was the firſt Place where the *Pretender* was ſo avowedly pray'd for and proclaim'd as King of theſe Realms. *Buxton's* Sermon gave mighty Encouragement to his Hearers, being full of Exhortations, flouriſhing Arguments, and cunning Inſinuations to be hearty and zealous in the Cauſe; for he was a Man of a comely Perſonage, and could humour his Diſcourſe to induce his Hearers to believe what he preach'd; having very good natural Parts, and being pretty well read.

On *Monday* the 10th of *October* they march'd to *Morpeth*, a very conſiderable Market-Town belonging to the Earl of *Carliſle*, and gives Title to his eldeſt Son. Upon their March to this Town their Number got a conſiderable Addition, at *Felton-Bridge* they were join'd by 70 *Scots* Horſe, or rather

Gentlemen

Gentlemen from the Borders; and they had been
considerably increafed before, in their March from
Warkworth, at *Alnwick*, and other Places; fo that
at their entring this Town they were 300 ftrong,
all Horfe, for they would entertain no Foot, elfe
their Number would have been very large; but as
they neither had nor could provide Arms for thofe
they had mounted, they gave the common People
good Words, and told them that they would foon
be furnifh'd with Arms and Ammunition, and that
then they would lift Regiments to form an Army.
This was upon the Expectation they had of furprizing *Newcaftle*, in which Cafe they did not queftion
to have had as many Foot as they pleas'd. Here
Mr. *Forfter* receiv'd an Account that Mr. *Lancelot
Errington* and fome others had furprized the Caftle
in the *Holy Ifland*, which is a fmall Fort guarded by
a few Soldiers fent weekly from the Garifon at
Berwick. *Errington* undifcover'd took Boat and
went to Sea, and with his Companions landed under
the Cover of the Wall, and got into the Fort by
Surprize; tho' he kept the Poffeffion but a very little while, for the Governor of *Berwick* having an
immediate Account of the Action, and refolving if
poffible to recover the Place before *Errington* could
be fupply'd with Men and Provifions, detach'd a
Party of 30 Men of his Garifon, with about 50
Voluntiers of the Inhabitants, and marching over
the Sands at Low-water-mark attack'd the Fort,
and took it Sword in Hand; *Errington* himfelf attempting to make his Efcape, was wounded and
taken Prifoner, with feveral others; he with his
Brother afterwards got out of *Berwick* in Difguife.
The Defign of taking this Fort was, to give Sig-
nals to any Ships that feem'd to make to the Coaft
to land Soldiers; for by the Affurances they had
from Friends beyond Sea, they expected them to
land on that Coaft with Supplies of Arms and Offi-

cers;

cers ; but they never came till they were gone for
Scotland, and then two Ships appear'd off at Sea,
and made their Signal ; but having no Answer from
the Shore, made sail Northward. The Rebellion
was now formed, and they were all in a Body at
Morpeth , promising themselves great Things at
Newcastle, and several Gentlemen join'd them there,
and several of the Country People came in and offer'd to list, but they still declin'd them, and prepared to march to *Newcastle*; but before they went,
Mr. *Buxton* the Clergyman taking on himself the
Office of a Herald as well as of a Churchman, proclaim'd the *Pretender*. They had a Party that went
and seized the Post at *Felton-Bridge* ; and one *Thomas Gibson*, a Blacksmith of *Newcastle*, whom they
apprehended and detained as a Spy, which it is
thought he was from Alderman *White* of *Newcastle*,
a zealous Gentleman for the Government, he afterwards became an Evidence against some of the Rebels at their Trials. Here it was that they receiv'd
their first Disappointment, *viz.* in the Affair of
Newcastle, which they expected should open its
Gates to them ; but finding some Delay in it, they
promised themselves to have it in a few Days ; and
in the mean time they turned a little to the Westward, and marched to *Hexam*, an ancient Town
famous for its Privileges and Immunities, and its
once stately, but now ruinous Cathedral, formerly
for many Years a Bishop's Seat, of which three
were canoniz'd. This Town is distant from *Morpeth* 14 long Miles; here they were join'd by some
more *Scots* Horse. From this Town they all marched, few or none knowing whither, and went three
Miles distant to a Heath or Moor adjoining to *Dilston*, the Seat of the Lord *Derwentwater*, and there
they made a Halt; this was with Design, as was
thought, to go to *Newcastle* for the Surprize of that
Town, which, as above, they hoped to have done
sooner :

fooner: It is certain they had a great many Friends there; and it was reported among them that Sir *William Blackett* would join them. If all that was faid of this Gentleman's Conduct was true, they were not in the wrong to have fome Dependance upon his Affiftance; but whether or not he was actually engag'd, remains a Secret; for he manag'd fo well as to keep out of the way. His Intereft is indeed very confiderable in the Town of *Newcaftle*, being one of their Reprefentatives in Parliament, and he has in his Service a great many Colliers and Keelmen, who in flat Boats call'd Keels convey the Coals from the Collieries to the Ships. He has likewife feveral Lead-Mines on that fide the Country, which employ a great many Hands. Whether his Intereft was fo ftrong among thefe People, as to bring them to take Arms, by his Order, againft their Sovereign, I will not fay, or whether they received any Orders of that kind from him; but this we had a certain Account of, *viz.* that thefe Men were order'd to provide themfelves with Arms, and to be ready to go with one who is a kind of Steward or Governor over them, wherever he fhould direct; but whether this was to be for the Service of the Government, or for the Service of the *Pretender*, is not certainly known; Charity bids us hope they were engaged by this Steward for the King's Intereft, efpecially becaufe he has always pretended to be engaged in the Intereft of his Majefty King GEORGE. The Rebels that had gone out of *Hexam* to the Moor, as above, returned again to their Quarters, having certain Intelligence from fome of their Friends in *Newcaftle*, that even before any regular Forces enter'd that Town, the Magiftrates and Deputy-Lieutenants having firft had fome Sufpicion, and foon after pofitive Intelligence of the Defigns of the Rebels to furprize the Town, had effectually prevented it, and had taken all imagina-

C   ble

ble Precaution for their Security, raifing immediately what Men they could, fecuring and imprifon-
ing all Papifts and fufpected Perfons, arming and
encouraging the Inhabitants for their own Defence.
Indeed the Magiftrates fhew'd a very commendable
Zeal in the Intereft of the King, and the Service of
the Town, and no lefs Courage in their Application
to the Defence of the Place. They got the Militia
and Train-bands, who about that Time were order'd
to mufter at *Killingworth-Moor* near the Town, to
be taken into it for its better Defence: At the fame
time the Earl of *Scarborough*, Lord Lieutenant of
the County of *Northumberland*, repaired with his
Friends to *Newcaftle*: And the Gentry of thofe
Parts, after his Lordfhip's Example, mounted their
Neighbours and Tenants on Horfeback, fo that
the Town was full of Horfes and Men, both Townf-
men and Countrymen unanimoufly declaring for
King GEORGE. However, the Chiefs of the Rebels having great Intereft in that Place, the Inhabitants were not altogether without Fear; nor were
the High Party in the Town without the Folly of
difcovering their Well-wifhes to the Rebels at *Hexam*, and even ufing fome threatning Expreffions,
which the other ought to underftand as fo many
Declarations of their Intentions, if the Power had
been in their Hands to have acted according to their
apparent Intentions. From this Town Lord *Derwentwater* had Intelligence, by an Upholfterer,
of the Meffengers coming there, in order to take
him.

This perhaps, was partly the Occafion of laying
afide the former Divifions and Prejudices between
one another as Churchmen and Diffenters; the latter chearfully offering, and the former freely accepting the Offer, an Affociation was entered into by
both Sides, for the mutual Defence of their Lives
and Eftates; and a Body of 700 Voluntiers were
arm'd

arm'd by the Town for their immediate Guard, without Diftinction; and the Keel-men, being moftly Diffenters, offered a Body of 700 Men more, to be always ready at half an Hour's Warning; which was alfo accepted; at the fame time the Affociation aforefaid was fign'd by the whole Body of Loyal Inhabitants. In the middle of this Hurry, alfo a Battalion of Foot, and part of a Regiment of Dragoons, being order'd out of *Yorkſhire* for the Security of the Town, having made long Marches, they came to *Newcaſtle*, and then all their Fears vaniſh'd: But they were all farther eas'd of thefe Diforders a few Days after; for Lieutenant-General *Carpenter* having been ordered by the Government to go in Purfuit of the Rebels, with *Hotham's* Regiment of Foot, *Cobham's, Moleſworth's*, and *Churchill's* Dragoons, for which Purpofe he fet out from *London* the 15th of *October*, and arrived at *Newcaſtle* the 18th, where he began to prepare for attacking the Gentlemen at *Hexam*, waiting a little for the coming up of the Troops. It is to be obferved, that the Town of *Newcaſtle* is not a Place to be entered as an open Village, but has an old and very ſtrong Stone-Wall about it, and very good Gates to defend it, tho' they had no Cannon planted: The Gates alfo were Walled up with Stone and Lime very ſtrong, in cafe of any Attempt; fo that without Cannon they could not have affaulted the Town. But the Rebels gave them no occafion to make ufe either of Walls or Gates, as we ſhall fee prefently. But firſt let us fee how they fpent their Time at *Hexam*. They ſtaid there but three Days, tho' they were not idle during that Time; for firſt they feized all the Arms and Horfes they could lay their Hands on, efpecially fuch as belong'd to thofe who were well-affected Subjects to the King. Next, here Mr. *Buxton* went to the Minifter of the Town, and defired him or his Curate

to read Prayers, commanding that in them he should mention the *Pretender* by Name, as King *James* III. The Minister modestly declined it, (for there was no speaking boldly to them;) so Mr. *Buxton* officiated, and performed as usual. It was reported, that the Curate Mr. *Richardson* had promised to join the Rebels, and there are strong Presumptions to believe that as Matter of Fact. The Night before they left the Town, they were all drawn round the *Cross* in the Market-Place, where the *Pretender* was proclaimed, and the Proclamation fixed to the *Cross*; which remain'd there several Days after the Rebels were gone; which some say, is an Evidence of that Town's good Inclination to His Majesty King GEORGE; and others added, that the Bailiff and Clerk were too much of the Principles of the Lord of their Manor, Sir *W—— Bla————*, else they would have exerted their Authority, and shewed their Loyalty, in pulling down that Proclamation. Here the Rebels had notice of the Viscount *Kenmure*, Earls of *Nithsdale*, *Carnwath*, and *Wintoun*, who had taken Arms in *Nithsdale*, *Dumfries-shire*, and other Places in the West of *Scotland*, having entred *England* to join them, and that they were come to *Rothbury*. The Viscount *Kenmure*, the only Nobleman in that part of *Scotland* capable of commanding Forces upon that Account, was solicited by the Earl of *Mar* to take up Arms for the *Pretender*, and to command such Forces as would join him on that side the *Forth*. At first, he refus'd this Offer, but being importun'd by the Jacobites in that Country, he, at last, was prevailed with to set up the *Pretender*'s Standard at a small Town in *Annandale*, called *Mophet*. This Standard, supposed to be made by his Lady, was very handsome, one side being Blue, with the *Scot*'s Arms done in Gold; the other side a Thistle, with this under, *No Union*; above the Thistle, the usual Motto, *Nemo me im-*
pune

pune laceſſet. This Standard had Pendants of white Ribbon; upon one of theſe was written, *For our Wronged King, and Oppreſſed Country*; the other Ribbon had thereon, *For our Lives and Liberties.* This Standard was ſet up the firſt Night they made their Appearance. Being late, next Day being the 13th of *October*, they marched towards *Dumfries*, with Deſign to ſurprize that Town; but the Marquis of *Annandale*, whom they had followed the Day before, having none but his Servants along with him, entred the Town, and concerted ſuch Meaſures as made that Deſign abortive; which obliged them to alter their Rout, tho' many Diſputes happened hereupon, but at laſt agreed to march to *Loughmaben* that Night, where next Day they ſet up their Standard, and proclaimed the *Pretender*. This Town was the firſt Place, on this Side the *Forth* of *Scotland*, where the *Pretender* was proclaimed, and his Standard ſet up. This Day the Standard was carried by *John Dalziel* Eſq; Brother to the Earl of *Carnwath*. On the 14th of this Month they march'd to *Achelfechen*. On their March thither, on a Common, being in all near 200 Horſe, they were formed into a Regiment. divided into two Squadrons. The chief Command to Viſcount *Kenmure*, that of each Squadron to the Earls of *Wintoun* and *Carnwath*. Hence they marched regularly, and ſent their Quarter-Maſter-General Mr. *Calderwood*, to take up Quarters for them. Next Day they continued their March to *Langholm*, behaving themſelves all along civil in their Quarters. From thence they continued their Rout to *Hawick*. Upon theſe Marches their Number increaſed. At this Place they were alarm'd, which raiſed ſome Diſputes whether they ſhould proceed. They agreed to return, but had an Expreſs from Mr. *Forſter* about two Miles from *Hawick*, towards *Langholm*. This Meſſenger, Mr. *Douglaſs*, had an Invitation from the *Northumberland*

C 3   General

General to my Lord *Kenmure* and his Followers, to meet him at *Rothbury:* So they faced about, and marched that Night to *Jedburgh.* Here they received Intelligence of the *Mackintosh*'s croffing the *Forth*, and the Duke of *Argyle*'s Refolution to attack them, which put them into mighty Pain how the Confequence would prove. It is to be obferved, that they were alarmed in marching to *Jedburgh:* Being late, their Advance Guard was furpriz'd by the Shouts of one who called out, That the Grey Horfe were ready to fall upon them, and had cut the Quarter-Mafter and thofe with him into pieces. Thofe acquainted with the Quarter-Mafter affured Lord *Kenmure*, that he would by no means be fo eafily enfnar'd, being better ufed to Military Affairs; fo they continued their March, and entred the Town without Oppofition. Here, as in moft other Towns, they proclamed the *Pretender*; next Morning proceeded to *Rothbury*, perhaps fuch a March as few People are acquainted with, being very mountainous, long, tedious, and marfhy. From *Rothbury* they difpatched Mr. *Burnett* of *Carlips* to *Hexam*, to Mr. *Forfter*, to know his Mind, whether he would come towards them, or they fhould advance? He returned an Exprefs, that he would join them. This Mr. *Burnett* afterwards carried the above-mentioned Standard; a Gentleman of comely Appearance; was afterwards Try'd, found Guilty, and Executed in *Lancafhire.* Upon this News, but more efpecially on the aforefaid News of General *Carpenter* preparing to attack them, they march'd out of *Hexam*, *Wednefday* the 19th of *October*, and making a long March, they joined them and their Men that Night; and both of them next Day march'd to *Wooler* in the County of *Northumberland.* Here they refted all *Friday*, where I, with fome Men which I had inlifted, being Keel-men, overtook them upon *Rothbury* Foreft: I fufpefted them for

some

fome of the Militia, and kept at a diſtance ; but diſcovering they had no Arms, made up to them, and aſked them what News, and whither they deſigned? They anſwered, (but eſpecially one, a brave ſtout young Fellow,) *We are* Scotſmen, *going to our Homes to join our Countrymen that are in Arms for King* James. I told him, *he was very bold. Sir,* (ſays he) *I'll drink his Health juſt now :* So with his Bonnet, which he dipt into a Runner, he ſaid, *Here is King* James's *Health* ; which all his Partners did. After this, I told them, *If they were ſincere, and would follow me; I would bring them to their Countrymen.* Which they promiſed to do. I gave each of them a Shilling. Drawing near the Town, I left them under a Hedge, 'till I could enquire what was become of the Rebels, and if we could by ourſelves lodge ſafely there. I enquired for the beſt Inn, being directed there, where I found Mr. *Charles Wogan*'s Man, who came with me from *Hexam,* but parted for fear of being taken. He gave me a Pair of Piſtols ; ſo I returned to my Companions, and brought them quietly into Town, both wet and weary, and immediately went to the Head Conſtable, and told him, that if he would give us no Diſturbance, we would ſtay all Night civilly, paying for what we had ; but if he intended to make a Prey of us, our Friends being gone, we would then follow them. He made fair Promiſes; but not daring to truſt him too much, made him ſure in his own Houſe; ſo that we watched him by turns 'till early next Day ; we ſet out from this Town *Rothbury* for *Wooler,* and there joined the *Engliſh* and *Scots* Horſe, and was kindly entertained by the Chiefs. Here Mr. *Errington* brought them an Account of the Highlanders being alſo coming to join them, and that they were advanced to *Dunſe,* of which a full Account has been given already. On this News they march'd for *Kelſo* in *Scotland.*

On

On this Day's March they seized several Horses, and made Mr. *Selbye* a Gentleman of that Country Prisoner. A little before they came to *Kelso*, they made a Halt upon a Moor ; and there the Gentlemen formed into Troops, were drawn out by themselves, and called over, not only by their Names, but by their design'd Offices for the several Troops : And it is to be observ'd, that to each Troop they assigned Two Captains, being the only way they had to oblige so many Gentlemen. Whilst they were thus employed, there came some Townsmen from *Kelso*, and acquainted the Rebels that Sir *William Bennet* of *Grubbet*, who had been in *Kelso*, and had barricado'd the Town, pretending to keep Post there, had gone off in the Night with his Men, who were only Militia and Servants, and that they might enter the Town without Opposition; so they continued their March, and crossing the River *Twede*, tho' very deep at that Time, and rapid, they entred the Town. The Highlanders came into the Town presently after from the *Scots* Side, with their Bag-pipes playing, led by old *Mackintosh* ; but they made a very indifferent Figure.; for the Rain and their long Marches had extremely fatigued them, tho' their old Brigadier, who march'd at the Head of them appear'd very well. Next Day being *Sunday* the 23d of *October*, my Lord *Kenmure* having the chief Command in *Scotland*, ordered me to preach at the Great Kirk of *Kelso*, and not at the Episcopal Meeting-House, and gave further Orders that all the Men should attend Divine Service. Mr. *Buxton* read Prayers, and I preached on these Words, *Deut.* xxi. 17. the latter part of the Verse, *The Right of the First-born is his.* All the Lords that were Protestants, with a vast Multitude of Papists attended, who have since told me, they were willing so to do, to grace the Cause ; but withal said, They did not see but they may be allowed so to do, for

they

they approved very well of our Liturgy, which 'till then they never heard. It may be said, that the Service of the Church of *England* had never been read in any Church on this side of the *Forth* in *Scotland* before. This Church in its former Days, has been very large, lofty, and beautiful, whose Porch, and other Remains, speak its former Splendor. The Church-yard is very large and neat. It was very agreeable, to see how decently and reverently the very common Highlanders behav'd, and answer'd the Responses according to the Rubrick, to the Shame of many that pretend to more polite Breeding. In the Afternoon Mr. *William Irwine* a *Scots* Clergyman and Nonjuror read Prayers, and preach'd a Sermon full of Exhortations to his Hearers, to be zealous and steady in the Cause: He told me afterwards that he had formerly preach'd the same Sermon in the Highlands of *Scotland*, to the Lord Viscount *Dundee* and his Men, when they were in Arms against King *William*, a little before the Battle of *Gillycranky*. The Sermon was very well digested, and suited fitly for the Men that heard it. I must take notice, that it has been reported that there were other Sermons preached on our Marches; and I have seen such Things written in the Publick Prints, with the Texts of Scripture alledged to have been the Subject of such Discourses; but nothing is more false, for other Sermons than these had we none. Next Morning the Highlanders were drawn up in the Church-yard, and so march'd in Order to the Market-place, with Colours flying, Drums beating, and Bag-pipes playing, and there formed a Circle, the Lords and other Gentlemen standing in the Centre: There was an inner Circle formed also by the Gentlemen Voluntiers: Then Silence being enjoined, the Trumpet sounded; after which the *Pretender* was proclaimed by one *Seaton Barnes*, who

assum'd

affirm'd the Title of Earl of *Dumferling*. The Proclamation was to this Effect :

    " Whereas by the Decease of the late King
" *James* the VIIth, the Imperial Crowns of these
" Realms did lineally descend to his lawful Heir
" and Son our Sovereign *James* the VIIIth : We
" the Lords, *&c.* do declare him our lawful King
" over *Scotland*, *England*, &c."

    Then was read the following *Manifesto* of the
Earl of *Mar*.

*MANIFESTO by the Noblemen, Gentlemen,
and others, who dutifully appear at this Time in
asserting the undoubted Right of their lawful Sovereign* James VIII. *by the Grace of God, King of
Scotland, England, France, and Ireland, Defender of the Faith, &c, and for relieving this his an-
tient Kingdon from the Oppression and Grievances it
lies under.*

    " **H**IS Majesty's Right of Blood to the Crowns
" of these Realms is undoubted, and has
" never been disputed or arraigned by the least Cir-
" cumstance of lawful Authority.
    " By the Laws of God, by the ancient Consti-
" tutions, and by the positive unrepeal'd Laws of
" the Land, we are bound to pay his Majesty the
" Duty of Loyal Subjects. Nothing can absolve
" us from this our Duty of Subjection and Obe-
" dience ; the Laws of God require our Allegiance
" to our rightful King ; the Laws of the Land se-
" cure our Religion and other Interests ; and his
" Majesty giving up himself to the Support of his
" Protestants Subjects, puts the Means of securing
" to us our Concerns Religious and Civil in our
" own Hands.
                                  " Our

" Our fundamental Conſtitution has been entirely
" altered and ſunk amidſt the various Shocks of
" unſtable Faction ; while in the ſearching out new
" Expedients, pretended for our Security, it has
" produced nothing but daily Diſappointments,
" and has brought us and our Poſterity under a
" precarious Dependance upon foreign Councils and
" Intereſts, and the Power of foreign Troops.

" The late unhappy Union, which was brought
" about by the miſtaken Notions of ſome, and the
" ruinous and ſelfiſh Deſigns of others, has prov'd
" ſo far from leſſening and healing the Differences
" betwixt his Majeſty's Subjects of *Scotland* and
" *England*, that it has widened and increaſed them ;
" and it appears by Experience ſo inconſiſtent with
" the Rights, Privileges, and Intereſts of us and
" our good Neighbours and Fellow-Subjects of
" *England*, that the Continuance of it muſt inevita-
" bly ruin us, and hurt them. Nor can any Way
" be found out to relieve us, and reſtore our an-
" cient and independent Conſtitution, but by re-
" ſtoring our rightful and natural King, who has
" the only undoubted Right to reign over us : Nei-
" ther can we hope that the Party who chiefly con-
" tribute to bring us into Bondage, will at any
" time endeavour to work our Relief ; ſince it is
" known how ſtrenuouſly they oppoſed, in Two
" late Inſtances, the Efforts that were made by all
" *Scotſmen* by themſelves, and ſupported by the
" beſt and wiſeſt of the *Engliſh*, towards ſo deſira-
" ble an End, as they will not adventure openly to
" diſown the Diſſolution of the Union to be.

" Our Subſtance has been waſted in the late
" ruinous Wars ; and we ſee an unavoidable Pro-
" ſpect of having Wars continued on us and our
" Poſterity, ſo long as the Poſſeſſion of the Crown
" is not in the right Line.

" The

" The Hereditary Rights of the Subjects, tho'
" confirm'd by Conventions and Parliaments, are
" now treated as of no Value or Force ; and paft
" Service to the Crown and Royal Family, are now
" look'd upon as Grounds of Sufpicion.

" A pack'd-up Affembly, who call themfelves
" a *Britifh Parliament*, have, as far as in them lies,
" inhumanly murder'd their own and our Sovereign,
" by promifing a great Sum of Money as the Re-
" ward of fo execrable a Crime.

" They have profcribed, by unaccountable and
" groundlefs Impeachments and Attainders, the
" worthy Patriots of *England*, for their honourable
" and fuccefsful Endeavours to reftore Trade, Plen-
" ty, and Peace to thefe Nations.

" They have broken in upon the Laws of both
" Countries, by which the Liberty of our Perfons
" was fecured ; they have empower'd a Foreign
" Prince (who notwithftanding his Expectation of
" the Crown for 15 Years, is ftill unacquainted
" with our Manners, Cuftoms, and Language) to
" make an abfolute Conqueft (if not timely pre-
" vented) of the Three Kingdoms, by invefting
" himfelf with an unlimited Power, not only of
" raifing unneceffary Forces at Home, but alfo of
" calling in Foreign Troops, ready to promote his
" uncontroulable Defigns : Nor can we be ever
" hopeful of its being otherwife, in the Way it is
" in at prefent, for fome Generations to come. And
" the fad Confequences of thefe unexampled Pro-
" ceedings have really been fo fatal to great Num-
" bers of our Kinfmen, Friends, and Fellow-Sub-
" jects of both Kingdoms, that they have been
" conftrain'd to abandon their Country, Houfes,
" Wives, and Children, or give themfelves up
" Prifoners, and perhaps Victims to be facrificed
" at the Pleafure of Foreigners, and a few hot-
" headed

" headed Men of a reſtleſs Faction whom they
" employ.

" Our Troops Abroad, notwithſtanding of their
" long and remarkable good Services, have been
" treated, ſince the Peace, with Neglect and Con-
" tempt, and particularly in *Holland*; and it is not
" now the Officers long Service, Merit, and Blood
" they have loſt, but Money and Favour, by which
" they can obtain Juſtice in their Preferments ; ſo
" that it is evident the Safety of his Majeſty's Perſon
" and Independency of his Kingdoms, call loudly
" for immediate Relief and Defence.

" The Conſideration of theſe unhappy Circum-
" ſtances, with the due Regard we have to com-
" mon Juſtice, the Peace and Quiet to us and our
" Poſterity, and our Duty to his Majeſty and his
" Commands, are powerful Motives that have en-
" gaged us in our preſent Undertakings ; which we
" are firmly and heartily reſolved to puſh to the
" utmoſt, and ſtand by one another to the laſt Ex-
" tremity, as the only ſolid and effectual Means of
" putting an End to ſo dreadful a Proſpect, as by
" our preſent Situation we have before our Eyes ;
" and with faithful Hearts, true to our only right-
" ful King, our Country, and our Neighbours,
" we earneſtly beſeech and expect (as his Majeſty's
" Commands) the Aſſiſtance of all our true Fellow-
" Subjects, to ſecond this our firſt Attempt ; de-
" claring hereby our ſincere Intentions, That we
" will promote and concur, in all lawful Means,
" for ſettling a laſting Peace to theſe Lands, under
" the auſpicious Government of our native-born
" rightful Sovereign, the Direction of our Do-
" meſtick Councils, and the Protection of our na-
" tive Forces and Troops.

" That we will in the ſame manner concur and
" endeavour to have our Laws, Liberties, and Pro-
" perties ſecured by the Parliaments of both King-
" doms :

" doms: That by the Wifdom of fuch Parliaments,
" we will endeavour to have fuch Laws enacted,
" as fhall give abfolute Security to us, and future
" Ages, for the Proteftant Religion, againft all
" Efforts of Arbitrary Power, Popery, and all its
" other Enemies. Nor have we any Reafon to be
" diftruftful of the Goodnefs of God, the Truth
" and Purity of our Holy Religion, or the known
" Excellency of his Majefty's Judgment, as not
" to hope that in due Time, good Example, and
" Converfation with our learned Divines, will re-
" move thefe Prejudices, which we know his Edu-
" cation in a Popifh Country has not riveted in
" his difcerning Mind ; and we are fure, as Juftice
" is a Virtue in all Religions and Profeffions, fo
" the doing of it to him, will not leffen his good
" Opinion of ours.

" That as the King is willing to give his Royal
" Indemnity for all that is paft, fo he will chear-
" fully concur in paffing general Acts of Oblivion,
" that our Fellow-Subjects who have been mifled,
" may have a fair Opportunity of living with us
" in the fame friendly Manner we defign to live
" with them.

" That we will ufe our utmoft Endeavours for
" redreffing the bad Ufage of our Troops Abroad,
" and bringing the Troops at Home to be on the
" fame Foot and Eftablifhment of Pay as thofe of
" England.

" That we will fincerely and heartily go into
" fuch Meafures as fhall maintain effectually, and
" eftablifh a right, firm, and lafting Union betwixt
" his Majefty's ancient Kingdom of *Scotland*, and
" our good Neighbours and Fellow-Subjects of the
" Kingdom of *England*.

" The Peace of thefe Nations being thus fettled,
" and we thus freed from Foreign Dangers, we will
" ufe our Endeavours to have the Army reduced
" to

" to the usual Number of Guards and Garisons,
" and will concur in such Laws and Methods, as
" shall relieve us of the heavy Taxes and Debts
" now lying upon us, and at the same time will
" support the Publick Credit in all its Parts.

" And we do hereby promise and engage, That
" every Officer who joins with us in our King and
" Country's Cause, shall not only enjoy the Post
" he now does, but shall be advanced and preferr'd
" according to his Rank and Station, and the Num-
" ber of Men he brings off with him to us ; and
" each Foot-Soldier so joining with us, shall have
" Twenty Shillings Sterling ; and each Trooper or
" Dragoon, who brings Horse and Accoutrements
" along with him, Twelve Pounds Sterling Gra-
" tuity, besides their Pay.

" And in general, we shall concur with all our
" Fellow-Subjects in such Measures, as shall make
" us flourish at Home, and be formidable Abroad,
" under our rightful Sovereign, and the peaceful
" Harmony of our ancient fundamental Constitu-
" tion, undisturbed by a *Pretender's* Interests and
" Councils from Abroad, or a restless Faction at
" Home.

" In so honourable, so good, and just a Cause,
" we do not doubt of the Assistance, Direction,
" and Blessing of Almighty God, who has so oft-
" en succour'd the Royal Family of *Stuarts*,
" and our Country, from sinking under Op-
" pression."

This *Manifesto* being ended, the People with loud
Acclamations shouted, *NO Union! NO Malt, NO
Salt-TAX!* Then the Highlanders returned to their
Quarters, where they continued till *Thursday*; du-
ring which time nothing material happened, but that
they failed not here, as well as in all Places, to de-
mand all the Publick Revenues, viz. of Excise,
Customs,

Cuftoms, or Taxes, and to fearch for Arms, of which they found very few, unlefs fome fmall Pieces of Cannon of different Size and Shape, which formerly belonged to *Hume-Caftle*, and had been employ'd in former Ages in that Strong-Hold againft the *Englifh*, but were at this time brought thence by Sir *William Bennet* aforefaid, to be placed at the Barricadoes which he had made in the Streets leading to the Market-Place : They likewife found fome broad Swords hid in the Church, and a fmall Quantity of Gunpowder. There happened a very uncommon Accident while they remained here, which is worth recording for the fingularity of it ; a Highlander having taken the Lock from his Mufket, he laid down the Barrel, &c. crofs the Arms of a Chair, whilft he at two Yards diftance having cleaned, and trying the Lock, a fpark of Fire flew from it directly, and moft exactly to the Touch-hole of the Piece which was loaded, and went off and wounded three Children fitting round the Fire ; And it was the more ftrange, that at fuch a Diftance, by meer Chance, a Spark fhould direct its way to the Touchhole, and the Bullet fhould wound all the three Children, who did not fit in a Line.

There were no Hoftilities ufed here, only the Horfe going out a Foraging, went to a Seat of the Duke of *Roxburgh*'s near the Town, and brought in fome Hay. While they continued here, Dr. *Arthur*, a Gentleman concerned in that defigned Attempt upon the Caftle of *Edinburgh*, of very good Parts, and generous Education, and one Mr. *Cunningham* of *Barnes*, came from the Earl of *Mar* with Intelligence, and returned to him again ; after which, the fame Gentlemen came again to the Rebels when at *Prefton*. Before I leave this Town, I fhall give fome Account of what Force the Rebel-Troops now confifted, as well becaufe they were more in Number at that time, and better armed

Men

Men than at any time after ; as also becaufe fo many different Accounts of their Numbers have been made publick, that it is not eafy to know what may be depended upon. The Lord Vifcount *Kenmure* had the chief Command whilft in *Scotland :* He was a grave, full-aged Gentleman, of a very ancient Family, and he himfelf of extraordinary Knowledge and Experience in Publick and Political Bufinefs, though utterly a Stranger to all Military Affairs ; of a fingular good Temper, and too Calm and Mild to be qualified for fuch a Poft, being both plain in his *Drefs*, and in his *Addrefs*. He made his firft Rendezvous at *Lochmabben :* He had a Troop of Gentlemen with him, which, as he was General, was call'd the Firft Troop, the Command of which he gave to the Honourable *Bazil Hamilton* of *Beldoun*, Son to the Lord *Bazil Hamilton*, Brother to the late Duke *Hamilton*, a very promifing Youth, and who behaved himfelf with a great deal of Courage in the Action at *Prefton*, tho' but very young.

The Second Troop was called the *Merfe* Troop, commanded by the Honourable *James Hume*, Efq; Brother to the Earl of *Hume*, who at that time was Prifoner in *Edinburgh* Caftle. This Youth is of a good Temper, but not very capable of having the Command of a Troop, as well on account of his Age, as other Incapacities. He was try'd at the *Marfhalfea*, and found Guilty.

The Third Troop, called the Earl of *Wintoun's* Troop, and commanded by himfelf. This Earl is of a very ancient Family, wants no Courage, nor fo much Capacity as his Friends find it for his Intereft to fuggeft, efpecially if we may judge by the Counfel he gave: He was always forward for Action, but never for the March into *England*; and he ceafed not to thwart the Scheme which the *Northumberland* Gentlemen laid down for marching into *England*, not fo much from the Certainty, which,

D   as

as he faid, there was of their being over-power'd, as from the greater Opportunity, which, as he in-fifted, there was of doing Service to their Caufe in Scotland; in order to which, he argued with and preffed them back into Scotland, and leaving Edinburgh and Stirling to their Fate, to go and join the Weftern Clans, attacking in their Way the Town of Dumfreis, and Glafgow, and other Places, and then open a Communication with the Earl of Mar and his Forces. Which Advice, if followed, in all probability would have tended to their great Advantage, the King's Forces being then fo fmall. However therefore fome People have reprefented that Lord, of which I fhall fay no more, all his Actions both before a Prifoner, and whilft fuch, till he made his Efcape out of the Tower, fpeak him to be Mafter of more Penetration, than many of thofe whofe Characters fuffer no Blemifh as to their Underftandings. The Command of this Troop he affigned, under himfelf, to Captain James Dalziel, Brother to the Earl of Carnwath, who had been in King George's Service formerly, and continued an Half-pay Officer for fome time; but upon engaging in the Rebellion, he threw up his Commiffion; which piece of Policy was the faving of his Life, and prevented his being fhot to death at Prefton by Sentence of the Court-Marfhal among the Half-pay Officers. He was a very bold and brave young Gentleman, and fhew'd it upon all Occafions.

The Fourth Troop belonged to Robert Dalziel, Earl of Carnwath: This Nobleman was brought up under the Tuition of One who made it his ftudy'd Care to inftill the Principles of Hereditary Right, Paffive Obidience, and Non-Refiftance into his Mind. He ftudy'd fome time at Cambridge, and there fucked in an entire Affection for the Liturgy and Worfhip in ufe in the Church of England, of
which

which he was a fincere Devotee. He is fingularly
good in his Temper, and of an agreeable Affabi-
lity, and delivers himfelf very handfomely in
his Difcourfe. The Command of this Troop he
gave over to his Uncle *James Dalziel*, Efq;. This
Gentleman has a very good Character, and gave
fufficient Demonftrations of his Affections to the
Pretender's Intereft, by his Courage and Conduct.

The Fifth Troop was under the Command of
Captain *Lockart*, Brother to Mr. *Lockart* of .*Carnwath :* He was a Half-pay Officer in the Lord
Mark Ker's Regiment, and as fuch try'd at *Prefton*
by a Court-Martial ; by which being found Guilty
of Defertion, he, with three more, were fhot to
death there. He was a young Gentleman of a
comely Appearance, and very handfome : He
gave feveral Inftances of his Bravery. He died very penitent for all his Sins, but would not acknowledge that to be one for which he fuffer'd. It is believed, and not without good Reafon, that this
Troop was rais'd by his Brother's Intereft, who is a
Gentleman of a good Eftate, one of the beft, perhaps, in *Scotland* poffeffed by a private Gentleman.
This Troop was compofed of feveral Servants belonging to the Laird of *Carnwath*, befides feveral
of his own Horfes : The Men were paid by Mr.
Auxton, a Merchant of *Edinburgh*, who was en-
trufted in all Mr. *Lockart's* Concerns : And to confirm this, the Quarter-Mafter of this Troop was
Mr. *Lamb*, a Servant of Mr. *Lockart's*, of good
Efteem with his Mafter. He himfelf was taken
into Cuftody upon fhrewd Sufpicions, and fent to
the Caftle of *Edinburgh*. If that Book was written by him, called, *The Memoirs of* Scotland, he
may be called a Gentleman of deep Penetration,
and fingular Affection for his native Country, elfe
he would not make fo free with the Characters
of a great many Noblemen and Gentlemen who

are

are very little fufpected to be the Men he makes them.

Thefe Troops were well mann'd, and indifferent-ly arm'd; but many of the Horfes fmall, and in mean Condition: Befides thefe Troops, there were a great many Gentlemen Voluntiers, who were not formed into any regular Troop.

The Foot defign'd to crofs the *Forth*, were Regimented under thefe Colonels, being Six Regiments in all.

The Firft, the Earl of *Strathmore*'s; but he and his Lieutenant-Colonel *Walkinfhaw* of *Barrowfield* were forced back in their Paffage by the King's Men of War, with feveral others, and obliged to go on fhore in the Ifle of *May*. This Regiment was not in Highland-Drefs, as the others were. This Lord was a hearty Friend of the *Pretender*'s, and had fome time before this Rebellion broke out, given it under his Hand that he would be ready the firft Opportunity to rife and affift to eftablifh him upon the Throne. This Paper, which was fign'd by feveral others, was lodg'd in the Hands of Colonel *Hookes*, to be by him tranfported into *France*.

The Second Regiment was the Earl of *Mar*'s. I fhall here add his Character, given him by his Countryman Mr. *Lockart*, in his *Memoirs of* Scotland.

" *John* Earl of *Mar* was defcended from, and
" the Reprefentative of a Family noted for its Loy-
" alty, on many Occafions both ancient and mo-
" dern, and much beholden to the Bounty of the
" Crown. It is true, his Father embark'd with the
" *Revolution:* But if all be true that is reported,
" his Lordfhip gave a particular, tho' fatal Sign of
" his Remorfe and Repentance, This prefent Gen-
" tleman's Fortune being in bad Circumftances,
" when he came of Age he devoted himfelf to the
" Duke of *Queenfberry*, and the Court Meafures,
" to

" to which he always ftuck clofe, till in the Year
" 1714, he headed fuch of the Duke of *Queenfber-*
" *ry*'s Friends as oppos'd the Marquis of *Tweedale,*
" and his Party's Defigns, and that with fuch Art
" and Diffimulation, that he gain'd the Favour of
" all the Tories, and was by many of them efteem'd
" an honeft Man, and well inclin'd to the Royal
" Family. Certain it is he vowed and protefted fo
" many times ; but no fooner was the Marquis of
" *Tweedale* and his Party difpoffefs'd, than he *re-*
" *turn'd as a Dog to the Vomit,* and promoted all
" the Court Meafures with the greateft Zeal ima-
" ginable. He was not a Man of a good *coram*
" *vobis,* and was a very bad, tho' frequent Speaker
" in Parliament ; but his great Talent lay in the
" cunning Management of his Defigns and Projects,
" in which it was hard to find him out when he
" aim'd to be *incognito* ; and thus he fhew'd himfelf
" to be a Man of good Senfe, but bad Morals.

His Regiment came not entire over the *Forth,*
for at *Prefton* there were only thefe Officers taken
Prifoners, *viz. Nathanael Forbes* Major, a Man fingularly brave, of pleafant Difcourfe, mixing the
Thread thereof with a great many *Scots* Proverbs,
which were very well apply'd, and gave great Entertainment to thofe that were acquainted with that
Dialect. He was very ftrong, and by the Help
thereof forced his way out of the *Marfhalfea.* The
other Officers were three Captains and three Lieutenants (whofe Names are in the Lift of Officers
hereafter memtioned ;) the reft were driven back by
the King's Men of War upon the Coaft of *Fife.*

The Third, *Logie Drummond*'s. This Regiment
came not entire over the *Forth,* being driven back
on the *Fife*-fide, with many more ; for of the 2500
defigned to crofs the *Firth,* the better Half were
prevented. He that had the Command of this
Regiment was one of thofe that figned an Anfwer

to

to Monfieur *de Torci*'s Queftions, which gave a diſtinct Refolution to each Query, containing a full Account of the State of Affairs; particularly an Account of the Inclinations of the People, to venture All for the *Chevalier*'s Service : This was when the People of *Scotland* were diſſatisfy'd about the Union, in the Year 1707. This Paper was likewife lodg'd in the Hands of Colonel *Hookes*, to be by him tranſported into *France*.

The Fourth, the Lord *Nairn*'s, Brother to the Duke of *Athol*; but by marrying an Heireſs, according to the Cuftom of *Scotland*, chang'd his own Name for hers : He came over the *Firth* with a good many of his Men. He is a Gentleman well belov'd in his Country, and by all that had the Advantage to be acquainted with him : He had formerly been at Sea, and gave fignal Inftances of his Bravery : He was a mighty Stickler againft the Union. His Son, who was Lieutenant-Colonel to Lord *Charles*, took a great deal of Pains to encourage the Highlanders, by his own Experience, in their hard Marches, and always went with them on Foot through the worft and deepeft Ways, and in Highland Dreſs.

The Fifth Regiment was commanded by Lord *Charles Murray*, a younger Son of the Duke of *Athol* : He had been a Cornet of Horfe beyond Sea, and had gained a mighty good Character for his Bravery, even Temper, and graceful Deportment. Upon all the Marches, he could never be prevailed with to ride, but kept at the Head of his Regiment on foot, in his Highland Dreſs without Breeches : He would fcarce accept of a Horfe to croſs the Rivers, which his Men in that Seafon of the Year forded above mid-thigh deep in Water. This powerfully gained him the Affection of his Men ; befides, his Courage and Behaviour at a Barrier, where his Majefty's Forces made a bold Attack, was fingularly

gularly brave. When the Rebels furrender'd at *Pre-ston*, he was made a Prifoner, and try'd for a De-ferter, being a Half-pay Officer, found guilty, and condemned to be fhot ; but he pleaded that he had given his Commiffion into the Hands of a Relation before he enter'd the Rebellion: This, tho' he could not bring any Proof of at that time, yet with his Friends Intereft and his Majefty's gracious Reprieve, makes him yet enjoy his Life. When he was fenfible that he was to die, being removed to the Houfe of Mr. *Wingilby*, with the other Half-pay Officers, he kept a true Decorum fuitable to the Noblenefs of his Mind and the Bravery of his Soul, and not un-fuitable to the Circumftance he was in.

The Sixth Regiment was called *Mackintofh's* Bat-talion, a Relation of the Brigadier's, who is Chief of that Clan. He is of an ancient Family, defcend-ed from the old *Thanes* of *Fife*. His Name, in the *Irifh* or *Highland* Language, difcovers his Defcent ; for *Tofh* fignifies *Thane*, and *Mac* Son. His *Motto* to his Coat of Arms is comical as well as remark-able ; *Touch not the Cat without your Glove*; which Coat of Arms is fupported by two wild Cats, and has a Cat for the Creft. The Earl of *Weems* is de-fcended from the fame *Thane* of *Fife*; and it is dif-puted whether he or *Mackintofh* are elder, tho' cer-tain it is that the Earl of *Weems* retains a confidera-ble Part of *Thane's* Eftate. Whether *Mackintofh* be elder or younger, he left *Fife*, and made a Purchafe in the North, where his Succeffors have lived for feveral Hundreds of Years in handfome and fplen-did manner, and married the Heirefs of *Clancattun*, whereof *Mackintofh* became the Head and Chief ; which has a great many Tribes, or Followers, *viz.* the *M^c^pherfon's*, the *Farquarfon's* of *Brae Mar*, the *M^c^gilwroy's*, the *Shaw's*, *M^c^beans*, *M^c^queens*, *Smith's*, and *Clark's*, &c. which joined together, make a numerous Clan. *Mackintofh*, in all old

Grants,

Grants, Charters, Patents, and Bonds, and several Letters from Kings, yet extant, is call'd Captain of *Clancattan :* And *Buchanan* in his Annals mentions him often, *Cateneorum Dux Tribus,* in other Places ſtiles them *Gens Ferox.* They had four hundred Years conſtant Wars and Broils with the *Camerons* and *Cumings,* of old very conſiderable in *Scotland,* whom he overcame. This Tribe, for their Loyalty and good Service at the Battel of *Wardlaw,* famous in *Scots* Hiſtory, got an Eſtate call'd *Brae Lochaber,* of which he is ſtill poſſeſſed. His Family is mentioned often by *Buchanan, Boëtius, Leſley, &c.* It is to be obſerved that the *M'pherſon's,* Part of this Tribe, out of ſome diſtant View, would not on this Occaſion follow their Chieftain, but formed themſelves into a ſeparate Regiment for their Maſter the *Pretender :* Tho' they promiſed great Things, yet it is well known how they behav'd at *Sheriff-Moor ;* for they ſtood within View of the Battel, but never drew a Sword or fired a Gun ; like the *M'gregors* under *Rob. Roy,* the *Stuarts,* and *Camerons. Seaforth's* Men, except thoſe of *Kintail,* miſbehav'd. *Stuart* of *Appin's* Men, and moſt Part of the *Frazers,* were at *Perth* with *Frazerdale ;* but upon Notice of *Lovat's* Arrival in the North they deſerted the *Pretender,* and returned to the Service of King GEORGE. This Regiment came entire over the *Forth.* He is a Gentleman that few People expected in the Rebellion, having always appeared on the other Side ; but the Perſuaſions of the Brigadier prevailed with him. He is a handſome brave young Gentleman, of a very conſiderable Intereſt in his own Country ; for he can bring into the Field upon any Occaſion 1000 ſtout, hardy, and well-armed Men.

Beſides theſe Six Regiments (a Liſt of whoſe Officers are hereafter inſerted) there were a conſiderable Number call'd The Gentlemen Voluntiers, commanded by Captain *Skeen* and Captain *Mac-Lean,*

Lieutenant

Lieutenant *David Stewart*, and Enfign *John Dunbar*, formerly an Excifeman.

The *English* were not altogether fo well regulated, nor fo well armed as the *Scots*. The Troops were thefe :

Firft, the Earl of *Derwentwater's*, commanded by his Brother *Charles Radcliffe* Efq; and Captain *John Shaftoe*. That Earl being a Papift, and a Relation of the *Pretender's*, having it feems had the Opportunity of being perfonally acquainted with him, all thefe Circumftances unhappily concurr'd to draw him into this Snare, to his Deftruction, and the utter Ruin of the moft flourifhing Family in that Part of *Britain*.

It was thought, however, that this Lord did not join either fo heartily or fo premeditately in this Affair as was expected ; for there is no doubt but he might have brought far greater Numbers of Men into the Field than he did ; the great Eftate he poffeffed, the Money he could command, his Intereft among the Gentlemen, and, which is above all, his being fo well beloved as he was, could not have fail'd to have procur'd him many hundreds of Followers more than he had, if he had thought fit ; for his Concerns in the Lead-Mines in *Alftone-Moor* are very confiderable, where feveral hundreds of Men are employ'd under him, and get their Bread from him, whom, there is no doubt, he might eafily have engaged : Befides this, the Sweetnefs of his Temper and Difpofition, in which he had few Equals, had fo fecur'd him the Affection of all his Tenants, Neighbours, and Dependants, that Multitudes would have liv'd and dy'd with him : The Truth is, he was a Man form'd by Nature to be generally belov'd ; for he was of fo univerfal a Beneficence, that he feem'd to live for others. As he liv'd among his own People, there he fpent his Eftate, and continually did Offices of Kindnefs and

Good-

Good-neighbourhood to every body, as Opportunity offer'd. He kept a House of generous Hospitality and noble Entertainment, which few in that Country do, and none come up to. He was very charitable to poor and diftreffed Families on all Occafions, whether known to him or not, and whether Papift or Proteftant. His Fate will be fenfibly felt by a great many, who had no Kindnefs for the Caufe he died in, and who heartily wifh he had not forwarded his Ruin, and their Lofs, by his Indifcretion in joining in this mad as well as wicked Undertaking. If the Warrant from the Secretary's Office for apprehending him had been made a greater Secret than it was, he might have been taken, and fo his Ruin have been prevented. His Brother is young and bold, but too forward: He has a great deal of Courage, which wants a few more Years, and a better Caufe to improve it; there is room to hope he will never employ it in fuch an Adventure again.

The Second Troop was the Lord *Widdrington's*, commanded by Mr. *Thomas Errington* of *Beaufront*. This Lord's Family has been famous in former Days for many noble Atchievements recorded in Hiftory; though there is but a fmall Part of that left in this Lord, for I could never difcover any thing like Boldnefs or Bravery in him, especially after his Majefty's Forces came before *Prefton:* But of this hereafter. Mr. *Errington* that commanded his Lordfhip's Troop, is a Gentleman of a very ancient Family in *Northumberland*, a younger Brother of the Family of *Errington:* He has very good natural Parts, and had been formerly an Officer in the *French* Service, where he had got the Reputation of a good Soldier. It is believed he would not have engaged in this Rebellion, had not the many Obligations he lay under to the Earl of *Derwentwater* prevailed with him.

The

The Third Troop was commanded by Captain *John Hunter*, born upon the River *North-Tyne* in the County of *Northumberland*: He had obtain'd a Commission in the latter End of Queen *Anne*'s Reign to raise an *Independent Company*, but never receiv'd any Pay, nor lifted any Men, but when he made use of that Commission now in the Rebellion. He was famous for running uncustomed Goods out of *Scotland* into *England*. He behav'd with great Vigour and Obstinacy in the Action at *Preston*, where he took Possession of some Houses during the Attack, and galled that brave Regiment of Brigadier *Preston*'s, making a great Slaughter out of the Windows: He has since made his Escape out of *Chester*-Castle, and, as is said, got over into *Ireland*, and from thence to *France*.

The Fourth Troop was commanded by *Robert Douglass*, Brother to the Laird of *Finland* in *Scotland*: He signalized himself upon several Accounts; for going so often, so privately, and expeditiously betwixt *England* and the Earl of *Mar*. He was the Man who brought Mr. *Forster* his Commission, and the Manifestoes and Declarations of the *Pretender*. He was indefatigable in searching for Arms and Horses, a Trade, some were pleased to say, he had follow'd out of the Rebellion as well as in it. He was also very vigorous in the Action at *Preston*; where he with his Men were possessed of several Houses, and did a great deal of Harm to his Majesty's Forces from the Windows. He also made his Escape when a Prisoner either at *Leuerpool* or *Chester*.

To this Account of these two Gentlemen, I shall add a pleasant Story, which one was pleased to remark upon them. When he heard that the former was gone with his Troop back into *England*, as was then given out, to take up Quarters for the whole Army, who were to follow, and to fall upon General

tal *Carpenter* and his small and wearied Troops; he
said, *Let but* Hunter *and* Douglass *with their Men
quarter near General* Carpenter, *and in faith they'll
not leave them a Horse to mount on.* His Reason is
supposed to be, because these, with their Men, had
been pretty well versed in Horse-stealing, or at least
suspected as such: For an old Borderer was pleased
to say, when he was informed that a great many, if
not all, the loose Fellows and suspected Horse-steal-
ers were gone into the Rebellion, *It is an ill Wind
blows no body Profit*; *for now*, continued he, *I can
leave my Stable-door unlock'd, and sleep sound, since
* Luck-in-a-Bag *and the rest are gone.*

The Fifth Troop was commanded by Captain
Nicholas Wogan, an *Irish* Gentleman, but descended
from an ancient Family of that Name in *Wales*; he
joined the Rebels at their first Meeting. He is a
Gentleman of a most generous Mind, and a great
deal of Bravery, unwearied to forward the good of
his Cause: His Bravery was made known by several Instances in the Action at *Preston:* His Generosity, as well as Courage, was most remarkable
in bringing off Prisoner Captain *Preston,* of *Preston*'s
Regiment of Foot, who was mortally wounded thro'
the Body by a Bullet from the Rebels, and just at
the Point of being cut in Pieces; he hazarded
his Life among his own Men, if possible, to save
that Gentleman, though an Enemy, and was wounded in doing it: He took also a great deal of Care
of him after he had brought him off; for which it
is hoped he has obtain'd His Majesty's Pardon.
Captain *Preston* himself having, before he died,
openly acknowledg'd the Gallantry and Generosity
of the Action, and made it his earnest Request that
Mr. *Wogan* should be civilly used, for his kind Behaviour to him. Besides these Troops, there were
a great many Gentlemen Voluntiers that were not
formed into any Troop. It is likewise to be obser-

* A Nick-name to a famous Midnight Trader among Horses. ved,

ved, as is noted before, that thefe Troops were all Double-officer'd, to oblige the feveral Gentlemen that were among them.

Having thus given an Account of their Troops and Foot Regiments, which might then amount to 1400; I fhall give a farther Account of their Marches, and what happened in the Way, till I bring them to the Place of Action. Having continued in *Kelfo* fo long as they did, which was from *Saturday* the 22d, to *Thurfday* the 27th of *October*, it gave general *Carpenter*, who, as is faid, was fent down to purfue them, the Advantage of time to advance by the eafier Marches, and to obferve their Motions: That General, with the Forces under his Command, *viz. Hotham's* Regiment of Foot, *Cobham's, Molefworth's*, and *Churchill's* Dragoons, had march'd from *Newcaftle*, and lay now at *Wooller* the 27th, intending to face *Kelfo* the next Day; of which Lord *Kenmure*, who, as I faid, commanded the Troops while on the *Scots*-Side of *Twede*, having Notice, called a Council of War, wherein it was ferioufly confidered what Courfe they fhould take. And here again my Lord *Wintoun*, as is obferv'd already, prefs'd them earneftly to march away into the Weft of *Scotland*; but the *Englifh* oppofed, and prevailed againft that wifer Opinion: Then it was propofed to pafs the *Twede*, and attack the King's Troops, taking the Advantage of the Weaknefs and Wearinefs of General *Carpenter's* Men, *who were indeed extremely fatigued, and were not above 500 Men in Number, whereof two Regiments of Dragoons were new raifed, and had never feen any Service.* This alfo was Soldier-like Advice, and which, if they had agreed to, in all Probability they might have worfted them, confidering how they were fatigued, and not half the Number the Rebels were. But there was a Fate attended all their Councils, for they could never agree to any one thing that tended to their

Advantage.

Advantage. This Defign failing, they decamped from *Kelfo*, and taking a little to the Right, marched to *Jedburgh*. Upon this March they were all alarmed; by miftaking a Party of their own Men for fome of General *Carpenter*'s Forces: The Particulars whereof were thus; A Party of their own Men appearing at a diftance, Captain *Nicholas Wogan* being defirous to know who they were, went off towards the River's fide which parted them, and left me to ftand at a convenient diftance from him, whilft he rid up to make a Difcovery; if they proved Enemies, he was to fire a Piftol, if Friends, he was to tofs up his Hat. Juft at the fame time, fome of thefe fufpected Enemies wanting to know who he was, galloping towards him, he miftook them, and fired a Piftol, fo the Alarm was taken; but the Diforder was not great, the Matter being foon difcovererd. Then they continued their March to *Jedburgh*: The Horfe having entred that Town, word was brought them again, that General *Carpenter* had fallen upon the Foot, who had not as yet reach'd the Town. This put them into the utmoft Confternation: However, not being difcouraged fo as to abandon their Fellows, they all mounted their Horfes, and marched out to relieve their Friends. I here had an Opportunity to look into the Faces and Countenances of moft of the remarkable Leaders, when they formed themfelves under the Cover of a Hill. I did then behold a great Palenefs in fome Faces, and as much Fire and Refolution in others. Whether of thefe Signs were then the true Tokens of Bravery, I would not then determine; but afterwards at *Prefton*, when the Alarm was not falfe, I ever believed that generally the fiery Eye and ftern Look were the Men of beft Courage; but we had moft of thefe Men out of Danger at *Prefton*, and the former moft active. This Miftake alfo was occafioned by another Party of their own Men, who had taken a dif-

ferent

ferent Rout: And this being likewife difcovered, they returned all to their Quarters, according to the *Scots* Proverb, *Worfe frighted than hurt*. They ftaid in this Town till *Saturday* the 29th. And here it being apparent that an Opportunity offering to get the Start of General *Carpenter*, who would be three Days March behind, and the *Englifh* Gentlemen earneftly preffing, it was refolv'd, in an ill hour for them, to crofs the Mountains, and march for *England*: Accordingly Captain *Hunter*, who was well acquainted with the Country, was order'd with his Troops to go into *North-Tynedale*, and there provide Quarters for them who would follow. But here began a Mutiny, the Highlanders could not be perfuaded to crofs the Borders; and tho' many Perfuafions were ufed with them, would not ftir a foot: Hereupon the firft Refolution was altered, and Orders were fent after Captain *Hunter* to countermand him. In this Town the Magiftrates had Orders to furnifh the Highlanders with a Quantity of Oatmeal, which they did, by obliging every Houfekeeper to pay a certain Quantity according to his Ability. They were joined in this Town by Mr. *Ainfley* of *Blackhill*, with fome others. From hence they marched to *Hawick*, a fmall poor Market-Town belonging to the Dutchefs of *Bucclugh*, at whofe Houfe the *Englifh* Lords, with their Relations, and Mr. *Forfter*, took up their Quarters. Upon this March to *Hawick*, the Highlanders fuppofing ftill that the March for *England* was refolv'd on, were difgufted, feparated themfelves, and went to the Top of a rifing Ground, there refted their Arms, and declared that they would fight if they would lead them on to the Enemy, but they would not go to *England*; adhering to the Lord *Wintoun's* Advice, that they would go through the Weft of *Scotland*, join the Clans there, and either crofs the *Forth* fome Miles above *Stirling*, or fend word to

the

the Earl of *Mar* that they would fall upon the Duke of *Argyle*'s Rear, whilst he fell on his Front, his Number being then very small. Whilst this Humour lasted among them, they would allow none to come and speak with them but the Earl of *Wintoun*, who had tutor'd them in this Project; assuring them, that if they went for *England*, they would be all cut in pieces, or taken and sold for Slaves; one part of which has proved too true. This Breach held a great while; however, at last they were brought to this, tho' not till after two Hours Debate, that they would keep together as long as they staid in *Scotland*; but upon any Motion of going for *England*, they would return back: So they continued their March to *Hawick*, where they were sore straitned for Quarters. Here the Highlanders, for they always had the Guard, and did all the Duty after they join'd the Horse, discovered from their advanc'd Guards a Party of Horse, who were Patroling in their Front, took them for Enemies, and gave the Alarm at Midnight; so all run immediately to Arms: The Moon gave light, and the Night proved very clear; so the whole Body formed themselves in very good Order to oppose any Attack that should be made. But in the end this proved another false Alarm; so they all returned to their Quarters. I have heard that this Alarm was designed to try the Highlanders, and to see how they would behave, and whether they would stand chearfully to their Arms if an Enemy appear'd. Mr. *Forster* at this Place sent for Mr. *Buxton*, and told him he had a mind to receive the Sacrament, and ordered him to provide and attend him at his Chamber next Morning before they marched, and to bring Mr. *Patten* along with him; so both of them obeyed and officiated. When the Service was over, he said, *The* Roman *Catholicks have had the Sacrament administred by a Priest; when Opportunity serves,*

we

we will have all the Protestants ordered to Communicate. Next Morning being *Sunday*, they made their March to *Langholme*, another small Market-Town belonging to the Dutchess of *Bucclugh* : From hence there was a strong Detachment of Horse sent in the Night for *Achilficban*, with Orders to go and block up *Dumfries*, till they could come up and attack it. This Town of *Dumfries* is a very rich Place, and situate very commodiously upon the Mouth of a navigable River on the *Irish* Sea; and maintains a considerable Trade with *England* and the West of *Scotland*; and had they been settled in their Resolutions, they might very easily have made themselves Masters of that Town, there being no regular Forces in it, but some Train-bands, Militia, and Townsmen, which would not have been able to hold out, nor any Fortifications to have assisted them in the Defence of it. Here also they might have furnished themselves with Arms, Money, and Ammunition, which were much wanted, and open'd a Passage to *Glasgow*, one of the best Towns in *Scotland*, or for *England* also if they thought fit. Here also they might have join'd the Highland Clans from the West, besides a great many Country Gentlemen, who on such an Appearance, would have come in to them ; so that they might soon have formed a considerable Army : Also here they might have receiv'd Succours from *France* and from *Ireland*, no Men of War being in all those Seas at that Time. In a word, nothing could be a greater Token of a compleat Infatuation, that Heaven confounded all their Devices, and that their Destruction was to be of their own working, than their omitting such an Opportunity of fixing themselves past the Possibility of being attack'd. They were also assured, that in this City there were a great many Arms in the Talbooth ready for all Occasions, in good Order, and a good Quantity of Gunpowder up in the

E   Tron

Tron Steeple; all which would have been their own. That as to the Duke of *Argyle*, he was in no Condition to have hurt them; but, on the contrary, would fcarce have thought himfelf fafe in *Stirling*, his Troops being not above 2000 Men; for he had not then been reinforced by the Forces from *Ireland*, nor the *Dutch* from *England*. But all thefe Arguments were in vain, the *Englifh* Gentlemen were pofitive for an Attempt upon their own Country, pretending to have Letters from their Friends in *Lancafhire*, inviting them thither, and affuring them that there would be a general Infurrection upon their appearing; that 20000 Men would immediately join them; and promifing them Mountains which they were to perform by Molehills. Whether they had any fuch Expreffes or no, is to this Day a Queftion; but they affirm'd it to their Army, and urged the Advantages of a fpeedy March into *England* with fuch Vehemence, that they turn'd the Scale, and fent an Exprefs after the Party of Horfe they had order'd to *Achilfichan*, for them to return and meet them at *Langtoun* in *Cumberland*. So the Defign of continuing in *Scotland* was quitted. But the Highlanders, whether dealt with underhand by the Earl of *Wintoun*, or whether being convinced of the Advantages they were going to throw away, and the Uncertainties they were bringing upon themfelves, halted a fecond time, and would march no farther. It is true, they did again prevail with their Leaders to march, making great Promifes, and giving Money to the Men: But many of the Men were ftill pofitive, and that to fuch an Extremity, that they feparated, and about 500 of them went off in Bodies, chufing rather, as they faid, to furrender themfelves Prifoners, than to go forward to certain Deftruction. All imaginable Means were ufed to have prevented this Defertion, but nothing could prevail on thefe Men to alter their Refolutions,

lutions, neither fair Promifes, nor any Arguments; fo they went their ways in Parties over the Tops of the Mountains; the Earl of *Wintoun* went off likewife with good part of his Troop, being very much diffatisfy'd at the Meafures, and declaring that they were taking the way to ruin themfelves: However, in little time he return'd and join'd the Body, tho' not at all fatisfied with their Proceedings; and afterwards was never called to any Council of War, which incenfed him mightily againft the reft of the Lords and commanding Officers, And in fhort, he was flighted, having often no Quarters provided for him, and at other times very bad ones, not fit for a Nobleman of his Family; yet being in for it, he refolved to go forwards, and diverted himfelf with any Company, telling many pleafant Stories of his Travels, and his living unknown and obfcurely with a Blackfmith in *France*, whom he ferved fome Years as a Bellows-blower and Under-Servant, till he was acquainted with the Death of his Father, and that his Tutor had given it out that he was dead: Upon which he refolved to return home; and when there met with a cold Reception. He was very curious in working in feveral Handicraft Matters, and had made good Proficiency in them, witnefs the nice way he had found to cut afunder one of the Iron Bars in his Window in the *Tower*, by fome fmall Inftrument fcarce perceivable. They left the fmall Pieces of Cannon which they had brought from *Kelfo* at *Langholm*, having nailed them up and made them unfit for Service; then they marched for that Night to *Longtoun*, which is within feven Miles of *Carlifle*, and was a very long and fatiguing March. Here they had Intelligence that Brigadier *Stanwix*, with a Party of Horfe from *Carlifle*, had been there that Day to get Intelligence of their Numbers and Motions; but that upon notice of their coming towards him,

he

he had retired to his Garifon, which then confifted
of but a very few Men, having made Mr. *Graham*
of *Inchbrachy* a Prifoner. This Night the Party
ordered to *Achilfichan*, returned and join'd us, fore
fatigued with their long and difmal March. Next
Day they entred *England*, and marched to *Brampton*, a fmall Market-Town, and the fecond they
came to on the *Englifh* fide, belonging to the Earl
of *Carlifle*. Here nothing happened but proclaiming
the *Pretender*, and taking up the Publick Money,
viz. the Excife upon Malt and Ale. Here Mr.
Forfter opened his Commiffion to act as General in
England, which had been brought him from the
Earl of *Mar* by Mr. *Douglafs* aforenam'd: And
from this Day the Highlanders had Sixpence a
Head *per* Day paid them to keep them in good
Order and under Command. Here alfo Mr. *Forfter*
and Lord *Kenmure* had the following Letters fent
them from the Earl of *Mar*, dated at *Perth*, *October* 21. The Duplicates of thefe Letters were it
feems intercepted, being thofe which came by Land,
and were made publick by the Government; but
thefe being brought by Sea, and landed near *Blith*,
came fafe to their Hands.

My Lord,

' I Long extremely to hear from you, you may
' be fure, fince I have not had the leaft Ac-
' counts almoft of your Motions fince I fent the
' Detachment over. I hope all is pretty right
' again, but it was an unlucky Miftake in Briga-
' dier *Metofh*, in marching from *Haddingtoun* to
' *Leith*. I cannot but fay though, that it was odd
' your Lordfhip fent no Orders or Intelligence to
' him, when they had Reafon to expect that Party's
' coming over every Day. His Retreat he made
' from *Leith*, and now from *Seaton*, with the help
' of the Movement I made from this, makes fome
' ' Amends

‘ Amends for that Miſtake ; and I hope that Party
‘ of Men with him will be of great Uſe to you
‘ and the Cauſe. I wiſh you may find a Way of
‘ ſending the incloſed to Mr. *Forreſter*, which I
‘ leave open for your Lordſhip to read ; and I
‘ have little further to ſay to you, than what you
‘ will find in it. I know ſo little of the Situation
‘ of your Affairs, that I muſt leave to yourſelf
‘ what is fit for you to do, as will moſt conduce
‘ to the Service, and I know you will take good
‘ Advice.

‘ My humble Service to all Friends with you,
‘ particularly Brigadier *Metoſh*; Lord *Nairn*, Lord
‘ *Charles Murray* and *Metoſh*, who, I hope, are
‘ joined you long e're now ; and indeed they all
‘ deſerve Praiſe for their gallant Behaviour. I muſt
‘ not forget *Kinackin*, who, I hear, ſpoke ſo reſo-
‘ lutely to the Duke of *Argyle* from the Citadel ;
‘ and I hope *Inercall*, and all my Men with him,
‘ are well ; and their Countrymen long to be at
‘ them, which I hope they and we all ſhall ſoon.
‘ I have ſent another Copy of the incloſed to Mr.
‘ *Forreſter* by Sea, ſo it will be hard if none of
‘ them come to his Hands.

‘ I know your Lordſhip will endeavour to let
‘ me hear from you as ſoon as poſſible, which I
‘ long impatiently for, and I hope you will find a
‘ Way of ſending it ſafe. In one of my former,
‘ either to your Lordſhip, or to ſome body to ſhew
‘ you, I told that a part of the Army would be
‘ about *Dumbartoun* ; but now I beg you would
‘ not rely upon that, for, till I hear from General
‘ *Gordon*, I am uncertain if they hold that Way.
‘ I have ſent your Lordſhip a Copy of my Com-
‘ miſſion, which perhaps you have not ſeen before.
‘ I have named the General Officers, and your
‘ Lordſhip has the Rank of Brigadier, of the
‘ Horſe.

‘ I am

'I am told the Earl of *Wintoun* has been very ufe-
'ful to our Men we fent over. I fuppofe he is now
'with your Lordſhip, and I beg you may make
'my Compliment to his Lordſhip, and I hope the
'King will foon thank him himſelf.

'I will trouble your Lordſhip no farther now,
'but all Succeſs attend you, and may we foon have
'a merry Meeting. I am, with all Refpect,

My Lord,

Your moft obedient and

moft humble Servant,

MAR.

From the Camp at *Perth,*
  October 21, 1715.

From the Camp at Perth, Oct. 21. 1715.

S I R,

'I Wrote to you of the 17th from *Auchterarder,*
'which I hope you got. I marched the fame
'Night, the Horfe to *Dumblain,* within four Miles
'of *Stirling,* and the Foot fome Miles fhort of that
'Place. Next Morning I had certain Intelligence
'of the Duke of *Argyle's* returning from *Edinburgh*
'with moft of the Troops he had carried there,
'and was on their March towards *Stirling*: I alfo
'had an Account of *Evans's* Regiment landed in
'the Weft of *Scotland* from *Ireland,* and were on
'their Way to *Stirling.* I had come away from
'*Perth* before our Provifions were ready to go
'with us, and I found all the Country about *Stir-*
'*ling,* where we were to pafs *Forth,* was intirely
'exhaufted by the Enemy, fo there was nothing
'for

' for us to subfift on there. I had no Account from'
' General *Gordon*, as I expected ; and the foonest I
' could expect him at the Heads of *Forth*, was two
' Days after that, and I could not think of paffing
' *Forth* till I was join'd by him. Under thefe Dif-
' ficulties, and having got one of the Things I de-
' figned by my March, *the Duke of* Argyle*'s with-*
' *drawing from our Friends in* Lothian, I thought it
' fit to march back to *Auchterarder*, which was a
' better Quarter, tho' not a good one neither. Next
' Morning I got Intelligence of the Duke of *Ar-*
' *gyle's* being come to *Stirling* the Night before, and
' that he had fent Exprefs upon Exprefs to *Evans's*
' Dragoons to haften up. I had a Letter alfo, that
' Morning from General *Gordon*, telling me that
' fome Things had kept him up longer than he ex-
' pected ; that it would be that Day e'er he could
' be at *Inverary* ; and that he could not poffibly
' join me this Week : Upon this I thought it better
' to return here, which is a good Quarter, and
' wait his coming up, and the Lord *Seaforth's*,
' than continue at *Auchterarder*, fince it would not
' a bit retard my paffing the *Forth* when I fhould
' be in a Condition to do it ; and in the mean
' time I could be getting Provifions ready to carry
' along with me in my March, which, as I have
' told, are abfolutely neceffary about the Heads of
' *Forth* : So I came Home laft Night.
' I very much regret my being oblig'd to this,
' for many Reafons, particularly becaufe of its keep-
' ing me fo much the longer from joining you ;
' but you eafily fee it was not in my Power to help
' it. However, I hope my Stay here will be very
' fhort, and you may depend upon its being no longer
' than it neceffarily muft. The Paffage over the *Forth*
' is now fo extremely difficult that it's fcarce pof-
' fible to fend any Letters that Way ; and within
' thefe two Days there were two Boats coming

' over

‘ over with Letters to me, that were so hard pur-’
‘ fued, that they were obliged to throw the Letters’
‘ into the Sea; so that I know very little of our’
‘ Friends on that side, and less of you, which is’
‘ no small Loss to me. I heard to Day, by word’
‘ of Mouth, that the Detachment I sent over are’
‘ marched and joined our Friends in the South of
‘ *Scotland*, so I hope they may be yet useful, but’
‘ I hope you know more of them than I do. I’
‘ have now writ to Lord *Kenmure*, but it is ten to
‘ one if it comes to his Hands. I know not what’
‘ he is doing, where he is, or what Way he in-’
‘ tends to dispose of his People; whether he is to
‘ march into *England*, or towards *Stirling*, to wait
‘ my passing *Forth*; and in the Ignorance I am in
‘ of your Affairs besouth the River, I scarce know’
‘ what to advise him. If you be in need of his
‘ Assistance in *England*, I doubt not but you have
‘ called him there; but if not, certainly his being
‘ in the Rear of the Enemy, when I pass *Forth*;
‘ or now that the Duke of *Argyle* is reinforced;
‘ should he march towards me before I am, it would
‘ be of great Service. I am forced in a great mea-
‘ sure to leave it to himself, to do as he finds most
‘ expedient.

‘ I am afraid the Duke of *Ormond* is not as yet
‘ come to *England*, else I should have had the Cer-
‘ tainty of it, one way or other, before now. I
‘ cannot conceive what detains him nor the King
‘ from coming here; however, I am sure it is none
‘ of their Fault, and I hope they will both surprize
‘ us agreeably very soon.

‘ I believe I told you in my last, of the Lord
‘ *Strathmore* and 200 of the Detachment that were
‘ going over *Forth*, and drove into the Island
‘ of *May* by three Men of War, who being got
‘ safe ashore on this Side, are now joined us again.
‘ There were but two of all the Boats taken; and
‘ I hear,

' I hear, fome of the Men that were in them, who
' were made Prifoners in *Leith*, were reliev'd by
' our Men, when they came there, but that their
' Officers were fent to *Edinburgh* Caftle; fo I
' want fome Reprifals for them, which I hope to
' have e'er long.

' Tho' *Metofh* Brigadier's Miftake in going to
' *Leith* was like to be unlucky to us and them, yet
' it has given the Duke of *Argyle* no little Trouble;
' and our March obliging him to let them flip, has,
' I am apt to believe, vex'd him.

' I beg you will find fome Way to let me hear
' from you. Ever fince my Detachments were in
' *Fyfe*, all the Men of War that cruifed on the
' North Coaft, betwixt *Peterhead* and the *Firth*,
' have been in the *Firth*, and, I believe, will con-
' tinue there, to prevent my fending more over that
' Way: So all that Coaft is clear, which I wifh to
' God the King knew; and you may eafily fend a
' Boat here any-where, with Letters from *England.*
' I hear there is one of the Regiments of Foot from
' *Ireland* come to *Stirling*.

' When you write to me, if by Sea, pray fend
' me fome News-Papers, that I may know what
' the World is doing, for we know little of it here
' thefe eight Days. Succefs attend you; and I am,
' with all Truth and Efteem,

Sir,

Your moft obedient

humble Servant,

M A R.

Direóted thus,
To Mr. *Forrefter* with the King's Forces in
Northumberlard.

They

They halted one Night at *Brampton*, to refreſh the Men after their hard Marches, having march'd above 100 Miles in five Days. The next Day they advanced towards *Penrith* : They expected to have met with ſome Friends here to join them ; for it was reported that Mr. *Dacre* of *Abbeylanner-Coaſt*, a Papiſt, had promiſed to raiſe 40 Men ; but he was taken with a fortunate Fever, which hindred him of his Deſign, and prevented him and his Family from Ruin: He died ſince ; his Name, which was very ancient, is now extinct in that Eſtate. As they drew near *Penrith*, they had notice that the Sheriff, with the *Poſſe Comitatus*, were got together, with the Lord *Lonſdale*, and the Biſhop of *Carliſle*, to the Number of 14,000 Men, who reſolv'd to ſtand and oppoſe their penetrating farther into *England*. The firſt part of this was very true, *viz.* That the *Poſſe* was drawn together, nor was their Number much leſs. But they gave the Rebel Army no occaſion to try, whether they would ſtand or no ; for as ſoon as a Party, who they ſent but for Diſcovery, had ſeen ſome of our Men coming out of a Lane by the Side of a Wood, and draw up upon a Common or Moor in Order, and then advance, and that they had carried an Account of this to their main Body, they broke up their Camp in the utmoſt Confuſion, ſhifting every one for themſelves as well as they could, as is generally the Caſe of an arm'd, but undiſciplin'd Multitude.

The Lord *Lonſdale*, whoſe Predeceſſors have been famous for their Loyalty as well as Antiquity, had had ſtill conſiderable Intereſt in that Country. This Nobleman, tho' young, has very valuable and endearing Accompliſhments, and no ſmall ſhare of Courage ; tho' ſome were pleaſed to reflect upon him for his Retreat from *Penrith* ; but thoſe that know how naked and unprepar'd that Multitude were of all warlike Arms and Stores, juſtly commend

mend his wife Conduct, to retreat and prevent the
Effufion of fo much Blood and innocent Lives,
which would have been of bad Confequence, and
no Service to his Mafter's Intereft, which, I am affured of, he prefers before his own Life, or the Prefervation thereof. He retired no farther than *Appleby*
Caftle that Night, but 10 Miles from the Rebels
Quarters, and lefs from a Detachment advanced to
his own Houfe ; fo if Fear or Cowardice had poffefs'd him, as one of *Appleby* hinted to the Rebel
Lords and *Forfter*, he might have, with a good
Retinue well mounted, with eafe gone over *Stone-
more* into *Yorkfhire :* But the brighteft Characters
are not befpattered or fullied with the faufty Breath
of Malice.

Altho' their coming together was very little to
the Purpofe, yet, as the Rebels were greatly animated
by their fudden and diforderly feparating over the
whole Country, the Horfe who were very near
them, made fome Booty among them, taking feveral Horfes, and a great many Arms. The whole
Body of the Rebels being now come up, made a
Halt upon the Moor near the Town, and drew up
in Order of Battle, that they might enter the Town
in a good Figure. Here Mr. *Patten*, being acquainted with the Country, and having formerly
been Curate of that Town, was ordered out with a
Party of Horfe to intercept the Bifhop of *Carlifle*,
of whom, it feems, they had fome Intelligence.
This Lord is known to be not only a compleat
Scholar in all manner of Learning, but likewife a
Man of Courage and brave Soul. I believe, if
there had happened any Conteft betwixt the two Parties, he would have been willing to have taken a
Share in the hotteft Part of the Difpute. He was
returning to his Seat of *Rofe-Caftle* when Mr. *Patten* was fent after him. But Mr. *Forfter*, upon o-
ther Information, fent an Exprefs after him, and
counter-

countermanded that Order, and directed him to march forwards quite through the Town of *Penrith* to *Emont-Bridge*; and there he had Orders to beset a House where he was told he should find his Brother-in-Law, Mr. *Johnston*, Collector of the Salt-Tax, whom he was ordered to make Prisoner, and to bring him, with his Books, Papers, and what Money he had belonging to the Government, to the Army: But Mr. *Johnston* gave them the slip, and had made his Escape before Mr. *Patten* came up with his Party. However, Mr. *Patten*, upon this little Expedition, took several of the *Posse Comitatus* above-named Prisoners, and committed them to the Guard, taking their Arms from them. Of all this Number of People, which, as is said, were got together upon the Moor by *Penrith*, there were none received any hurt, but one Man that was shot through the Arm; for Orders were given not to fire upon them, unless they resisted, which they were wiser than to do. In this Town, which is the richest and most plentiful of that part of the Country, they refreshed themselves very comfortably; tho' the Inhabitants cannot charge them with any Rudeness, Violence, or Plunder in the least. The *Pretender* was proclaimed, and the Excise and other publick Money was taken up, as had been the Usage all along, and all the Arms they could get were seiz'd. Tho' this Town is very Loyal, yet still there were some that informed where they might be furnished, inasmuch, that they were acquained where Mr. *John Pattefon*, an Attorney, had hid some Arms of his own, and others belonging to Sir *Christopher Musgrave* of *Edenhall*. The chief People of this Town, with Mr. *Whelpdale*, one of his Majesty's Justices of the Peace, agreed, when they heard of the Rebels Advance, wisely to consult their own Interest and Safety, by shewing all manner of Civility to their Enemies; Prudence and Necessity obliging
them

them to act that Part, which Force conftrain'd them unwillingly to comply with. In this Town there is a *Preſbyterian* Meeting-Houſe, which ſome deſired Leave or Encouragement from Mr. *Forſter* to pull down, or burn: But he would not condeſcend thereto, adding, *That he was to gain by Clemency, and not by Cruelty.* There was one *Oſſington*, formerly an Excife-man, that performed both theſe Offices whilft in *England*; and what Money he receiv'd, he paid to Mr. *William Tunſtall*, who was conftituted their Pay-Maſter General. While they continued here, they began to look into the Country a little, as well for their Friends, as to furniſh themſelves with Arms and Horſes; for of the latter they were in great Want: And firſt, there was a Party ſent to *Lowther-Hall*, the Seat of the Viſcount *Lonſdale*, three Miles diftant from *Penrith* in the County of *Weſtmoreland*, to ſee for his Lordſhip, if he could have been found, and to ſearch for Arms, but they found neither. They ftay'd all Night at the Houſe, where, to do them Juſtice, they behav'd very civilly, though it was otherwiſe reported; particularly, I have heard it was complained of, that the Rebels were rude, in defacing ſome Statues, and ſpoiling the Gardens and Trees; but nothing is more falſe, for they were commanded by Colonel *Oxburgh* an old Soldier, and a Man whoſe generous Temper would not allow him to do any thing ſo baſe. Having ftay'd at *Penrith* that Night, and, as is ſaid, refreſh'd themſelves very well, the next Day they march'd for *Appleby*. It is to be obſerv'd, that there were none of any account had yet join'd them on this March; for all the Papifts on that Side the Country were ſecur'd beforehand in the Caftle of *Carliſle*, viz. Mr. *Howard* of *Corbee*-Caftle, a Papift, Mr. *Warwick* of *Warwick*-Hall, a Papift, converted to that Church ſome Years ago, and lately made Steward to a Lord in the *North*; which occaſioned a merry Rogue to ſay,

when

when he saw this Gentleman proclaiming a Fair at the Head of the Tenants, that it was a monstruous Sight, to see a Popish Head upon an *English* Body; and *James Graham* of *Inchbracky*, a Gentleman of *Scotland*, who had fled his Country for killing the Lord *Rollo*'s Brother. He was a Relation to the Lord *Nairn*; and therefore there was a Proposal sent to Brigadier *Stanwix*, Deputy-Governor of *Carlisle*, a very good Soldier, to acquaint him, That if he would discharge this Gentleman out of the Castle, that then Mr. *Wyburgh*, one of the Militia Officers taken by the Rebels, should be set at Liberty; but the Brigadier return'd an Answer, That he would hear no Terms from Rebels, &c. Besides these, there was Henry *Curwen*, Esq; of *Workington*, a Gentleman of a plentiful Estate in that Country, &c. secured himself likewise in the Castle of *Carlisle*. Now, instead of increasing, the Rebels Number decreased; for Mr. *Aynsly* who joined them at *Jedburgh*, not liking the Prospect of their Affairs, nor their Management, deserted them, and several with him. Here Mr. *Patten* was in great Danger of being taken by the Sheriff of the County; and had he stay'd a quarter of an Hour longer than he did, he had certainly fallen into their Hands; for being engag'd with some Acquaintance who stopt him some time after his Rebel Friends were march'd, the Sheriff, who had got notice of him, spar'd no Diligence to have taken him, but came a little too late. On the March to *Appleby*, the Highlanders, who are exceeding good Marksmen, shot several Rabbets, and two or three Deer in *Whinfield*-Park, very well stock'd with both, belonging to the Earl of *Thanet*. Mr. *John Hall*, who was not much respected by the Chief of the Rebels, stay'd behind them at Mr. *Hall*'s of *Temple-Sowerby*, which gave suspicion to some to believe that he was gone off. Whatever were his Reasons for this, and the like, next Night, whilst

at

at *Appleby*, none knows ; for he went off some Miles
to a Clergyman's House in the Commission for the
Peace, who might have secur'd him, so that the
Rebels would not have known thereof: Yet as all
his Plea at his Trial was, "That he was willing to
"make his Escape, but was so narrowly look'd to,
"that he never could get an Opportunity," may be
a standing Evidence, that he valu'd not what he said.
A short Abstract of his Life shall be added among
the List of the rest of the Gentlemen at the End
of the *First Part.*

Being come to *Appleby* the 3d of *November*, they
halted again, and stay'd there till the 5th. This is
an ancient Corporation, and the head Town of the
County of *Westmoreland*: The Assizes are held here.
It was formerly a famous *Roman* Station. Here,
during their Stay, nothing material happen'd but as
usual, Proclaiming the *Pretender*, and taking up
the Publick Money. Here taking possession of the
Church, Mr. *Patten* had Orders to read Prayers,
if the Parson or Curate refused ; but they were not
very backward as to the thing itself, though they
thought it their safest way modestly to excuse themselves, testifying, however, their Satisfaction, in
giving Orders for the Bells to ring, and having all
things made ready for the Service ; nor did the Parson and his Curate scruple to grace the Assembly
with their Presence, or to join in the Prayers for
the *Pretender* ; which encourag'd the Highlanders to
believe the High-church Party were entirely theirs,
and would join in a little time. Whilst here, they
made Mr. *Thomas Wyburgh*, a Captain of the Train-
Bands, a Prisoner, and carry'd him, Mr. *Senhouse*,
and some others suspected as Spies, to *Preston*, and
there they continued as such till his Majesty's Forces
set them at Liberty. They kept Mr. *Baines* some
time a Prisoner in the *Mute-Hall*, being inform'd
against by some in the Town, for knowing where
the

the Excife-Money was lodg'd, and obnoxious to the Malice of the Tory Party, as Bailiff to the Earl of *Wharton*: He was afterwards difcharg'd. Whilft at this Place, they might have made themfelves Mafters of two Companies of Invalids then upon their Rout to *Carlifle*, and were fore fatigued with a long March in that Seafon of the Year, whofe Arms would have been of fingular Ufe to the Rebels; though thefe *Chelfea-Collegians* were old and well difciplin'd, and refolv'd to make a vigorous Defence, if affaulted, by forming themfelves into a hollow Square, under the Conduct of undaunted Officers, whom they affured they would live and die by. They were within three Miles of the whole Rebel Army, the latter knowing nothing of them, whofe Horfe and fuperior Numbers would certainly have over-power'd them.

On the 5th they fet out for *Kendal* a Town of very good Trade. Here they remain'd all Night; and the next Morning, being *Sunday* the 6th, they fet forward for *Kirbylonfdale* a fmall Market-town in *Weftmoreland*. This Day's March was fhort, fo they came early to their Quarters, and had time to proclaim the *Pretender*, and in the Afternoon to go to Church, where Mr. *Patten* read Prayers, the Parfon of the Place abfconding. There was one Mr. *Guin*, who went into the Churches in their Way, and fcratched out His Majefty King GEORGE's Name, and placed the *Pretender*'s fo nicely, that it refembled Print very much, and the Alteration could fcarce be perceiv'd. In all the March to this Town, which is the laft in *Weftmoreland*, there were none joined them but one Mr. *John Dalfton*, and another Gentleman from *Richmond*, though we had now march'd through two very populous Counties; but here Friends began to appear, for fome *Lancafhire* Papifts with their Servants came and join'd them. Next Day, being the 7th of *November*, they march'd to *Lancaster*, a Town of very good Trade, very pleasantly seated, and which, had they thought fit to have held it, might easily have been made strong enough to have made a Stand for them ; and having an old Castle for their Arms, Stores, and Provisions, and a Sea Port to have received Succours, it might have been very useful to them ; but our Infatuations were not yet over.

In the March from *Kendal* to *Lancaster*, the whole Army drew up upon a Hill, and lay some time upon their Arms, to rest the Men. During which time, Mr. *Charles Widdrington*, second Brother to the Lord *Widdrington*, came from *Lancashire*, whither he was sent some Days before the Rebels advanc'd, to acquaint the Gentlemen of that County with their marching that way ; he return'd with the News of their Chearfulness, and Intention to join them with all their Interest, and that the *Pretender* was that Day proclaim'd at *Manchester*, where the Town's-People had got Arms to furnish a Troop of Fifty Men at their sole Charge, besides other Voluntiers. This rouzed the Spirits of the Highlanders, and animated them exceedingly ; nor was it more than needed, for they had often complain'd before, that all the Pretences of Numbers to join were come to little, and that they should soon be surrounded by numerous Forces. But on this News they pluck'd up their Hearts, gave three Huzza's, and then continu'd their March into *Lancaster*. Colonel *Chartres*, and another Officer who was then in the Town, would have blown up the Bridge which leads into the Place, to hinder us from entring ; but the People of the Town shewing their Unwillingness, and especially because, as they said, it would no wise hinder our Entrance into the Place, seeing the River at Low-water was passable by Foot or Horse, and that we could easily find Boats to pass into the Town ; and that as it would be a vast

F Charge

Charge to rebuild the Bridge so strong and fine as before, so it would be a Loss to no manner of End. Then these two Gentlemen finding a Quantity of Powder in some Merchants Hands, order'd it to be thrown into a Draw-well in the Market-place, left it should fall into our Hands.

In this Town Sir *Henry Haughton*, Member of Parliament for *Preston*, a Gentleman of known good Intentions and steddy Loyalty to the Protestant Succession, used his best Endeavours to have all Things put out of the way that might be serviceable to the Rebels. In the River which runs by *Lanca-ster* there lay a Ship of about 500 Tons, belonging to Mr. *Hisham* of *London*, and Mr. *Lawson* an eminent Quaker in Town, on board of which there were six Pieces of Cannon, some Blunderbusses, and small Arms : Sir *Henry* thought it convenient that these Arms should be brought from the Ship, and made use of for his Majesty's Service (having then a Resolution to defend the Bridge ;) to this End he sent for *Lawson*, and requested that the Cannon might be brought from the Ship, then five Miles distant from the Town, to be used as aforesaid ; which he positively refused : But being still pressed to grant that Demand, he at last came to this Resolution, That he would by no means part with the Cannon, unless Sir *Henry Haughton* would give him a Bond of 10000 Pounds to insure the Ship against any Damages she might sustain from the Rebels, who, he said, would not forbear to burn the Ship and Cargo, upon the least Notice that he had parted with the Cannon to oppose them. But it is more probable that the Ship would have been rifled or destroy'd if Sir *Henry* had given his Bond, he being very obnoxious to the Rage of the Rebels for his Vigilance and Care. Upon this Refusal, Sir *Henry* desired that the Mayor, Aldermen, and Common-Council

Council might meet in the Afternoon, to confult about this important Affair; which they did accordingly. Being met, it was then propofed by Sir *Henry Haughton*, *Charles Rigby* Efq; and *Francis Chartres* Efq; who were alfo zealous for his Majefty's Intereft, that the Cannon on board the Veffel then in the River fhould be deliver'd for his Majefty's Service: Which was refufed. But thefe three Gentlemen being in the Commiffion for the Peace, produced a Warrant ready drawn up for feizing the Cargo and Arms on board the Veffel above-mention'd. *Lawfon* finding this to prefs hard, acquiefced. At this time there were fome Dragoons in *Prefton*, who were advifed to advance to *Lancafter*; but having no Orders for that March, continued there till they were order'd to *Wigan*. Upon this, Sir *Henry Haughton* having Intelligence that the Rebels were within 16 Miles of him, he went from *Lancafter* with 600 Militia, and with them retired to *Prefton*. Before he left *Lancafter*, finding that the Cannon already mention'd could be of no Ufe to him, having not a fufficient Number of Men to cover that Town, he order'd Mr. *Lawfon* to fall down the River with his Veffel, out of the reach of the Rebels, fo that his Cannon might not fall into their Hands. Which Mr. *Lawfon* did not obey; for the Rebels having enter'd *Prefton*, they had Intelligence, by a Gentleman of no mean Figure, of the Cannon, and of all that paffed in the Town.

After all this, as faid, we enter'd the Town without Oppofition in very good Order, and march'd to the Market-place, where the whole Body was drawn up round the Crofs, and there with Sound of Trumpet proclaimed the *Pretender*: Then the Men were billeted and quarter'd in every Part of the Town; which was very well able to entertain them all. The fame Night a Party of Horfe were fent to Colonel *Chartres*'s Houfe, which is a few Miles from *Lan-*

cafter,

caster, belonging to a fine Estate which he has lately purchased there, called *Hornby-Hall*; this Party
were detached thither before we entered *Lancaster*,
by another Way, under the Command of Colonel
Oxburgh: They did no Harm to the House, nor
to any thing about it, tho' it was reported, and that
presently by himself, to ingratiate himself with the
Government, that they committed several Disorders,
to the Owner's great Loss. But he could never
make out the Loss; nor was there any Truth in
the Charge, for they behaved very civilly, only
made free with a few Bottles of his Wine and strong
Beer. When this Colonel demanded of one that had
the Care of the House, how much he did insist upon
for what the Men and Horses had received, he
brought in a Bill of 3 *l.* 6 *s.* 8 *d.* for which the Colonel gave his Note, payable when his Master's
Concerns were settled. On the other hand, if these
Men had not been sent thither, but that the *Scots*
had been allow'd to pay their Countryman's House
a Visit, they would not have scrupled to have set
it on fire, so well is he respected by them; and that
not on account of his Affection or Disaffection to
one Side or other, but on account of his own per-
sonal Character, which is known not to have been
very acceptable to those who are acquainted with
him. They continued at *Lancaster* from *Monday* the
7th to *Wednesday* the 9th, during which time they
seized some new Arms which were in the Custom-
House, and some Claret, and a good Quantity of
Brandy, which was all given to the Highlanders
to oblige them: They likewise took up all the Money belonging to the Revenue, which was either in
the Excise-Office or Custom-House, six Pieces of
Cannon, which they seized, and mounted upon new
Carriages (the Wheels that mounted these Cannon
belong'd to Sir *Henry Haughton's* Coaches) and carried them to *Preston*; of which hereafter. During
their Stay at *Lancaster* they had Prayers read in this
Church

Church by Mr. *Patten*, the Parfon of the Place ex-
cufing himfelf. It feems he was not fo averfe to it,
any more than fome of his Brethren ; but he wanted
to fee how the Scales would turn before he could
think of venturing fo far. From this Town Mr.
Buxton a Clergyman was fent off with Letters to
fome Gentlemen in *Derbyſhire*, where his Acquaintance lay. It was a lucky Errand for him, for by
that means he had the good fortune to efcape being
taken at *Preſton*. He was a well-bred and good
humour'd Gentleman, but his Conftitution could
not bear the Hardſhips of fuch an Undertaking
as this, efpecially of the long Marches in that
Seafon of the Year. He went to his own Country,
and there fell ill of the Small-Pox ; but hearing that
narrow Search was made for him, he was obliged
to remove, even in that Condition, and has not
fince been heard of.

As the old Saying goes, *Uno avulſo non deficit
alter :* So it was here ; for that very Day Mr.
Buxton went from *Lancaſter*, the unhappy Mr. *Paul*
came thither.

The Life and Cháraɛler of Mr. Paul.

William Paul Clerk, who liv'd and dy'd a Bat-
chelor was the Son of *John Paul*, of *Little Aſhby*
near *Lutterworth* in the County of *Leiceſter*, lately
deceas'd ; his Mother was Daughter of Mr. *Barfoot*
of *Streetfields* in *Warwickſhire :* They had a Free-
hold Eftate of about 60 or 70 *l. per Annum*, liv'd
in good Repute, and had five Children, of which
William was Eldeft, and born at *Aſhby* aforefaid,
about the Year 1678 ; brought up at School, the
greateft part of his time, by the Reverend Mr. *Thomas Seagrave* Reɛtor of *Leir* in *Leiceſterſhire*. About
the Year 1697 he removed to a School at *Rugby* in

War-

Warwickſhire, and remained there, under the Care of Mr. *Holyoak* Maſter thereof, for near two Years; and from thence he went to *Cambridge*, and was admitted into St. *John's College*, about *May* 1698, and Mr. *John Harris* Fellow of the ſame, where he contracted his Acquaintance with Mr. *Forſter*. He was at firſt a Sizer, and then made Scholar; ſoon after which his Tutor died, and he (as they ſay in *Cambridge*) became Servitor to Mr. *Edmundſon* and Mr. *Lambert*, and not long after went into Orders. He was Curate at *Carlton Curlieu* near *Harborough*, *Leiceſterſhire*, and at the ſame time Chaplain to Sir *Geoffry Palmer*. From thence he went to *Tam-worth* in *Staffordſhire*, and was Curate and Uſher of the Free-School there. He went from thence to *Nun-Eaton* in *Warwickſhire*, and was Curate to Mr. *Foxcraft*. From thence he removed, being pre-ſented to the Vicarage of *Horton on the Hill*, *Lei-ceſterſhire*, by the late Lord Biſhop of *Oxon*. The Village is ſituate in the South-weſt Corner of the County, both in the Deanry and Hundred of *Spar-kenboe*; it is valued in the King's Books at 6 *l.* 12 *s.* 6 *d.* and the improved Rents are near 60 *l. per An-num*. He was inſtituted into the aforeſaid Vicarage by his Grace the preſent Lord Arch-Biſhop of *Can-terbury*, then Biſhop of *Lincoln*, on the 5th of *May* 1709; to qualify himſelf for which, he took the uſual Oaths to Queen *Anne*, and abjured the *Pre-tender*. He went down with Mr. *Gaſcoign*, Mr. *Cotton*, and ſome Others to meet the Rebels at *Pre-ſton*; was ſeized on the Way by one commonly called Major *Bradſhaw*, and Mr. *Matthews*, a Clergyman; and ſet at Liberty again by one Colonel *Noel* a Juſtice of the Peace: But being born for his Deſtiny, he goes to *Lancaſter*, there join'd the Rebels, and at *Preſton* importuned Mr. *Patten* that he might read Prayers; which was granted him, tho unwillingly, becauſe he was in a Lay-Dreſs:

There

There he read Prayers thrice for the *Pretender* as
King. Juſt before the King's Troops inveſted that
Town, he went out, borrowing Mr. *Patten*'s black
Coat, and leaving a Blue one; he ſaid he had Letters to a Lord in *Staffordſhire.* He was taken by
General *Wills*, but diſcharged. He called in his
own Country, in his way to *London*, where he appear'd in colour'd Cloaths, laced Hat, and long
Wig, and a Sword by his Side; but he was acci-
dentally met near *Montague*-Houſe by *Thomas Bird*
Eſq; Juſtice of the Peace for the County of *Leiceſter*, who knew him, and took him Priſoner,
Decemb. 12. 1715. He was carried to the Duke
of *Devonſhire*'s, afterwards Lord *Townſhend*'s, Principal Secretary of State, there examin'd, and put
into a Meſſenger's Houſe, and 14 Days after was
ſent to *Newgate.* He was arraigned at *Weſtminſter*
on *May* 31. pleaded at firſt, Not Guilty: Afterwards he withdrew his Plea; was found Guilty,
and *July* 13. 1716. Drawn, Hang'd and Quarter'd
at *Tyburn.*

At firſt, when Mr. *Paul* intended to engage, he
came boldly up to Mr. *Forſter*, as he was at Dinner
with Mr. *Patten* at the Recorder of *Lancaſter*'s
Houſe; he entred the Room in a Blue Coat, with
a long Wig and a Sword, and Mr. *John Cotton* of
Cambridgeſhire with him. They let him know who
they were, and in a flouriſhing way made a tender
of their Services for the Cauſe; which Mr. *Forſter*
accepting, they withdrew. Then Mr. *Forſter* told
Mr. *Patten* that the Taller of the two Gentlemen
was a Clergyman, and was of St. *John*'s College in
Cambridge, and that he had given him a perfect
Account of General *Carpenter*'s Marches, and that
he was then at *Bernard*'s-Caſtle in the Biſhoprick of
Durham, that his Men and Horſes were ſore fatigued, and the like. All which was true enough;
tho' their being ſo fatigued, did not hinder their

March

March after us. While we were in this Town our
Number increased confiderably; and had we ftaid
here, or kept Garifon here, they would have continued fo to do. For in that time a great many
Lancafhire Gentlemen joined us, with their Servants
and Friends. It's true, they were moft of them
Papifts; which made the *Scots* Gentlemen and the
Highlanders mighty uneafy, very much fufpecting
the Caufe; for they expected all the High-Church
Party to have joined them. Indeed, that Party,
who never are right hearty for the Caufe, 'till they
are Mellow, as they call it, over a Bottle or two,
began now to fhew us their Blind-fide; and that it
is their juft Character, that they do not care for
venturing their Carcaffes any farther than the Ta-
vern. There indeed, with their *High-Church* and
Ormond, they would make Men believe, who do
not know them, that they would encounter the
greateft Oppofition in the World; but after having
confulted their Pillows, and the Fume a little eva-
porated, it is to be obferved of them, that they generally become mighty Tame, and are apt to Look
before they Leap, and with the Snail, if you touch
their Houfes, they hide their Heads, fhrink back,
and pull in their Horns. I have heard Mr. *Forfter*
fay he was bluftered into this Bufinefs by fuch People as thefe, but that for the time to come he would
never again believe a drunken Tory.

Having now received what addition of Force
they could expect in that part of the Country, and
having firft difcharged fome Prifoners of their
Friends who were in the Caftle, particularly the
famous *Tom Syddal*, a Mob Captain, who was in
this Goal for the Riot at *Manchefter*, when the
Meeting-Houfe was pull'd down; tho' all or moft
of the Prifoners, who were a confiderable Number,
got upon the Leads of the Caftle, and feeing us
advance, gave loud Huzza's. I went to view that
ancient

ancient Place, so famous in our History, where the
Prisoners desired me to represent their Case to Mr.
Forster, which I did; but was told by him, That
they should have his Master's Pardon speedily, and
in the mean time ordered *Syddal*, and another Prisoner for Treasonable Words, to be discharged. It
was time now to advance and open the Way for
their other Friends to come in; for as they had News
daily of Troops gathering to oppose them, it was
time to extend themselves, that they might join all
those who had promised their Assistance. To this
end, they moved from *Lancaster*, taking the Road
to *Preston*, and designing to possess themselves of
Warrington-Bridge, and of the Town of *Manchester*,
where they had Assurances of great Numbers to join
them; and by this means they made no doubt of
securing the great and rich Town of *Liverpool*,
which would be cut off from any Relief, if they
were once possess'd of *Warrington*-Bridge. According to these Measures the Horse reach'd *Preston*
that Night: The Day proving rainy, and the Ways
deep, they left the Foot at a small Market-Town
called *Garstang*, half-way between *Lancaster* and
Preston: Here the unfortunate Mr. *Muncaster* join'd
us, who was afterwards executed, yet died very
Penitent, and own'd King GEORGE for his only
lawful Sovereign; but the blazed Rumor of *the
Church's being in Danger*, hasten'd him to the fatal
Tree. He was of very good Sense and Natural
Parts, brought up an Attorney. The Foot were
order'd to advance early next Morning to *Preston*,
which they did accordingly. The Horse, as is said,
entred *Preston* that Night, and found that two
Troops of *Stanhope's* Dragoons, formerly quartered
there, had removed upon their Approach. This
encouraged them exceedingly, and made them imagine that the King's Forces would not look them
in the Face. The Foot coming up next Day,
being

being *Thursday* the 10th of *November*, they marched
straight to the Crofs, and were there drawn up
as ufual, whilft the *Pretender* was proclaimed.
Here they were alfo joined by a great many Gentlemen, with their Tenants, Servants, and Attendants; and fome of very good Figure in the Country; but ftill all Papifts. They once refolved to
have marched out of *Prefton*, and Order was given
to get ready on the *Friday*; but that Order was
countermanded, and they refolved to continue till
the next Day, and then to advance. All this while
they had not the leaft Intimation of the Forces that
were preparing to oppofe them, much lefs of the
near approach of the King's Army: And as it is
a Queftion often afked, and which very few can
anfwer, *viz.* How they came to be fo utterly void
of Intelligence at that time, as to be fo ignorant of
the March of the King's Forces, and to know nothing of them till they were within Sight of *Prefton*,
and ready almoft to fall upon them? It may be very
proper to give a plain and direct Anfwer to it,
which will in fhort be this, *viz.* That in all their
Marches Mr. *Forfter* fpared neither Pains nor Coft
to be acquainted with all General *Carpenter*'s Motions, of which he had conftant and particular Accounts every Day, and fometimes twice a Day; but
the *Lancafhire* Gentlemen gave him fuch Affurances
that no Force could come near them by Forty Miles
but they could inform him thereof, this made him
perfectly eafy on that fide, relying entirely on the
Intelligence he expected from them: And therefore,
when on the *Saturday* Morning he had given Orders
for his whole Army to march from *Prefton* towards
Manchefter, it was extremely furprizing, and he
could fcarce credit the Reports that General *Will's*
was advancing from *Wigan* to attack them: But
he was foon fatisfied of the Truth of it by Meffengers on all hands. That Morning Mr. *Paul* the

Clergy-

Clergyman went off with Letters, *as he then said,* to a Noble Lord in *Staffordshire,* and some Friends in *Leicestershire:* He met General *Wills* and his Troops on the Road, who stopped him and asked him some Questions; but not suspecting he was one of the Rebels, he himself also putting on a contrary Face, let him go: But I shall have occasion to say more of him. The Alarm being now given, a Body of the Rebels marched out of the Town as far as *Ribble-*Bridge, posting themselves there; and Mr. *Forster,* with a Party of Horse, went beyond it to get a certain Account of things; when discovering the Vanguard of the Dragoons, he returned another Way, not coming back by the Bridge. He ordered Mr. *Patten* with all haste to ride back, and give an Account of the Approach of the King's Army, and to give Orders to prepare to receive them, whilst he went to view a Ford in the River, in order for a Passage to come behind them. The Foot that were advanced to the Bridge were about 100; but they were choice, stout, and well-armed Men, and commanded by Lieutenant-Colonel *John Farquharson* of *Innercall,* belonging to *Mackintosh's* Battalion: He was a good Officer and a very bold Man, and would have defended that important Pass of the Bridge to the last Drop, and till the rest had advanced and drawn themselves out of the Town; but he was order'd to retreat to *Preston:* This Retreat was another wrong Step, and has been condemned on all hands as one of the greatest Oversights they could be guilty of; for the River is not fordable but a good way above and below the Bridge, which they might have made impassable also, by several Methods practised on like Occasions. As for the Bridge, they might have barricado'd it so well, that it would have been impracticable to have pass'd there, or to have dislodg'd them from it; also they had Cannon, which General *Wills* wanted. And here alone indeed it might be

said

said they were in a Condition to have made an effectual Stand; for here the King's Forces would have been entirely expofed to their Fire, having no Cover; whereas the Rebels could have very much fecured themfelves againft the others Fire by the Bridge, and by the Rifing-Ground near it. General Wills did indeed expect fome Difficulty and Oppofition at this Place, believing, by their Situation, that the Rebels would have made their greateft Effort at that Place; but underftanding by his Advance-Guard that the Rebels had abandon'd that Poft, he was furprized, and fufpected that then they had fome Stratagem in hand, and perhaps had lined the Hedges, and fo made the Lane unpaffable for his Men. The Lane is indeed very deep, and fo narrow that in feveral Places two Men cannot ride a-breaft. This is that famous Lane, at the end of which Oliver Cromwell met with a ftout Refiftance from the King's Forces, who from the Height rolled down upon him and his Men (when they had entred the Lane) huge large Mill-ftones; and if Oliver himfelf had not forced his Horfe to jump into a Quick-Sand, he had luckily ended his Days there. General Wills, on thefe Suppofitions, proceeded with Caution, and caufed the Hedges and Fields to be view'd, and the Ways laid open for his Cavalry to enter; but finding the Hedges alfo clear, he concluded then the Enemy was fled, and expected that they had abandon'd the Town and all, and would endeavour by their long Marches to return to Scotland, tho' he thought it impoffible for them to do it: But he was foon inform'd that they were retreated to the Town only, and that they refolv'd to receive him there with a refolute Countenance; fo he had nothing to do but to prepare for the Attack, which he went about immediately. Having advanced nearer the Town, he ordered his Troops to pafs at a Gate which leads into the Fields which lie on the back

of

of the Town, and immediately spreading the Enclosures with the utmost Expedition and Diligence, so disposed of his Forces as best to be able both to attack them in the Town, and to prevent them from Sallying or making a Retreat.

During this time, the Rebels were not idle in the Town, nor did they appear in the least discourag'd, but applied themselves resolutely to their Business; barricadoing the Streets, and posting their Men in the Streets, by-Lanes, and Houses, to the greatest Advantage, for all Events. The Gentlemen-Voluntiers were drawn up in the Church-yard, under the Command of the Earl of *Derwentwater*, Viscount *Kenmure*, Earls of *Wintoun* and *Nithsdale*. The Earl of *Derwentwater* signally behav'd, having stript into his Wastcoat, and encouraged the Men, by giving them Money to cast up Trenches, and animating them to a vigorous Defence of them: When he had so done, he order'd Mr. *Patten* to bring him constantly an Account from all the Attacks, how things went, and where Succours were wanted; which Mr. *Patten* did, till his Horse was shot under him. The Rebels formed four main Barriers; one a little below the Church, commanded by Brigadier *Mackintosh*; the Gentlemen in the Church-yard were to support that Barrier in particular, and Lord *Charles Murray* that which was at the end of a Lane leading to the Fields: The third Barrier was called the Windmill; this was commanded by Colonel *Mackintosh*: And the fourth was in the Street which leads towards *Liverpool*, commanded by Major *Miller* and Mr. *Douglass*. The three former were all attack'd with great Fury by his Majesty's Forces: The first Attack was made upon that Barrier below the Church, commanded by Brigadier *Mackintosh*; but they met with such a Reception, and so terrible a Fire was made upon them; as well from the Barricado as from the Houses on both Sides, that they were obliged to retreat back

to

to the Entrance of the Town. During the Heat of this Action, some of *Preston*'s Officers being inform'd that the Street leading to *Wigan* was not barricado'd, and that the Houses were not possess'd on that side, they presently entered that Street with great Bravery, pushing all before them. *Preston*'s Regiment of Foot were commanded upon this Service, supported by *Honeywood*'s Dragoons. It is true, the Rebels had at first taken Possession of that Street, and posted Men in the Houses on both Sides; but were, against their Inclination, called off to other Service; nor were they left, as some desir'd, to post themselves at the extremest Ends of the Town, even at that End which leads to the Bridge, where the first and hottest Attack was made. Several Houses were left, particularly one which belonged to Sir *Henry Haughton*: Captain *Innis* with Fifty Highlanders had taken Possession of this House; and had he been allowed to have continued there, he would have given a good Account of it; but he being obliged to leave that Post, some of *Preston*'s Men got Possession of that too, tho' it cost them dear, for many of their Men were kill'd there from other Houses. It is a high House, over-looking the whole Town: There was also another House opposite to it, which they entered, and posted several of their Men in it. And from these two House came almost all the Loss the Rebels sustained during the Action. Mr. *Forster* cannot be blamed for this Oversight, but it must be charged upon the Brigadier, who, when the Regiment of *Preston*'s Foot made this brave and bold Attack and Attempt, withdrew his Men from those Houses. The Attack was thus, *Preston*'s Men, led by their Lieutenant-Colonel the Lord *Forrester*, did not come up the Head of the Street, but marched into a straight Passage behind the Houses, and then made a Halt till their Lieutenant-Colonel the Lord *For-*
rester

rester came into the open Street with his drawn
Sword in his Hand, and faced *Mackintosh's* Barrier,
looking up the Street and down the Street, and
viewing how they were posted. There were many
Shots fired at him, but he returned to his Men, and
came up again at the Head of them into the Middle of the Street, where he caused some to face the
Barricade where the Brigadier was posted, and ply
them with their Shot, at the same time commanding
another Party to march cross the Streets, to take
Possession of those Houses. It was a very desperate
Attempt, and shews him an Officer of an undaunted
Courage. Whilst this was doing, the Rebels from
the Barrier, and from the Houses on both sides,
made a terrible Fire upon them, and a great many
of that old and gallant Regiment were kill'd and
wounded : The Lord. *Forrester* received several
Wounds himself. Besides the Damage they received
on that side, they were sore galled from some Windows below them, by Captain *Douglass* and Captain
Hunter's Men. *Preston's* Foot fired smartly upon
the Rebels, but did little Execution, the Men being
generally cover'd from the Shot, and delivering their
own Shot securely, and with good Aim ; yet some
were kill'd, and some also wounded, particularly
two very gallant Gentlemen were wounded here;
and both dy'd of their Wounds ; the one was Captain *Peter Farquharson* of *Rochaley,* a Gentleman of
an invincible Spirit, and almost inimitable Bravery.
This Gentleman being shot through the Bone of his
Leg, endured a great deal of Torture in the Ope-
ration of the Surgeon. When he was first brought
into the Inn call'd the *White-Bull,* the House where
all the wounded Men were carry'd to be dress'd, he
took a Glass of Brandy, and said, *Come, Lads,
here is our Master's Health ; tho' I can do no more, I
wish you good Success.* His Leg was cut off by an
unskilful Butcher, rather than a Surgeon, and he

presently

presently died. The other Gentleman was Mr.
Clifton, Brother to Sir Jervas Clifton; he was also a
gallant and thoroughly accomplished Gentleman;
he received a Shot in his Knee, of which he died
some Hours after. There was another Gentleman
call'd Colonel Brereton, who had formerly serv'd in
the Army; he had many Wounds, one of which,
by the vast Flux of Blood, was not discover'd soon
enough by his Surgeon, or else it's thought he might
have out-liv'd his Fate that Day: After he was bury'd, he was taken out of his Grave, to satisfy the
Curiosity of a Commanding Officer, who could not
be persuaded that this Gentleman was in the Rebellion.

The next Barrier which was attack'd, was commanded by Lord Charles Murray: He behav'd
very gallantly, but being very vigorously attack'd,
wanted Men, and order'd Mr. Patten to acquaint
the Earl of Derwentwater therewith; who immediately sent back Mr. Patten with Fifty Gentlemen
Voluntiers from the Church-yard to reinforce him,
who came in very good Season. Immediately Mr.
Patten was order'd over the Barrier to view the King's
Forces, who appearing in a Clergyman's Habit,
was not suspected, nor fired on. He soon returned
back, and gave Lord Charles an Account, that by
what he saw, they were resolved to attack him again;
whereupon Lord Charles gave Orders to his Men to
be ready to receive them; and accordingly they
came on very furiously: And tho' the King's Forces
that made this Attack, were, for the most part,
raw, new-listed Men, and seem'd unwilling to fight;
yet the Bravery and good Conduct of experienc'd
Officers supply'd very much that Defect. However, Lord Charles Murray maintain'd the Post, and
oblig'd them to retreat with Loss; nor, had they
been all old Soldiers, could they have beaten Lord
Charles from that Barrier, which was very strong;
the

the Number they had flain from the Barn-holes and Barrier itfelf added very much, fo that at laft the Officers themfelves thought fit to give it over. And however fome, in their dying Speeches afterwards, were pleafed to leffen the Bravery of the King's Forces ; this may be offered in Anfwer, That not-withftanding the Afperfion we all know that he that publickly difplay'd it, could not be a Judge of the Faft ; for no Body ever faw him at any Poft of Danger himfelf. On the contrary, the Author here-of, who was an Eye-witnefs to the Three Attacks, can affure the World, he faw that very Gentleman who left that Afperfion in his *Dying Speech*, placed very fecurely out of all Danger, in an Ale-houfe, where, he was affur'd, he remain'd during the whole Aftion.

Hitherto the Rebels feem'd to have had fome Ad-vantage, having repulfed the King's Forces in all their Attacks, and maintained all their Pofts ; and Night drawing on, no new Aftion happen'd ; but during all this time, and all *Saturday*-Night and *Sunday*, and good part of that Night, the King's Forces kept inceffantly Plattoons firing upon the Rebels from Sir *Henry Haughton*'s and Mr. *Ayre*'s Houfes. It's true, they kill'd but very few ; thofe of Note were, one Mr. *Hume* a Cornet, one Mr. *Scattery*, and a Highland Gentleman belonging to the Lord *Nairn*. There were feveral Houfes and Barns fet on fire by both Parties, both for covering themfelves among the Smoak, and diflodging Men ; fo that if the Wind had blown almoft from any quarter, that Town had been burnt to the Ground, and the Rebels had been burnt to Afhes in it. I fhall, as I defign'd, impartially hint at all the Mi-ftakes on both Sides ; and this was one, the King's General had order'd Illuminations to be fet in all the Windows of the Houfes where they had Poffeffion, which, as long as they continued burning, expofed

the

the Rebels that were croffing the Streets upon all Occafions, to the plain View of thofe poffeffed of the
Houfes aforefaid, and gave them a good Aim at
their Mark. This was the Occafion of the Death
of fome, and Wounds of others, even on both
Sides; fo that after a fhort time, Orders were given
for fome to go to all the Houfes, and call aloud to
the People to put out their Candles. Which being
fhouted aloud (as is faid) in the Streets, for the
People had fhut all their Doors, they miftook the
Command, and inftead of putting out or extinguifh-
ing their Lights, fet up more; which amufed both
Sides, but did no harm to either.

The third Attack was at the Windmill in the
Street which leads to *Lancafter*, where the Barrier
was defended by near 300 Men, under the Command of Mr. *Mackintofh*, who, with his Men, behaved very boldly, and made a dreadful Fire upon
the King's Forces, killing many on the fpot, and
obliging them to make a Retreat; which, however,
they did very handfomely. This was owing to the
common Men, who were but new lifted; though
the Officers and old Soldiers behav'd themfelves with
great Bravery. After this, the Rebels began to fee
their Error, by being impos'd on to give Credit to
the many Falfhoods told them, of which this was
one, That they might be affured that the King's
Forces would all come over to them: Yet not one
Man offer'd to do fo; for of feveral private Men
made Prifoners, being wounded, not one of them
would liften to the Offers made to Enlift, but chofe
rather to be fhut up in clofe Prifon, than to forfake
their King and Country's Caufe. One private Man
belonging to Brigadier *Prefton's* Foot, that was
wounded, and laid in Bed with two others, when
Mr. *Patten* went to that Bed where they were, which
was at the *White-Bull*, having afked them feveral
Queftions, told them he was ready to pray with
them,

them, as he was a Clergyman ; that Soldier above-
mentioned answered, *If you be a Protestant, we desire your Prayers, but name not the* Pretender *as King.*
A sufficient Demonstration that the common Impo-
sition was false ; and a very sure Sign that King
GEORGE's Forces were not merely Mercenary.
Nay, Major *Preston* and Captain *Ogleby*, as well as
several common Soldiers that were made Prisoners,
being wounded, assured us, that not one Man belonging to the King's Forces but would die in their
Country's Cause ; and told us we could not be able
to hold out, for that more Forces were also coming
from all Quarters ; they inform'd us of the Arrival
of General *Carpenter* with three Regiments of Dragoons to surround us.

This brave General, after his long, troublesome,
and dismal Marches after the Rebels, had very much
weary'd his Men, but more the Horses, for want of
good Forage, returned to *Newcastle*, having Intelligence that the Rebels were gone over the Mountains to join *Mar*, which was impracticable for his
heavy Horse. Having scarce refreshed himself, he
had an Express from Sir *Henry Haughton*, that the
Rebels were marching towards *Lancaster*. Upon
which, with all imaginary Speed, over high Mountains and deep Ways, he at last came to *Clithero*, a
Town 12 Miles from *Preston*, on *Saturday* Night
that the Action was begun. Whilst he was here, he
receiv'd another Express from Sir *Henry Haughton* of
all the Affair ; which made him use his wonted Vigilance to have the Horses taken care of, so that they
might be able early in the Morning to hasten towards *Preston*; which they performed with the
greatest Expedition, for they came before *Preston*
betwixt Nine and Ten on *Sunday* Morning. The
Prisoners acquainted us likewise with the Dispositi-
ons he had taken, and the Alterations he had made
in the Posts, to prevent our Escape.

And

And now our People began to open their Eyes, and to fee that there was nothing but prefent Death before them, if they held out longer; and that there was no Remedy, but, if poffible, to make Terms, and get a Capitulation for Life, and lay down their Arms. But of this, it is neceffary that a gradual Account be given in the Order in which it happen'd; for it was not all done in a Moment.

General *Carpenter*, I fay, was now arriv'd with *Churchill*'s, *Molefworth*'s, and *Cobham*'s Dragoons, and a great many Gentlemen of the Country with him, as the Earl of *Carlifle*, Lord *Lumley*, Colonel *Darcy*, and others.

The General having an Account from General *Wills* of what had pafs'd, approved very well of what had been done, but found it neceffary to make fome fmall Alterations in the Difpofitions of the Troops: He found three Attacks had been made, though not with the defir'd Succefs, and yet that the Rebels would be forced to furrender at laft, or be taken Sword in Hand.

Here it is neceffary to obferve, as part of the Reafon why the firft Attack was not immediately fuccefsful, *viz.* becaufe of the Barricado's and Cannon which the Rebels were poffeffed of. But by the way, I muft obferve, that the Rebels, though they had fix Pieces of Cannon, did not much ufe them, except at firft only; in fhort, they knew not how, having no Engineers among them; and a Seaman who pretended Judgment, and upon his own Offer took the Management of the Cannon at the Brigadier's Barricado, acted fo madly, whether it was that he had too little Judgment, or too much Ale, or perhaps both, that in levelling one of the Pieces to cut off *Prefton*'s Foot, who advanc'd to attack us, the Ball brought down the Top of a Chimney. It is true, the next he fired did Execution, and oblig'd the Regiment to halt; though upon all Occafions

cafions they behav'd with a great deal of Bravery and Order. But this by the way. Lieutenant-General *Carpenter* was, as I have faid, now arriv'd, and had view'd the Pofts and the Situation of the Rebels; and finding moft part of the Horfe and Dragoons of the King's Troops pofted on one fide of the Town, very incommodioufly on many Accounts, being crouded in a deep narrow Lane near the End of the Town, and befides that, fo inconvenient for the Service, that it was impoffible to draw up above three or four in the Front, he brought them off in Parties to feveral other Places. Alfo, going to view the Ground towards the River, he found, to his great Surprize, that no Troops were pofted at the End of *Fifhergate-ftreet*, to block up that part of the Town; and that for want of it, feveral of the Rebels had efcaped there, and more rid off that Way even before his Face. This Street leads to a Marfh or Meadow which runs down to that part of the River *Ribble* where there are two good Fords, being the High-way towards *Liverpool*. At the upper End of this Street there was another Barricade, with two Pieces of Cannon, (as is already faid:) But no Attack had been made on this Side; nor indeed could it be fo, the few Troops confider'd. Here the Lieutenant-General order'd Colonel *Pitt* to poft his two Squadrons of Horfe, and extend themfelves into that Marfh, in order to prevent any more efcaping that Way; as it effectually did; for fome bold Fellows attempting to efcape after this, were all cut to Pieces by the Horfe: Alfo the General caufed a Communication to be open'd through the Inclofures on that Side, that his Poft might be relieved, in cafe the whole Body fhould attempt to force their Retreat that Way, as it was given out they would, and as indeed they might have done; but they had no fuch good Meafures in their Heads.

G 3

The

The Rebels being thus invested on all Sides, so
that they found themselves entirely block'd up, and
being now sensible, tho' too late, of their Condition,
and also that they were short of Powder for an ob-
stinate Resistance, began to consider what to do.
The Highlanders were for sallying out upon the King's
Forces, and dying, as they call'd it, like Men of
Honour, with their Swords in their Hands ; but
they were over-rul'd, and were not allow'd to stir :
Nor was the Motion communicated to the whole
Body ; but General *Forster*, prevail'd upon by my
Lord *Widdrington*, Colonel *Oxburgh*, and some few
Others, resolv'd upon a Capitulation, flattering them-
selves with obtaining good Terms from the King's
Officers. Colonel *Oxburgh* pretending Acquaintance
with some of the Officers, made an Offer to go out
and treat of a Surrender.

As this was done without the Knowledge of the
Rebel Army, the Common Soldiers were told that
General *Wills* had sent to offer honourable Terms to
them, if they would lay down their Arms ; so
blinded were we with their Tory Lies to the last :
But certain it is, that Gentleman, had his Design
been known, had never seen *Tyburn*, for he had
been shot dead by the Consent of all the Common
Men, before he had gone out of the Barrier. However, go he did, and made such a Bargain for them,
as the Circumstances of Things might easily tell
them they could expect no other ; and which, had
not the Gentlemen thus abandon'd them, the Soldiers would not have yielded to. But be that as it
will, he went with the Trumpet to the General,
who allow'd him to come and go freely ; but told
him, They might expect no other Terms, than to
lay down their Arms, and surrender at Discretion.
The Colonel, to give him his due, urg'd all the
Arguments he could for better Terms ; but was
told, That they must submit to the King's Mercy,

there

there was no other Terms could be made with them. The General told Colonel *Oxburgh*, He knew that in the Cafe of a Rebellion reduced, it was not rational to expect, or ufual to give other Terms. The Colonel coming back with this Anfwer, a fecond Meffage was fent out by Captain *Dalziel*, to defire Time to confider of it. About Three in the Afternoon, Colonel *Cotton*, with a Dragoon, and a Drum beating a Chamade before them, came up the Street from the King's General: The Colonel alighted at the Sign of the *Mitre*, where the Chief of the Rebel-Officers were got together, and told them he came to receive their pofitive Anfwer. 'Twas told him, There were Difputes betwixt the *Englifh* and *Scots*, that would obftruct the Yielding, which Others were willing to fubmit to ; but if the General would grant them a Ceffation of Arms till the next Morning at Seven, they fhould be able to fettle the Matter, and that the Gentlemen promifed they would then fubmit. Colonel *Cotton* fent the Drum to beat a Chamade before the Doors of fome Houfes where the King's Men continued firing, to caufe them to ceafe, on account of the Ceffation which was agreed to, and to order them to withhold till they had Notice from the General ; but the poor Fellow was fhot dead upon his Horfe as he was beating his Drum. It is faid this was not done by the King's Men, (for they muft needs know him to be one of their own Drums, by his Livery and Mounting) but that it was done by fome of the Rebels who were averfe to all Thoughts of Surrender.

And here, becaufe the Rebels and their Friends have given it out fince, that they had fuch Terms granted them at this fhort Treaty which would fecure their Lives, and that the Terms of Surrender ought fo to be underftood, I fhall give you a true and faithful Account of the Capitulation itfelf, with

its Circumſtances, as it was given upon Oath by
General *Wills* himſelf at the Lords Bar at the Earl
of *Wintoun's* Trial : The General there declared,
" That having the Honour to command his Ma-
" jeſty's Troops that attack'd the Rebels at *Preſton*,
" he came before that Town on the 12th of *No-*
" *vember* laſt about One o'Clock, and order'd two
" Attacks upon the Town ; the Attack which led
" to *Wigan* being commanded by Brigadier *Honey-*
" *wood*, who beat the Rebels from their firſt Bar-
" ricade, and took Poſſeſſion of ſome of the Houſes
" in the Town ; the other Attack which led to
" *Lancaſter*, under the Command of Brigadier *Dor-*
" *mer*, who lodg'd his Troops nigh the Barricade
" of the Rebels. The next Day about Two of the
" Clock Mr. *Forſter* ſent out one Mr. *Oxburgh* an
" *Iriſhman*, offering to lay down their Arms and
" ſubmit themſelves, and hoped this Deponent
" would recommend them to the King's Mercy.
" Which this Deponent refuſed, and told him, he
" would not treat with Rebels, for that they had
" kill'd ſeveral of the King's Subjeſts, and they
" muſt expeſt to undergo the ſame Fate. That
" upon this *Oxburgh* ſaid, That as this Deponent
" was a Man of Honour and an Officer, he hoped
" he would ſhew Mercy to People that were wil-
" ling to ſubmit. Upon this the Deponent ſaid,
" All he would do for them was, That if they laid
" down their Arms, and ſubmitted Priſoners at
" Diſcretion, he would prevent the Soldiers from
" cutting them in Pieces till he had farther Orders ;
" and that he would give them but an Hour to
" conſider of it. That he ſent *Oxburgh* back into
" the Town to acquaint *Forſter* of it ; and before
" the Hour was expired they ſent out Mr. *Dalziel*,
" Brother to the Earl of *Carnwath*, who wanted
" Terms for the *Scots*. That this Deponent's An-
" ſwer was, That he would not treat with Rebels,
" nor

" nor give them any other Terms than what he had
" before offered them. Upon which it was defired
" that this Deponent would grant farther Time,
" till Seven o'Clock next Day, to confult the beft
" Method of delivering themfelves up. That this
" Deponent agreed to grant them the Time defi-
" red, provided they threw up no new Intrench-
" ments in the Streets, nor fuffered any of their
" People to efcape, and that they fent out the Chief
" of the *Englifh* and *Scotch* as Hoftages for the Per-
" formance: And this Deponent fent in Colonel
" *Cotton* to bring them out; who brought out the
" Earl of *Derwentwater* and Mr. *Mackintofh*. That
" the next Day, about Seven o'Clock, Mr. *Forfter*
" fent out to let this Deponent know that they
" were willing to give themfelves up Prifoners at
" Difcretion, as he had demanded. That Mr. *Mac-
" kintofh* being by when the Meffage was brought,
" faid, He could not anfwer that the *Scotch* would
" furrender in that manner, for that the *Scots* were
" People of defperate Fortunes, and that he had
" been a Soldier himfelf, and knew what it was to
" be a Prifoner at Difcretion. That upon this the
" Deponent faid, Go back to your People again,
" and I will attack the Town, and the Confequence
" will be, I will not fpare one Man of you. That
" *Mackintofh* went back, but came running out im-
" mediately again, and faid, That the Lord *Ken-
" mure*, and the reft of the Noblemen, with his
" Brother, would furrender in like manner with
" the *Englifh*.

General *Wills* farther depofed, " That when the
" Attack was made by the King's Forces, between
" 60 and 70 Men were kill'd; and that there were
" kill'd and wounded about 130. And being afk'd
" by the Attorney-General whether he gave the
" Rebels any Encouragement to hope for Mercy?
" he again declared, That all the Terms he gave
                                    " them

" them was, that he would save their Lives from
" the Soldiers till farther Orders, if they surren-
" der'd at Discretion ; (the Meaning of which was,
" That by the Rules of War it was in his Power
" to cut them all to Pieces, but he would give them
" their Lives till farther Order ;) and if they did
" not comply, he would renew the Attack, and
" not spare a Man.

This Deposition was confirmed by Colonel
Churchill, Colonel *Cotton*, and Brigadier *Munden*.
Besides this, I can assure the World that I heard the
Answer which Colonel *Cotton*, whilst he was at the
Mitre, gave to a Gentleman among the Rebels,
who ask'd if they might have Mercy? he told him,
Sir, that I cannot assure you of, but I know the King
to be a very merciful Prince ; and that then he demanded of all the Noblemen and Gentlemen to give
their Parole of Honour to perform what they on
their Part promised.

Having thus set this Matter in a clear Light, I
shall now give a farther Account of what happen'd
in the Town : The common Men were one and all
against capitulating, and were terribly enrag'd when
they were told of it, declaring that they would die
fighting ; and that when they could defend their
Posts no longer, they would force their way out,
and make a Retreat. It is true this might have been
attempted, and perhaps many would have escap'd ;
but it could not have been perform'd without the
Loss of a great deal of Blood, and that on both
Sides ; and it was told them that it would be so,
and that if they did get out, they would be cut off
by the Country People : But their Madness was
such, that nothing could quiet them for a great
while ; and it was astonishing to see the Confusion
the Town was in, threatning one another, nay killing one another but for naming a Surrender ; one
was

was fhot dead, and feveral wounded. In this Dilemma many exclaim'd againft Mr. *Forfter*, and had he appear'd in the Street he would certainly have been cut to Pieces; but as he did not appear publickly, yet he had been actually kill'd in his Chamber by Mr. *Murray*, had not I with my Hand ftruck up the Piftol with which he fired at him, fo that the Bullet went thro' the Wainfcot into the Wall of the Room. And fince I mention Mr. *Forfter*, I cannot but juftify him againft the many Afperfions he lies under in this Part of the Action, I mean, *as a Coward*. It muft be own'd he was no Soldier, nor was the Command given to him as fuch, but as he was the only Proteftant who could give Repute to their Undertaking, being of Note in *Northumberland*, of an ancient Family, and having for feveral Years been Member of Parliament for that County, and therefore very popular: For if the Command had been given to either of the two Lords, their Characters, as Papifts, would have difcouraged many of the People, and been improved againft the Defign in general. As to Matters of Conduct, Mr. *Forfter*, tho' he was call'd General, yet he always fubmitted to the Counfel of Colonel *Oxburgh*, who was formerly a Soldier, and had obtain'd a great Reputation; tho' it is manifeft in our Cafe that he either wanted Conduct or Courage, or perhaps both: He was better at his Beads and Prayers than at his Bufinefs as a Soldier; and we all thought him fitter for a Prieft than a Field Officer. It muft be own'd he was very devout in his Religion, and that is all the Good we can fay of him; and that Devotion he has fince had great occafion for in another Place. Befides the Influence of Colonel *Oxburgh*, my Lord *Widdrington* had too great Prevalency over Mr. *Forfter*'s eafy Temper; and this Lord we thought underftood fo little of the Matter, that he was as unfit for a General as the other; for tho' the Family of

Widdrington

Widddrington be fam'd in History for their Bravery and Loyalty to the *English* Crown, yet there is little of it left in this Lord, or at least he did not shew it, that ever we could find, unless it consisted in his early Persuasions to surrender; for he was never seen at any Barrier, or in any Action but where there was the least Hazard. He was wonderfully esteem'd at Home by all the Gentlemen of the County, and it had been happy for him, and so we thought it would have been better for us (the Rebels) if he had stay'd at Home. I heard a Gentleman say, " He was vex'd to be under the Com-
" mand of an Officer that could not travel without
" strong Soup in a Bottle; for his Officer never
" wanted strong Broth wherever he came, both be-
" fore and after he was Prisoner". An Account of his Family is inserted in the *Appendix*.

But to return to Mr. *Forster:* He shew'd several times Forwardness enough for Action, and particularly that he was very far from being a Coward, by his riding up to *Mackintosh's* Barrier twice, in the very Face of the King's Troops; and when he was exposed to the Shot of those possessed of the Houses on both Sides of the Street, where I heard him command the Brigadier to advance without the Barricado, and make a Sally; which he positively refused. What Reason he gave I know not; Mr. *Forster*, however, warmly told him, He would have him try'd by a Court-Martial, if he out-liv'd the Service of the Day, and if ever his King came; This occasioned the Grudge which still continued betwixt them even in *Newgate*. The Brigadier has got the Character of Brave and Bold: He has given signal Instances thereof beyond Seas; but we all must say, we saw very little of it at *Preston*. Another Scandal upon Mr. *Forster*, is, That he betray'd them to the King's Troops: And this I must needs observe to be a very evident Slander, and was set

on

on Foot here by a Party, who did not do it fo
much to injure Mr. *Forſter*, as with another and
baſer Deſign, *viz.* that by having this credited, they
might blaſt the Reputation of the Commanding
Officers of his Majeſty's Troops, and of the Troops
themſelves; alſo ſuggeſting, that if the Rebels had
not been fold, the King's Forces could not have
reduced them; and alſo, that if they had not been
fure of *Forſter*, they would have given better Terms
to them when they did ſubmit. The contrary appears by the Uſage Mr. *Forſter* had receiv'd afterwards when a Priſoner; which tho' it may be ſaid
it was good enough for a Rebel, yet will make it
evident that he was no way favoured, as ſhall appear
farther hereafter. The ſame People who contrived
the firſt Story, have added at laſt, when he made
his Eſcape, that it was by Concert from the Government; as if the King would agree to ſuch a mean
Piece of Policy, as rather to wink at his Eſcape,
than to give him a Pardon; a thing which could
not lie hid long without being diſcovered, becauſe
ſeveral muſt be concerned, nay, common Servants,
Turnkeys, &c. muſt have their Share in ſuch a Deſign. After all, if the Truth was known, or when
the Truth ſhall be known, it may perhaps appear
that it was contrived and procured by the Tory Party, among whom there were many, doubtleſs, who
were afraid he would Squeak, and make ſome concern'd in Contributions, and Under-hand Aſſiſtances
in the Rebellion, be brought to Juſtice. I conclude
his Caſe with ſaying, that after ſeveral Affronts
which he receiv'd, and the Calumnies he lies under
for ſubmitting, yet we ſoon found they all came into his Meaſures, and tamely ſubmitted at Diſcretion.
Thus they were all made Priſoners next Morning at
Seven, being the 14th of *November*, and being diſ-
armed, were all at once put into the Power of the
King's Troops. And here it may not be improper

to observe what a fatal Day the 13th of *November*
proved to the *Pretender* and his Friends. For as
Preston was taken, and the Rebels in *England* sur-
render'd to the King's Troops in *Lancashire*; so the
Battle of *Dumblain*, as it was called here, or of
Sheriff-Moor, as in *Scotland*, was fought and lost in
Scotland by the Earl of *Mar*. And to add to the
Remark, in the North of *Scotland*, the Town of
Invernefs was retaken by the good Conduct of the
Lord *Lovat*, and the House of *Grant*, and their
Assistants : So that this Day seemed to determine
the Fate of the *Pretender*. But I return to the Ac-
count of the Surrender at *Preston*. Before the ap-
pointed Hour came, several of the King's Forces
entred that part of the Town which the Rebels held,
and began to plunder, looking upon what they got
their own, by Rule of War. But Complaint being
made, they were stopped for some time. At last
the two Generals entred the Town in Form, at the
Head of the Troops ; one Party under General
Wills, entred at that End which leads to *Lancaster* ;
Brigadier *Honeywood* at the Head of the remaining
Part of the Troops, entred at that End which leads
to *Manchester*. They came in with Sound of Trum-
pets and Beat of Drums, both Parties meeting at
the Market-Place. Here the Highlanders stood
drawn up with their Arms ; the Lords, Gentlemen,
and Officers were first secured, and placed under a
Guard in several Rooms in the Inns, where they
remained some time. The Highlanders laid down
their Arms in the Place where they stood drawn up,
and then were put into the Church under a sufficient
Guard. When all was safe, by the Rebels being
thus disarmed and secured, General *Carpenter* seeing
there would not be room enough in the Town for
near the Number of Horse which were there, and
considering the three Regiments that came with him
had been extremely harrass'd by above a Month's

continual

continual long Marches, he, to preferve the Regiments, fent them the fame Day to *Wigan*, there to reft a Day or two, and then move on by gentle Marches to their feveral Quarters; leaving the Care of the Prifoners to General *Wills*, who, tho' he was not the Commander in Chief, yet as he had been the firft Manager of the Work, the General would not take from him any part of the Honour of the Victory, or leffen him upon any Account. It is true, it was the Misfortune of thefe two brave Generals to differ about fome Punctilio's in this Cafe fome time after, and that fome would have it to be upon the Account of leffening one another in the Affair of *Prefton*; yet I have been informed that Difpute was rather upon fome other account, a former Mifunderftanding having been between them when beyond Sea. But to let that fall, as not to our prefent Purpofe. General *Carpenter*, as I have faid, went off the 15th with the Earl of *Carlifle*, Lord *Lumley*, Colonel *Darcy*, and the reft of the Gentlemen, who having been now with him ten Days, had been very ferviceable in procuring conftant Intelligence of the Rebels, by the great Intereft they have in that Country. The Slain on both Sides were buried, and then General *Wills* prepared to march: Thofe that were killed or wounded belonging to the King's Forces, were as follow; viz. the Wounded, Brigadier *Honeywood* received a Contufion on the Shoulder by a Mufket-fhot: Major *Bland* received a flight Wound in the Arm; his Horfe was fhot thro' the Neck: He is a brave and generous Officer, which all the Prifoners that were under his Command muft gratefully acknowledge. Lord *Forrefter*, Lieutenant-Colonel of *Prefton*'s Regiment, had two or three Wounds: An Officer worthy the Command of good Soldiers. Major *Prefton* was fhot thro' the Body a little above the Breaft, and taken Prifoner by Mr. *Wogan*; He

was

was a Man of great Gallantry and compos'd Courage, as was vifible by his expofing himfelf in the Danger and in the Manner he did, for he was fpent in a long languifhing Confumption, even to a Skeleton, and told us (the Rebels) That the Wound he received had only fhortened his Days two or three Months, which feeing it was in the Service of his King and Country, he faid he far preferr'd it to the lingring Death he expected. He died in our Hands. Captain *Ogleby* receiv'd a Wound in his Side ; the Bullet was lodg'd a good way in his Body, wrapt in part of his Scarf: He is a fine Gentleman, of a good Family in *Scotland*, and Son to the Lord *Ogleby*. He recover'd of his Wound. Major *Lawfon* was likewife wounded ; and Brigadier *Dormer* had a Contufion in his Knee. There were three other Captains wounded, two Lieutenants, one Cornet and four Enfigns. Killed, three Captains, and one Enfign. There were a great many private Men of his Majefty's Forces kill'd ; how many it is hard to determine, but the Number has been efteem'd above 200, tho' the publick Lifts fay not fo many.

Of the Rebels, there were 17 kill'd, and 25 wounded, and no more, for they were every where under Cover. I fhall take notice of one that was kill'd, tho' a Perfon of no Note, yet he is not to be forgotten, feeing the Bravery of mean Perfons ought not to buried: He was a lame Man, and had the care of the Gunpowder, which he carried under him on a Horfe from one Poft to another. He was told that they wanted Powder at *Mackintofh's* Barrier ; but if he went, they told him he would certainly be fhot. He anfwer'd, I know I cannot avoid that, if I go ; but fince they want, if I cannot carry it quite up to them, I'll carry it as far as I can; and fo fet forwards, and both he and his Horfe were fhot dead.

There

There were taken at *Preston* seven Lords, besides
1490 other, including the several Gentlemen, Officers, and private Men, and two Clergymen.
There was a Popish Priest, called *Littleton*, among
them : But having a great deal of the Jesuit, he
contriv'd a most excellent Disguise ; for he put on
a Blue Apron, went behind an Apothecary's Counter, and passed for an Assistant or Journeyman to
the Apothecary, and so took an Opportunity of
getting off. He took care of his own Tabernacle,
but left his Wafer Gods to be ridicul'd by the
Soldiers.

The Rebels being thus made Prisoners, I shall
add an Account how they were dispos'd of afterwards, which take as follows.

For the better preventing Escapes, they were
order'd to several Places of Confinement : The Lords
were secured in the most commodious Houses or
Inns. The *Scotch* Officers and Gentry, divided
into three Parties, were set under a Guard at the
Sign of the *Mitre*, the *White-Bull*, and the *Wind-Mill*. The Highlanders and common Men were
put into the Church, where they continued about
a Month, the Town's People being obliged to find
them Water and Bread ; whilst they took what care
of themselves they could, unripping all the Linings
from the Seats or Pews, and making thereof Breeches
and Hose to defend themselves from the Extremity of
the Weather. Several of them were sent under Guard
to *Wigan* the 23d of *November*, and afterwards sent
to *Chester*, whilst others were sent to *Lancaster*-Castle,
till their Trials came on ; when some were found
guilty, and executed, others transported by their
own Choice, others acquitted, others repriev'd ;
and those untried, or repriev'd, continued as Objects of His Majesty's most gracious Clemency. A
great many of the *Northumberland* and *Lancashire*
Gentlemen were confin'd in Mr. *Wingleby's* House

H

'till

'till *Sunday* the 21ft, when a great part of the chief Officers, and all the Lords were sent to *Wigan*. The *Lancashire* Gentlemen followed them on *Tuesday* the 23d, and continued there till *Thursday*; when all of them being divided into four Parties, were sent under the Guard of several Detachments to *Warrington*. It will please the Reader, I hope, to hear what happen'd at *Wigan* : Whilst we were there, we were allow'd to go with Centinels to visit our Friends; so Brigadier *Mackintosh* took an Opportunity to pay his Respects to the Lords at their Quarters. Entring the Room where they and several Gentlemen were got together, the Lord *Widdrington* called to him, and desired him to sit by him. Which done, my Lord seeing a Gentleman ready to leave the Chamber, he said, *Cousin* Tom, *pray stay a little; for I have a mind to ask some Questions of the Brigadier.* And thus begun : *Brigadier, the Reason why I did not expose myself as I ought to have done, was owing to my Indisposition, occasion'd by the Gout : But pray, you that had been at the Head of your Men, and had view'd the Bridge over* Rible, *why did you not defend it, being a Matter of no great Difficulty to have maintain'd that important Pass?* The Brigadier replied, *It was not maintainable, because the River was fordable at several Places.* Lord *Widdrington* asked him again, *Why he did not make his Barricade at the extreme End of the Street leading to the Town, which would have prevented the King's Forces from taking Possession of those Houses below his Barrier, which was a great way up the Town?* To this he answer'd, *My Lord, at the extreme End of the Town there were so many Lanes and Avenues, that to defend them would have required more Men than I had.* That Lord continued to demand of him, *Why he did not sally out himself with his Men? or why he would not obey Mr.* Forster, *who would have had the Horse to have sallied out?* To this he gave
Answer,

Anfwer, *That if his Foot had fallied out, they might by that means been parted from the Horfe, and fo left naked to have been cut off:* Befides, nothing more frightens the Highlanders than Horfe and Cannon. *As for obeying Mr.* Forfter, *in letting the Horfe fally out,* he faid, *If the Horfe had attempted any fuch Thing, they would have gone through the Fire of his Men; for they were afraid the Horfe defign'd fuch a Thing, and would have been able to have made a Retreat, and left them pent up in the Town.* This Difcourfe ending, they parted without Shew of much Concern for the Lofs of each other's Company. The Lord *Derwentwater* took little or no Notice of the Brigadier; but turn'd to a Gentleman in Company, and told him, *You fee what we have brought ourfelves to, by giving Credit to our Neighbour* Tories, as Will. Fenwick, Tate, Green, *and* Allgood. *If you out-live Misfortune, and return to live in the North, I defire you never to be feen to converfe with fuch Rogues in Difguife, that promifed to join us, and animated us to rife with them.* The Gentleman promifed that Lord to obey him. But that Lord anfwer'd, *Ah! I know you to be of an eafy Temper.* Having continued at *Warrington* all Night, they march'd forwards for *London* by eafy Marches; nothing material happening, only a Detachment of *Stanhope's* Dragoons were ordered to return; and whilft we were marching over a Heath, one of the Highlanders told the Country People that came to view us, *Where are all your High-Church* Tories? *If they would not-fight with us, why do they not come and refcue us?* Which indifcreet Words made the commanding Officer make him difmount, and walk on Foot pinion'd. Thefe Detachments of Horfe and Dragoons that guarded us, were relieved by a Squadron of *Lumley's* Horfe, under the Command of Brigadier *Panton,* who look'd more nearly to us than we had been formerly. At

Daventry

Daventry he fingled Mr. *Forfter* and me from among the reft, and confined us in the Guard-Room all Night (which was continued in all our Quarters till we came to *Newgate*) under a fufficient Watch, allowing none to fpeak with us.

Here I muft relate how Mr. *Forfter* catch'd Cold, by lying on the Ground in a Corner very damp, which indifpofed him very much all along, fo that at St. *Alban's* he was not able to ride, but was allowed a Coach. Upon this it was reported he had taken Poifon. Which was very falfe; for Lieutenant *Bifhop*, who had the Care of us, advifed him to take a little *Diafcordium*, which brought upon him a great Fit of Vomiting. From *Daventry* to *London*, he and I were diftinguifh'd from the reft, by our Halters being led by two Troopers, with Halters upon our Horfes Heads; which gave the People, as we paffed along, an Opportunity to compliment us with Encomiums upon a Warming-pan. At *Barnet* we were all pinion'd, more for Diftinction than any Pain that attended: And at *Highgate* we were met with a ftrong Detachment of Horfe-Grenadiers and Foot-Guards, each Man having his Horfe led by one of the Foot. Setting forward from *Highgate*, we were met by fuch Numbers of People, that it is fcarce conceivable to exprefs, who with, *Long Live King* G E O R G E! *and down with the* Pretender! ufhered us throughout to our feveral Apartments. I fhall add a very pleafant Story: A Quaker fix'd his Eyes upon me, and diftinguifhing what I was, faid; *Friend, Verily thou haft been the Trumpeter of Rebellion to thefe Men; thou muft anfwer for them.* Upon this, my Grenadier gave him a Pufh with the But-end of his Mufket, fo that the Spirit fell into the Ditch. Whilft fprawling on his Back, he told the Soldier, *Thou haft not us'd me civilly; I doubt thou art not a real Friend to King* G E O R G E. Mr. *Forfter* thought ftill to

have

have been releafed by a *Tory Mob*, and told me, that he had Affurances thereof from a Gentleman at *Highgate*. But thofe Bravaders will not hazard themfelves, tho' they fpeak great Things. He was likewife troubled that he fhould be fent to *Newgate*, being unexpelled the *Houfe of Commons*; and like- wife mortify'd, when he underftood that *Gordon*, *Carr*, and *Dorrel* were executed a Day before, and their Quarters then in a Box juft by, in order to be fet upon the Gates; which fpoiled his Stomach, fo that he could not eat with his then unhappy Companion.

The Names of the Lords, Prifoners, are well known, *viz.*

James Radcliffe Earl of *Derwentwater*, Beheaded on *Tower-Hill*, *February* 24. 1715-16.

William Widdrington Lord *Widdrington*.

William Maxwell Earl of *Nithfdale*, made his Efcape out of the *Tower*, *Feb*. 23. 1715-16. drefs'd in a Woman's Cloak and Hood, which fince are called *Nithfdales*.

[Thefe three were Papifts.]

George Seaton Earl of *Wintoun*, made his Efcape alfo out of the *Tower*, *Aug*. 4. 1716.

William Gordon Vifcount *Kenmure*, Beheaded with Lord *Derwentwater*.

William Nairn Lord *Nairn*.

I fhall here add a Lift of the reft in general, of thofe who were taken that were of any Note; which I fhould not do, it being fo often publifhed, but that it fhall be done in a different manner, adding a fhort Account of fo many as came within my Knowledge, as to their Circumftances, the Pofts they bore, and what Kingdom, County, and Re- ligion they were of, and the Fate that followed them.

Mr.

Mr. *Thomas Forster* jun. of *Etherston* in the County
of *Northumberland*, Proteſtant, Member of Parliament for the ſaid County, was made General :
Eſcaped out of *Newgate*. I ſhall here inſert : On
Saturday, April 7. 1716, a Bill of Indictment was
found againſt him ; he was to have been arraign'd,
in order to his Trial, on the 14th of *April* ; but on
Wedneſday Morning all were ſurpriz'd, to hear that
he had found Means to make his Eſcape the Night
before. Upon Notice of this, a Proclamation was
publiſh'd for apprehending *Thomas Forster* Eſq; with
a Deſcription of his Perſon, as one of a Middle-
Stature, inclining to be Fat, well-ſhap'd, except
that he ſtoops in the Shoulders, fair Complexion'd,
his Mouth wide, his Noſe pretty large, his Eyes
Grey, ſpeaks the Northern Dialect, with a Reward
of a Thouſand Pounds to any who ſhould apprehend him. The Grand-Jury of *Middleſex* having
enquir'd into the manner of his Eſcape, thought fit
to preſent Mr. *Pitts* Keeper of *Newgate*, for a very
high Neglect and Miſdemeanor in his Office, who
was afterwards committed to the Cuſtody of a Meſſenger, and then brought to his Trial, where he
made the manner of Mr. *Forster*'s Eſcape appear :
(He was acquitted.) Which is as follows. Mr.
Forster, for ſome time after his Commitment to
Newgate, was confin'd in a Chamber in the *Preſs-
yard*, but was removed into a ſtrong Room in Mr.
Pitts's Houſe, as likewiſe Mr. *Anderton* to another.
Mr. *Forster* hearing ſome-body upon the Stairs one
Night, opened his Door, (being allowed the Li-
berty to walk in the *Preſs-yard*) which was Mr.
Anderton, whom he invited to come and take a
Glaſs, 'till ſuch time as they were lock'd up. Mr.
Pitts entred the Room, and found them over a
Flaſk of Wine ; when it was ſomething above half
gone, Mr. *Forster* went up (as Mr. *Pitts* thought)
to the Neceſſary-houſe ; upon which his Heart miſ-
gave

gave him, and therefore Mr. *Pitts* went up after Mr. *Forster* ; but, to his great Surprize, found he was not there, and going down, he found the fall of the Latch deadned by a piece of Lift, and a Peg in the Kitchen-door, by which his Servant was confined ; for Mr. *Forster's* Man being below Stairs, asked for some Small-beer. Whilst the Servant was drawing him some, he fix'd the Peg, and secured him. Mr. *Forster* left his Night-Gown upon the Steps. Mr. *Pitts* called out for his Man, but he could not get out ; but finding the Peg, he pulled it out. Upon which he called aloud, *I am undone !* Forster *is gone !* then calling for the Key, there was another, a false one, in the other side of the Door, and the Door double-lock'd. Thus Mr. *Forster*, and his Man *Thomas Lee*, found Means to escape, leaving their Keeper a Prisoner.

Mr. *Edward Howard* Brother to the Duke of *Norfolk*, try'd and acquitted; a Papist.

Mr. *Charles Radcliffe* Brother to the late Earl of *Derwentwater*, try'd and found Guilty, and afterwards escaped out of *Newgate, December* 11. 1716. He lay under Condemnation.

Charles Widdrington Esq; Brother to the Lord *Widdrington* of *Northumberland*, Papist, pleaded Guilty. Since removed into the Custody of a Messenger, in order for a Pardon.

Per. Widdrington Esq; third Brother to this Lord, and *Aid de Camp* to General *Forster*, Papist : Removed out of *Newgate* into the Custody of a Messenger, in order for a Pardon.

Walter Tancred Brother to Sir *Thomas Tancred* of *Yorkshire*, Papist, pleaded Guilty. He was Companion to the Lord *Widdrington* in all his Country Diverfions.

John Thornton of *Netherwitton* in *Northumberland* ; has a good Estate there, pleaded Guilty; a Papist.

John

John Clavering, a Papiſt, of *Northumberland*. This Gentleman, by the Intereſt of my Lord Chancellor's Lady who is his Kinſwoman, had a *Noli proſequi*.

John Clavering Brother to *William Clavering*, both Papiſts, in *Northumberland*.

Nicholas Wogan Captain, an *Iriſhman*, who for his generous Uſage to Major *Preſton* whom he made a Priſoner, is in a fair way of being pardon'd, being now removed from *Newgate* into the Cuſtody of a Meſſenger : He ſtood his Trial, and was brought in Guilty of High-Treaſon. He is a Papiſt.

Charles Wogan an *Iriſhman*, behav'd very well at *Preſton* ; Mr. *Forſter* called him his *Aid de Camp :* He made his Eſcape out of *Newgate*. He was a Papiſt.

John Talbot of *Cartington* in *Northumberland*, a brave young Gentleman ; his Father made himſelf famous for his Courage at the Siege of *Buda*, but was killed : This Gentleman made his Eſcape from *Cheſter*.

Robert Talbot an *Iriſhman* and Papiſt, formerly an Officer in the *French* Service ; he was accounted a very good Soldier : He was found Guilty of High-Treaſon.

Roger Salkeld of *Cumberland*, a Papiſt, ſecond Son to Sir *Richard Salkeld* of *Whitehall* in the ſaid County : He made his Eſcape from *Cheſter*.

George Collingwood of *Northumberland*, a Papiſt, of a valuable Eſtate : He was ordered for *London*, but was ſeiz'd with the Gout at *Wigan*, and from thence was carried to *Liverpool*, and there found Guilty, and afterwards Executed there the 25th of *February*. He was a very pious Gentleman, and well beloved in his Country.

John Hall : This Gentleman has been very unlucky the whole time of his Life ; he was born to a handſome Eſtate in *North-Tine*, but his Indiſcretion

tion

tion and Forwardnefs reduced it to a low Ebb. He married a Gentlewoman of *Newcaftle*, againft the Confent of her Father Alderman *Hutchinfon.* His Misfortunes, or unfettled Humour, made him fhift from his own Seat to feveral other Places, as *Hexam* and the Borders of *Scotland,* where he farmed an Eftate, and cultivated the fame with a great deal of good Management ; being fkill'd in Hufbandry, he had reap'd a very good Crop of all manner of Grain from this Farm, and had them well gather'd together into Barns and Stack-yards ; but an unexpeeted Fire broke out, of which no Account can be given how, in the middle of the Night, and with Violence not to be conquer'd, confumed the Houfe he lived in, all the Stables and Cow-houfes, Barns, and Stacks of Corn, with the Oxen, Cows and Horfes, himfelf and Family narrowly efcaping. He return'd fome time after to his own Eftate, whither hard Fortune had purfued him ; for having the Profpeet of a plentiful Increafe of Corn which he had got cut down, and near ready to get together, in the Night there fell fuch a Flood of Rain as carried all his Crop along with the over-flowing Stream. Thefe two Misfortunes were look'd upon as Judgments upon him, for being concern'd, if not acceffory, to the Death of two Gentlemen, which was thus : At *Newcaftle upon Tyne* there happen'd a Quarrel betwixt Mr. *Septimus Forfter* Member of Parliament for the County of *Northumberland,* and one Mr. *Fenwick :* Mr. *Hall* was made privy to the Quarrel, and acquainted with their Refolution to fight ; which he might have prevented : But Mr. *Fenwick* efpying Mr. *Forfter* in the Street, without being hinder'd by Mr. *Hall,* went with hafte to the other, and both drawing their Swords, Mr. *Forfter,* who was generally efteem'd, was run through the Body, and inftantly died : The other was apprehended, and prefently brought to his Trial, the

Judges

Judges being then in Town, found guilty of Wilful Murder, and executed where he committed the Fact. Mr. *Hall* has been blamed for this by a great many People: If he was any way acceſſory, it ſeems the two mentioned ſtrange Fates that attended theſe worthy Gentlemens Deaths, ſhewed a purſuing Judgment. When Mr. *Fenwick* was try'd, he appear'd as an Evidence for him; but it was little regarded by the Jury, and he met with a ſevere Reprimand from the Judge. By what Intereſt, ſome Years after this, he came to be in the Commiſſion of the Peace, and an Officer of the Train'd-bands, I ſhall not hint; but, to ſhew the Indiſcretion of the Man, I muſt inform you, that when he was ſiting upon the Bench at the Quarter-Seſſions held for the County at *Alnwick*, all on a ſudden he left his Brethren the Juſtices in ſuch Precipitation, that he left his Hat, but got it again, and with haſte went to the Rebels, deſiring Mr. *Forſter* to go and ſeize on the Juſtices, and the County Clerk and his Books; which was refuſed. He was never much eſteemed by the commanding Rebels, being known to be of a fierce and paſſionate Temper, which got him the Name of *Mad Jack Hall of Otterbourn*. Thus you ſee that Fate never left him till ſhe purſued him to his untimely Death, where he denied his Faith, and made a ſtrange Exit. He has left Children born to him by his virtuous good Wife of very good Parentage, and no ſmall Fortune.

John Hunter a Farmer at *Callylee* in *Northumberland*, reputed very rich; he made his Eſcape.

Edward Ord.

William Tunſtall Pay-Maſter General and Quarter-Maſter General, a *Yorkſhire* Man, ſecond Son to a Gentleman of that County, of a plentiful Eſtate. He has had all the Advantages of a generous Education, which he has improved by his good and agreeable Converſation and Learning; for he made ſeveral

Copies

Copies of Verses after he was a Prisoner, which gain'd Applause from good Judges of Poetry: They shew the Man, tho' Old, and under Sentence of Death, not to despond; and it is hoped he will receive his Majesty's Pardon. He is a Papist.

William Shaftoe of *Bavington*, formerly a Justice of Peace for the County of *Northumberland*; has a plentiful Estate: There he was brought in to the Rebellion through the Instigation of his Lady, and Mr. *John Shaftoe* who was shot at *Preston*. He was once a Papist, but returned to the Church of *England*. He is a Gentleman of an easy Temper, and so too easily prevail'd with to join in the Rebellion. I shall add a Story of him, when in *Newgate* with Mr. *John Hall*, who was afterward Executed, which has something diverting in it. He says seriously to Mr. *Hall, Cousin* Jack, *I am thinking on what is told us, That* God *will visit the Sins of the Fathers unto the third and fourth Generation. I am of Opinion that it is so with us; for your Grandfather and mine got most of their Estates as Sequestrators, and now we must lose them again for being Rebels.*

John Shaftoe his Son, a Papist: He was but lately come from beyond Sea. He is a most violent Bigot to his Faith; was formerly Page to the Duke of *Wolfembottle.*

Edward Shaftoe, an old Grey-headed Gentleman, Father to *John Shaftoe* shot at *Preston* as an Half-pay Officer. This old Man became an Evidence for the King at *Liverpool* and *London.*

John Shaftoe Captain, shot, as mentioned before: He was made early acquainted with the Rebellion, and would have saved his Life by Impeaching others, but was too far from the Court to have his Mind known: This would have been of good Service. He died very Penitent.

Edward

Edward Swinbourn and *James Swinbourn*, both of them Papifts, and Brothers to Sir *William* of *Caph-eaton*; both found Guilty. The former a very handfome Gentleman, and of good Parts; dy'd in *Newgate*. The other, thro' long Confinement, or, as fome alledge, an hereditary Diftemper, which fome of that Family have been fubjeét to, became Penfive and Melancholy.

George Gibfon of *Stonecroft*, *Northumberland*, a Papift: A Gentleman well belov'd in his Country. Dy'd in *Newgate*.

Edward Byras of *Northumberland*, belonged to Lord *Widdrington*'s Troop, made his Efcape on the Road to *London*.

Richard Stokoe, formerly in the *Scots* Grey Regiment of Dragoons, was made a Quarter-Mafter in the Earl of *Derwentwater*'s Troop. He lived in *Northumberland*; a Proteftant. He was taken out of the *Fleet*, and put into the Cuftody of one of the King's Meffengers, in order to become an Evidence, but made his Efcape.

Richard Chorley of *Chorley* in *Lancafhire*, a Papift: A Gentleman of fingular Piety and Parts, was order'd for *London*; but falling fick at *Wigan*, was left behind, and was try'd at *Liverpool*, found Guilty, and Executed at *Prefton*, February 9. 1715-16.

Charles Chorley Son to *Richard Chorley*, was a young Gentleman of very good Parts, was try'd at *Liverpool*, found Guilty; but died in Goal.

Ralph Standifh of *Standifh*, a Papift in *Lancafhire*, a Gentleman of very good Repute; having a plentiful Fortune, marry'd into the Duke of *Norfolk*'s Family: He was found Guilty of High-Treafon at *Weftminfter*: fince removed into the Cuftody of a Meffenger, in order for a Pardon.

Sir *Francis Anderton* of *Loftock*, a Papift of *Lancafhire*: He has an Eftate of 2000 l. *per Annum*.
He

He was Indicted as a Baronet ; but he pleaded that false, because his Elder Brother, a Popish Priest beyond Sea, was alive. He was afterwards found Guilty, and received Sentence. This Gentleman is of pleasant and diverting Conversation : He is reported to say, He lost a good Estate for being with the Rebels but One Day. Taken out of *Newgate* into the Custody of a Messenger, in order for a Pardon.

Dr. *Walker*, alias *Alcock*, Physician, skill'd in that Practice. A little before the Rebellion broke out, on a Rejoicing-Day, he made an Entertainment for his Friends at his Chamber in *Alnwick*; but becoming somewhat overtaken with Liquor, instead of Loyal Words, he spoke some that amounted to Treason. He was afterwards call'd to answer for his Expressions, but he put in Bail for his Appearance ; tho' he did not think convenient to stay till the Assizes, but absconded, and joined the Rebels. Being of a frank and comical Disposition, he told his Rebel Friends, *That his Bail should not suffer; for he would write to the Judge, that he was now at* Hexam, *ready to pay his Fine.* He made his Escape from *Preston*.

Richard Townley of *Townley*, a Papist in *Lancashire*; he marry'd Lord *Widdrington*'s Sister. This Gentleman's Servants were found Guilty of High-Treason, for being in the Rebellion with their Master, and some of them afterwards Executed in *Lancashire*; but he was Acquitted by the Jury at the *Marshalsea*. After which, endeavouring to go beyond Sea, he was retaken into Custody, but soon discharged.

John Dalton a Papist of *Lancashire*, of a good Estate, was try'd at the *Marshalsea*, and found Guilty. Since removed into the Custody of a Messenger, in order for his Pardon.

John Leybourn a Papist, *Lancashire*.

Gabriel

Gabriel Hesket Father, and *Cuthbert Hesket* Son, both Papists, *Lancashire.*

Thomas Walton of *Winder*, *Lancashire*, a Papist.

Edward Tildesly of the *Lodge*, a Papist, *Lancashire*, was acquitted by the Jury at the *Marshalsea*, tho' it was proved he had a Troop, and entred *Preston* at the Head of it with his Sword drawn. But his Sword had a Silver Handle.

Thomas Errington of *Beaufront*, a Papist, *Northumberland:* At his Trial pleaded Guilty; and is since removed from *Newgate* into the Custody of a Messenger, in order for an Enlargement.

Philip Hudson of *Sandow*, a Papist, *Northumberland*; by Marriage, Uncle to the Lord *Widdrington.*

James Talbot an *Irish* Papist, made his Escape from *Newgate*; but a Reward of 500 Pounds being set forth, he was retaken in *London.*

Alexander Deasines.

Lyonel Walden of *Westminster*, an *Oxford* Student; joined in the Rebellion with his Uncle Mr. *Robert Cotton.*

John Masterson.

George Sanderson of *Highlee*, a Papist of *Northumberland.*

George Budden an Upholsterer of *London*, Protestant; made his Escape from *Newgate.*

William Charleton, Son to Mr. *Charleton* of the *Bower* in *Northumberland*, lately pardon'd by Queen *Anne* for murdering Mr. *Widdrington.* His Brother *Edward Charleton* is a Doctor of Physick, and lately turn'd Papist, having marry'd one of that Church.

Robert Cotton, a Gentleman of very good Fortune: He is a Nonjuror. This Gentleman is of good Repute for his Life and Conversation; is agreeable to all that have the Advantage of being

acquainted

acquainted with him ; he is very much given to Hofpitality ; and has a tender Regard to every unfortunate Perfon's Condition ; and, like a good Chriftian, thinks his plentiful Fortune put only into his Hands, that he might be ferviceable in his Generation.

John Cotton his Son, both Proteftants. He was liberally educated under the watchful Care of an affectionate Parent, who gave him all the Advantages to accomplifh a Gentleman ; which he improved fo, as to be capable of living either at Court as a Gentleman , with the Learned as a Scholar, or with his Country Neighbours as one of them ; to give him his due, he is of a Soul that is not lofty and afpiring, and yet not bafe or mean, and, which ftill adds, gives all that due Obedience and profound Refpect that is juftly owing to a kind Father.

Richard Gafcoine an *Irifh* Papift, executed at *Tyburn, May* 25. This Gentleman was born in *Ireland,* and defcended from a good Family, that had been very ferviceable to the Crown in *Oliver's* Rebellion. He was bred a *Roman* ; according to his Principles was zealous for the *Chevalier*, and a declar'd Enemy to the *Revolution.* His Grandfather was kill'd in the Service of King *Charles* I. and his Father in the Service of the unfortunate King *James* II. at the Siege of *Limerick.* He was Heir to an Eftate of about 200 *l. per Ann.* which he converted into Money. He came to *London,* and being a tall handfome Man, of an engaging Converfation, foon got Acquaintance in Town, and with them indulged himfelf in all youthful Follies and Vices, which reduc'd him to mean Circumftances ; but the Cards and Dice, his great Companions, in a little time made him Reparation, for he became a great Proficient that way ; fo being reinftated in *Fortune's* Favour, which, together with his good natural Parts, civil

Behaviour,

Behaviour, and political Principles, foon brought him acquainted with the beft Quality among the *Tories*, by whom he was intrufted with the principal Management at the *Bath*; from whence he fled as foon as he heard that his Majefty's Meffengers were in queft of him, and fo fteer'd towards the *North* to find out the Rebels, whom he joined at *Prefton*, and with thofe of Note was brought up to *London*, and confin'd to *Newgate*; whilft there he gave the greateft Demonftration of a true Penitent, and gave himfelf folely up to his Devotion, and dy'd with the greateft Unconcernednefs of any of the unfortunate Rebels.

John Hunter of *Northumberland*, executed at *Liverpool*, a Proteftant; he was fhot thro' the Leg at *Prefton*.

William Hardwick.

Richard Butler of *Racliffe*, *Lancafhire*, a Papift, found guilty, and dy'd in *Newgate*.

Robert Patten, one of the Chaplains, Minifter of *Allandale*, *Northumberland*; he fav'd his Life by being an Evidence for the King.

William Crafter of *Crafter*, *Northumberland*, came with Mr. *Forfter*, and two others, into the Rebellion; thefe being all that Gentleman brought into the fame Fate with himfelf.

Thomas Lifle of *Northumberland*, Proteftant, very young.

Thomas Forfter, a Relation of Mr. *Forfter's*; he was try'd and found guilty at *Liverpool*.

William Raine of *Newcaftle* upon *Tyne*, a Quarter-Mafter.

Thomas Riddle, Son to Mr. *Riddle* of *Swinbourn*-Caftle, *Northumberland*, a Papift, pleaded guilty; he was, a little before the Rebellion, come from the College beyond Sea.

Henry Widdrington, Quarter-Mafter.

Richard Ord, with two Brothers, of *Weetwood*; one dy'd.
William

William Sanderson of *Highlee*, *Northumberland*, a Papift, made his Efcape from *Chefter*. This Gentleman has many valuable and endearing Accomplifhments.

John Towle, an *Irifh* Papift.

Edward Mackay.

Henry Oxburgh, an *Irifh* Papift, and call'd Colonel, executed at *Tyburn.* He was born in *Ireland* to a plentiful Eftate, had ferved in the late King *James*'s Army for a confiderable Time, was of a good, mild, and merciful Difpofition, very thoughtful, and a mighty zealous Man in his Religion, quiet in his Converfation, and more of the Prieft in his Appearance than the Soldier : He dy'd very penitent. There came a Letter from *Ireland* to one in the Secretary's Office, to acquaint General *Stanhope*, Secretary of State, with this Gentleman's Character, and Inclinations to the *Pretender* ; which made him appear as irreconcilable to the Proteftant Intereft.

William Dobfon.

John Beaumont, a Papift, and Lieutenant, made his Efcape in *Lancafhire.*

John Crofts of *Wooler*, *Northumberland*, Adjutant.

William Calderwood, Quarter-Mafter-General to the *Scots*, formerly an Officer in *Douglafs*'s Regiment on the *Dutch* Eftablifhment, being in *Scotland* when the Rebellion began, was prevail'd with by Lord *Kenmure* to join the Rebels.

Englifh Followers, or Servants.

Robert Brufe,	*Corn. Stewart*,	*James Robfon*,
Val. Errington,	*Luke Blacket*,	*William Hardy*,
Edward Tinklar,	*Thomas Dixon*,	*James Mills*,
John Atkinfon,	*Oliver Hamilton*,	*John Brady*,
John Militfon,	*William Anfley*,	*Robert Brown*,
John Patrick,	*Robert Stubs*,	*James Wilkinfon*,
		J. Bywater,

I

J. Bywater,
Jonnage Aron,
Henry Masson,
William Smell,
John Holt,
Andr. Thompson,
James Shaw,
John Burtham,
Nicholas Doyle,
Thomas Holling,
Edward Bullock,
John Omfield,
Thomas Moore,
John Rowland,
Nicholas Wilson,
John Thornton,
William Young,
Henry Wilson,
Cuthbert Hasket,
Thomas Bell,
Mr. Hilyard Gentleman to Lord Widdrington,

Henry Rowley,
Ralph Lorrain,
Garret Nangle,
William Purdy,
Thomas Lee,
Mr. Wesby, Gentleman to the Earl of Derwentwater,
John Todd,
William Stewart,
Roger Balson,
John Wilson,
Thomas Smith,
John Thornton,
Wil. Dixson,
Leonard Ord,
William Scot,
Thomas Fareburn,
James Richmond,
James Asington,
Albert Hacksel,
John Tasker,

John Clarke,
Mich. Mosses,
Wil. Farnworth,
John Farnworth,
William Wilson,
William Tash,
Henry Gardiner,
John Steele,
Ra. Todd,
Henry Todd,
John Todd,
Charles May,
Henry Ashley,
William Ratcliff,
William Wilson,
Tim. Flanakan,
Charles Bartes,
Ro. Finkle,
James Wilson,
William Todd,
William Read,
R. Wilson.

A LIST of the *Scots* Officers.

M'intosh's Battalion consisted of thirteen Companies, fifty Men in each Company before the Desertion at *Langholm*.

——*Ferguson* Lieutenant-Colonel of *Invercall*, pardon'd by the Prince.
John M'intosh Major, Brother to the Brigadier, escap'd.

Laughlan M'intosh senior, Capt.
Farquhar M'gilroy Capt.
Angus M'bean Capt.
Robert Shaw Capt.
Duncomb M'intosh Capt.
William

William M'intosh Capt.
Angus M'intosh Capt.
Laughlan M'intosh junior,
Capt.
Francis Farquharson of
Whithouse, acquitted.
Laughlan M'clean Capt.
William M'gilroy Lieut.
John Farquharson of Kirk-
toun, acquitted.
John M'intosh Lieut.
Farquhar M'gilroy Lieut.
John M'bean Lieut.
Angus Shaw Lieut.
Benj. M'intosh Lieut.
James M'intosh Lieut.

William Maquin Lieut.
John M'intosh Lieut.
Duncan, M'intosh Lieut.
John Abercromby Lieut.
and Aid de Camp.
———— Skeen Lieut. and
Aid de Camp.
David Stuart Lieut.
Will. M'intosh Lieut.
Jo. M'intosh Aid de Cong.
Daniel Grant Adjutant.
Dav. M'quian Pay-Ma-
fter.
William Shaw Quarter-
Mafter.

Strathmore's Regiment: A great Part of them were
prevented from crossing the Forth by the KING's
Ships: but these did ;

William Duglass Capt.
William Miller Capt.
John Screnger Capt.
James Balfewer Capt.
William Lyon Lieut.
Alexander Murray Lieut.
Alexander Orrack Lieut.
John Burnes Lieut.

Patrick Duglass Ensign.
Hugh Ken Ensign.
Alex. Magiven Ensign.
Andrew Ramsey Ensign.
Henry Ogilvey Ensign.
Will. Henderson Quarter-
Mafter.

Logie Drummond's Regiment: Better Part hereof
were prevented from crossing the Forth, and some
of them left in Leith.

David Drummond Capt.
John Carnagy Capt.
Alex. M'grudder Capt.
James Drummond Lieut.

Alexander Drummond.
Archibald M'laughlan.
William Grudder.

Lord

Lord *Nairne*'s Regiment: Several were kept from crossing the *Forth*.

Lord *Nairne* Colonel.
John Stuart Lieut. Col.
————*Blair* Major.
Alex. Robertson Capt.
James Stuart Capt.
James Robertson Capt.

John Stuart Capt.
Robert Stuart Capt.
Arch. Butler, the Lady's
Darling, tho' *mangy* in
the Rebellion,

Mar's Battalion: Several left on the other side the *Forth*.

Nathanael Forbes Major.
John James Capt.
Donald Ferguson Capt.
John Gordon Capt.

John Cattanack Lieut.
Henry Lamsden Lieut.
Robert Gordon Lieut.

Lord *Charles Murray*'s Regiment.

Lord *Murray* Colonel.
Master of *Nairn* Lieutenant-Colonel.
James Stuart Major.
James Mineries Capt.
Alex. Mineries Lieut.
Adam Reid Lieut.
John Stuart.
John Ratson.
Alexander Stuart.

Alex. Mineries Capt.
Don. Robertson Capt.
John Robertson Capt.
Patrick Robertson Capt.
John M'kevan Lieut.
Dun. Campbell Lieut.
John Robson.
James Raton.
John Stuart.

English

Engliſh Noblemen and Gentlemen } ———— 75
taken Priſoners ———— ———— ————

Their Servants, or Followers, ———— ———— 83

Private Men in the Church ———— ———— ———— 305

Total *Engliſh* 463

Scots Noblemen, Officers, and Gen- } ———— 143
tlemen, taken Priſoners ————

Their Vaſſals, *&c.* ———— ———— ———— 862

Total *Scots* 1005

Re-taken ———— ———— 21

In all 1489

A great many found Means to eſcape.

THE

THE

HISTORY

OF THE

REBELLION

IN

SCOTLAND.

PART II.

THE Earl of *Mar* upon the Death of Queen *Anne*, whose Secretary of State he was, as it is believ'd, had no Rebellious Designs then in his Head; nor, could he have had his selfish Views answer'd, would he perhaps ever have embark'd as he did; as may seem by a Letter he sent to His Majesty King GEORGE with a tender of his Duty, and expressing himself in the most passionate Terms, as a Person full of Loyalty and Affection to his Person and Government, ready to serve his Interest, and defend his Succession; the Copy of which it is very necessary to put in the Front of what offers concerning him, and is as follows: to

SIR,

S I R,

'HAving the Happiness to be your Majesty's
'Subject, and also the Honour of being one
'of your Servants, as one of your Secretaries of
'State, I beg leave to kiss your Majesty's Hand,
'and congratulate your happy Accession to the
'Throne; which I would have done myself the
'Honour of doing sooner, had I not hop'd to
'have had the Honour of doing it personally e'er
'now.

'I am afraid I may have had the Misfortune of be-
'ing misrepresented to your Majesty; and my Reason
'for thinking so, is, because I was, I believe, the
'only one of the late Queen's Servants, whom your
'Ministers here did not visit; which I mentioned
'to Mr. *Harley,* and the Earl of *Clarendon,* when
'they went from hence to wait on your Majesty;
'and your Ministers carrying so to me, was the
'Occasion of my receiving such Orders as depriv'd
'me of the Honour and Satisfaction of waiting on
'them, and being known to them.

'I suppose I had been misrepresented to them by
'some here, upon Account of Party, or to ingra-
'tiate themselves by asperfing others, as our Parties
'here too often occasion; but I hope your Majesty
'will be so just as not to give Credit to such Mif-
'representations.

'The Part I acted in the bringing about and
'making of the Union, when the Succession to the
'Crown was settled for *Scotland* on your Majesty's
'Family, where I had the honour to serve as Se-
'cretary of State for that Kingdom, doth, I hope,
'put my Sincerity and Faithfulness to your Majesty
'out of Dispute.

'My Family hath had the honour, for a great Tract
'of Years, to be faithful Servants to the Crown,
'and have had the Care of the King's Children
'(when

‘ (when Kings of *Scotland)* intrufted to them. A
‘ Predeceffor of mine was honour'd with the Care
‘ of your Majefty's Grandmother when young;
‘ and fhe was pleafed afterwards to exprefs fome
‘ Concern for our Family in Letters which I ftill
‘ have under her own Hand.

‘ I have had the honour to ferve her late Majefty
‘ in one Capacity or other, ever fince her Acceffion
‘ to the Crown. I was happy in a good Miftrefs,
‘ and fhe was pleafed to have fome Confidence in
‘ me, and Regard for my Services: And fince
‘ your Majefty's happy Acceffion to the Crown,
‘ I hope you will find that I have not been wanting
‘ in my Duty, in being inftrumental in keeping
‘ Things quiet and peaceable in the Country to
‘ which I belong, and have fome Intereft in.

‘ Your Majefty fhall ever find me as faithful
‘ and dutiful a Subject and Servant as ever any of
‘ my Family have been to the Crown, or as I have
‘ been to my late Miftrefs the Queen. And I beg
‘ your Majefty may be fo good, not to believe any
‘ Mifreprefentations of me, which nothing but Party
‘ Hatred, and my Zeal for the Intereft of the Crown
‘ doth occafion; and I hope I may prefume to lay
‘ Claim to your Royal Favour and Protection.

‘ As your Acceffion to the Crown hath been quiet
‘ and peaceable, may your Majefty's Reign be long
‘ and profperous: And that your People may foon
‘ have the Happinefs and Satisfaction of your Prefence
‘ among them, is the earneft and fervent Wifhes of
‘ him, who is with the humbleft Duty and Refpect,

S I R,

Your Majefty's moft faithful,

moft dutiful, and moft obedient

Subject and Servant,

M A R.

Now

Now altho', befides this, he had, upon fome Reafons beft known to himfelf, prevail'd with himfelf,
perhaps againft Principle, to take the Oaths to his
prefent Majefty, he took another Liberty afterwards
more wicked and equally harden'd, (*viz.*) to forget
and caft off the Obligation of thofe Oaths, and refolve upon Rebellion againft that very Prince he
had fworn to. In order to this, he concerted Meafures with the Jacobites and Papifts to form a Rebellion, and by Force of Arms to make way for
the *Pretender*, as well to bring him in, as to eftablifh him upon the Imperial Throne of thefe Kingdoms: In which Concert, he for his part took
upon him to draw the chief of the Clans in the
Highlands of *Scotland* to Arms, and with them to
enter into open Rebellion. Accordingly, about the
Month of *Auguft*, 1715. he fet out for *Scotland*,
where he made, for a Pretence, a great Hunting.
This proclaiming a Hunting, is a Cuftom among
the Lords and Chiefs of Families in the Highlands,
and on which Occafions they invite their Neighbour-
ing Gentlemen and Vaffals to a general Rendezvous, to hunt or chafe the Deer upon the Mountains, of which they have there great Plenty. The
Ufage on thefe Occafions is, that all the People
round the Country, being well arm'd, affemble upon the Day appointed ; and after the Diverfion is
over, the Perfons of Note are invited to an Entertainment ; which the Earl of *Mar* obferved, and
having got his Friends together, he made his Intention known to them in a publick Speech full of
Invectives againft the Proteftant Succeffion in general, and againft King George in particular. It
is true, that at firft he gained little or no Credit
amongft them, they fufpecting fome piece of Policy
in him to enfnare them : But fome were weak
enough to fuck in the Poifon, and particularly fome
of thofe who were with him at his Houfe, called

Brae-

Brae-Mar. These listening to him, embrac'd his Project, and, as is reported, engag'd by Oath to stand by him, and one another, and to bring over their Friends and Dependants to do the like.

Previous to this, it will be necessary to give a full Account of the general Humour of the *Scots*, and their Inclinations to fix the *Pretender* upon the Throne of *Scotland*, which the Union so universally disliked both by the Presbyterians and Episcopal Party in general; but the Presbyterians in a great measure had heightned them to such a Resentment, that the designing Party in the *Pretender*'s Interest made it the main Bait to catch the unthinking People, who imagin'd themselves enslav'd to *English* Bondage by the Union. How far this was cultivated, is plainly laid down by the ingenious Author of the Memoirs of the Affairs in *Scotland*, of which I shall give a short hint, to shew how artfully the *Pretender*'s Interest was advanced in that Kingdom: There was one Colonel *Hook* sent from *France*, who landed in the North of *Scotland* about *March* 1707. He conversed with the Countess of *Errol*, Sister to the Duke of *Perth*, who told him who were proper Persons for him to converse with to promote his Master's Interest. He then came to the Shires of *Perth* and *Angus*, and avowed himself an Ambassador.

After he had found the People's Pulses, he produced a Letter from the *Pretender*, and another from the *French* King, empowering him to treat with the People of *Scotland*, for establishing the Chevalier St. *George* upon the Throne, and recovering the Nation's Sovereignty and ancient Privileges: He likewise produced several Queries from Monsieur *de Torci*, relating to the Number of Men that could be raised in *Scotland*; the Conveniency of subsisting Troops, besides the Number of Men, Sum of Money, and other War-like Matters to be

fent from *France* ; thefe Matters being adjufted, an
Anfwer to Monfieur *de Torci*'s Queftions was com-
piled, with a full Account of the Pofture of Affairs,
particularly the People's Inclinations, and Forwardnefs of the very Prefbyterians ; and fo figned Papers
which were lodged in the hands of Colonel *Hook*,
to be tranfported to *France*, fubfcribed by fixteen
Peers. This gave Encouragement for the Court of
France to fit out a Fleet to tranfport the Chevalier
St. *George* to *Scotland*, which was done accordingly,
but without any Refult, but returning in hafte home ;
yet this early Engagement to the *Pretender*, tho'
then croffed, was ftill maintain'd till the Rebellion
broke out ; tho' fome that were then very forward,
acted now in Difguife, as a certain Duke in the
North has done ; yet his Vaffals encouraged by his
Son, made themfelves a very great part of thofe in
Rebellion.

The Highlanders in *Scotland* are, of all Men in
the World, the fooneft wrought upon to follow
their Leaders or Chiefs into the Field, having a
wonderful Veneration for their Lords and Chief-
tains, as they are called there : Nor do thefe People ever confider the Validity of the engaging Caufe,
but blindly follow their Chiefs into what Mifchief
they pleafe, and that with the greateft Precipitation
imaginable.

They are fo entire at the Devotion of their Chiefs,
that formerly, when one Clan fell out with another,
they formed Bodies, and invaded each other's Terri-
tories, fpoiling and plundering each other's Lands ;
and publick Rencounters follow'd not eafily to be
appeafed, the Grudges for many Generations, of
which there are ftill fome remaining.

The Earl of *Mar*, to glofs his Actions with a
feeming Reflection as of Sorrow for what was paft,
told them, that tho' he had been very inftrumental
in forwarding the Union of the Two Kingdoms, in
the

the late Reign of Queen *Anne*, yet now his Eyes were open, and he could fee his Error, and would therefore do what lay in his Power to make them again a Free People, and that they fhould enjoy their ancient Liberties, which were by that *curfed Union*, as he call'd it, deliver'd up into the Hands of the *Englifh*; whofe Power to enflave them farther was too great, and their Defigns to do it daily vifible, by the Meafures that were taken, efpecially by the Prince of *Hanover*; who ever fince he had afcended the Throne, regarded not the Welfare of his People, nor their Religion, but folely left it to a Set of Men, who, while they pufh'd on his particular Intereft to fecure his Government, made fuch Alterations in Church and State as they thought fit; and that they had already begun to encroach upon the Liberties of both; which, he affured them, had already given Occafion to fome to confult their own Safety, and who were actually refolved vigoroufly to defend their Liberties and Properties againft the faid new Courtiers, and their Innovations, and to eftablifh the Perfon called the Chevalier St. *George*, who, he faid, had the only undoubted Right of the Crown, upon the Throne of thefe Realms; which Perfon, he told them, had promifed to hear their Grievances, and would redrefs their Wrongs. Farther he added, That Thoufands were in League and Covenant with him, and with one another, to Rife and Depofe King GEORGE, and eftablifh the faid Chevalier; and that the Duke of *Ormond* and the Lord *Bolingbrook* were gone over to *France* to engage the Regent of *France* to be aiding and affifting with Men and Money, and that they would not fail, with a good Force, to land, together with the Duke of *Berwick* to command them, in the Weft of *England*.

This, and much more he faid to them with a popular infinuating Air, which prefently took with

the

the unthinking People in the Highlands, who being alfo perfuaded by fome of their Leading Men, eafily gave Credit to what he faid ; when having before obtained the *Pretender*'s Commiffion to act as Lieutenant-General, immediately took upon him to exercife the Authority of a Military Officer ; and accordingly upon the 9th of *September*, 1715. fet up the *Pretender*'s Standard at a Town called *Kirk-Michael*, and there proclaimed him King of *Scotland*, *England*, *France*, &c. Having continued here four or five Days, he, with this fmall Beginning, for he had not then above 60 Men with him, marched to *Moulin*, thence to *Logaret*, increafing daily, and being then near 1000 Men ; thence he marched to *Dunkeld*, and was by that time increafed to 2000. With thefe he fet forwards to *Perth*, having ordered that Town to be feized, as it was by Mr. *John Hay*, Brother to the Earl of *Kinnoul*. This was done on the 16th of *September*, with a Party of about 200 Horfe : The Earl of *Rothes* being at the fame time marching with a Body of 500 Men of King GEORGE's Friends to have done the fame. He ftaid at this Town fome time, expecting the Clans to join him, and fent out Parties to feveral Quarters, to bring in what Ammunition and Arms they could find, and of which they really brought in a great many : Several Pieces of Cannon were alfo brought hither to him from *Dunotter*-Caftle, and from *Dundee* : He likewife having Intelligence of a Ship's loading of Arms which lay at *Brunt-Ifland*, bound for the North to the Earl of *Sutherland*, he detached a Party of 800 Men, who went and feized the Veffel, and found therein 306 compleat Stands of Arms, defign'd, as before is faid, for the Earl of *Sutherland*, who was juft then gone to his own Country, to raife his Tenants and Vaffals for the King's Service, and, if poffible, to hinder the Northern Clans from joining the Earl of *Mar*.

By

By this time however the Clans began to ftir :
And firft of all, the Laird of *Mackintofh*, Chief
of the Name of *Mackintofh*, and who are a confiderable and numerous Clan, by the Perfuafion of
his Kinfman the Brigadier of that Name, commanded his Vaffals to attend him to the *Pretender's*
Standard then at *Perth*. And here it is obfervable,
that tho' thefe Men were always noted to be on the
other Side, and were always for the *Revolution*; yet
without examining the Caufe, feveral of them obey'd
his Orders, and blindly engaged. The Brigadier
placed himfelf at their Head, formed them into a
Regiment, and regulated them very well, being no
lefs than 500 ftout Men. Thus they marched with
their Chief to *Perth*, where they found the Earl
of *Mar* with his Forces.

They were no fooner advanced to that Town,
but he fingled them out, and the Brigadier at the
Head of them, for that defperate Attempt of paffing
the *Firth* of *Edinburgh*, and landing in *Lothian*, (of
which I have fpoken at large.) Accordingly they
march'd to the Sea-Coaft of *Fife*, and there, with
other five Regiments, *viz. Mar's* own, Lord *Strathmore's*, Lord *Nairn's*, Lord *Charles Murray's*, and
Lord *Drummond's*; making in all 2500 Men;
having feized all the Boats they could find upon
that Coaft, they all embark'd. His Majefty's Ships
then in the *Firth* made up to them, as well as the
Circumftances would permit, but could not hinder
1500 from croffing, and getting fairly afhore, tho'
they fired hard upon them; (of all which a full Account is already given in the *Englifh* Part of the
Story.)

I therefore go back to the Earl of *Mar's* Proceeding: The Account of the taking the Ship with
Arms, gave fome Reputation to his Conduct. The
Manner was thus; the Arms that were taken, were
ordered from *Edinburgh* Caftle for the Earl of *Su-
tberland*,

therland, and were shipped off at *Leith*; but the
Master of the Ship called at *Brunt-Island* to see his
Wife and Family, the Earl of *Mar* having notice,
detach'd from *Perth*, *October* 2. in the Evening,
400 Horse, with as many Foot behind them, who
arrived at *Brunt-Island* about Midnight; and having
press'd all the Boats in the River, boarded the Ves-
sel, and seiz'd the Arms. They also found about
100 Arms in the Town, and 20 or 30 in another
Ship; all which they took and carried off, and so
returned to *Perth* undisturb'd: For the Duke of
Argyle had no notice of them till it was too late;
on the contrary, the Duke had notice that the Earl
of *Mar* designed to be at *Aloway*, his own House,
four Miles from *Stirling*, with a strong Detachment.
Upon which Advice, he order'd out the Picquets
of Horse and Foot, and had all the Troops ready
to march to sustain them, if there had been occasion; but none of the Rebels appearing, the Picquets returned to the Camp. For indeed this was a
false Alarm, design'd by the Earl of *Mar* on purpose to amuse the Duke. The Success the Rebels
found at *Brunt-Island* mightily encouraged them
and their Friends: Also in every Place after, they
not forgetting to range about the Towns and Coast
of *Fife* in quest of Arms, and in part made themselves amends for their being disappoined in those
they expected from *France*; which, by the Care of
Sir *George Bing*, were about this time discovered,
and by the earnest Application of the Earl of *Stair*,
were stopt at *Havre-de-Grace*.

The same Day that the Earl of *Mar* went from
Dunkeld to *Perth*, Mr. *James Murray*, second Son
to the Viscount of *Stormount*, arrived *incognito* at
Edinburgh from *France*, by way of *England*, and
crossing the *Firth* at *Newhaven* above *Leith*, got
undiscover'd into *Fife*, and so to *Perth*. His Arrival gave another Occasion of great Rejoicings a-
mong

mong the Rebels ; for he brought large Promiſes
from the *Pretender*, and from the Court of St. *Ger-*
main's, and took to himſelf the Character of Secretary of State to the *Pretender*. About this time
alſo, a ſtrong Party of the *Mac-Donald's*, *Mac-*
Clean's, and *Cameron's* in Rebellion, attempted to
ſurprize the Gariſon of *Inverlochy*, and ſucceeded
ſo far as to take two Redoubts at ſome Diſtance, in
one of which were an Officer and twenty Men, and
another a Serjeant with five : But the main Gariſon
being upon their Guard, the Rebels marched off to
Argyleſhire.

Before I proceed any further in this Part, the
Order of Things calls me back to give an Account
of a Deſign to ſurprize the Caſtle of *Edinburgh*. It
was on the 9th of *September* that the Attempt was
made ; the Lord *Drummond* was the Perſon chiefly
concern'd, but it was communicated to ſeveral o-
thers, and there were no leſs than Ninety choice
Men pick'd out for the Enterprize, all Gentlemen.
They had corrupted one *Aineſly* a Serjeant, who was
afterwards hang'd for it ; a Corporal, and two Centinels, within the Caſtle : Theſe were to be ready
to aſſiſt at a certain Place upon the Wall near the
Sally-Port ; where, having contived a Scaling-Lad-
der made of Ropes and with Pulleys, which being
faſtened to the Top of the Wall by the Conſpirators, the Centinel was to draw up with a ſmall Rope
provided on Purpoſe. This Engine was ſo contrived, that it could draw up ſeveral Men a-breaſt :
all the Joints or Lengths of this Ladder not coming
at once, it proved too ſhort in Length for any to
get over the Wall. While this was doing, the Officers of the Gariſon got Intelligence of the Deſign,
and having got their Men together ſilently, they
diſcover'd the Ladder, unlooſed it at the Top of
the Wall, and let it fall, and immediately ordered
the Centinel to diſcharge his Piece. Upon this,

K   the

the Rounds alfo fired upon the Gentlemen at the Foot of the Ladder, who immediately difpers'd themfelves, four only of their Number being taken. This Project's failing, is attributed to the Gentleman's Neglect in not bringing all the Lengths of the Ladder at once, and the Centinel's fixing of it at a Place fome Diftance from that firft refolv'd on: For Lieutenant *Lindfey* going the Rounds, as above, found that the Ladder was actually drawn up, and fixed on the Top of the Wall; upon which, he ordered the next Centinel to fire, (as above.) The Confpirators finding the Plot was difcover'd, fled, as is faid; but a Party of the Town-Guard, which, at the Requeft of the Lord Juftice *Clerk*, the Provoft, had been fent out to Patrole with fome refolute Voluntiers, coming up, found one *Mac-Lean*, formerly an Officer, fprauling on the Ground, and bruifed with a Fall from the Wall; whom they fecur'd, with Mr. *Lefly*, Mr. *Ramfey*, and Mr. *Bowwell*; the laft two, Writers; the firft, formerly Page to the Dutchefs of *Gordon*. They likewife found the Ladder, and one Dozen of Fire-Locks and Carbines. Each Perfon concern'd was to have 100 *l.* Sterling, and a Commiffion in the Army. The Number of Soldiers engag'd in this Confpiracy were, a Serjeant who was to have a Lieutenant's Place; the Corporal an Enfign's; and one of the Soldiers had eight Guineas, and the other four. The Lord *Drummond* was to be Governor of the Caftle, as being Contriver of the Defign. If this Defign had fucceeded, the Confpirators were to fire three Rounds in the Caftle, which was to be a Signal for their Friends.

But to return to the Earl of *Mar*, who having poffeffed *Perth*, and being greatly encouraged by fome Proceedings, he ordered the *Pretender* to be proclaimed there; which was done by Colonel *Balfour*, and at feveral other Places, as at *Aberdeen*;

by

by the Earl of *Marifchal* at *Dundee* ; by one created
Vifcount of *Dundee* by the *Pretender*, at *Montrofe* ;
by the Earl of *Southefk*, at *Forrefs* ; by Mr. *Cum-
ming*, at *Alter*.

By this time the Earl of *Mar* alfo had taken upon him the Title of Lieutenant-General of the *Pretender*'s Forces, and ordered the following Declaration to be publifhed ; and alfo a Letter to the Bailiff of *Kildrummy*, as follows :

The Earl of M A R's *Declaration.*

‘ OUR Rightful and Natural King *James* the
‘ Eighth, by the Grace of God, who is now
‘ coming to relieve us from our Oppreffions, having
‘ been pleas'd to entruft us with the Direction of his
‘ Affairs, and the Command of his Forces in this
‘ his ancient Kingdom of *Scotland:* And fome of
‘ his faithful Subjects and Servants met at *Aboyne,*
‘ *viz.* the Lord *Huntley,* the Lord *Tullibardine,* the
‘ Earl *Marifchal,* the Earl of *Southefk, Glingary*
‘ from the Clans, *Glenderule* from the Earl of *Broad-
‘ albine;* and Gentlemen of *Anglefhire,* Mr. *Patrick
‘ Lyon* of *Auchterboufe,* the Laird of *Auldbair,* Lieu-
‘ tenant-General *George Hamilton,* Major-General
‘ *Gordon,* and myfelf, having taken into Confide-
‘ ration his Majefty's laft and late Orders to us,
‘ find, that as this is now the Time that he ordered
‘ us to appear openly in Arms for him, fo it feems
‘ to us abfolutely neceffary for his Majefty's Service,
‘ and the relieving our Native Country from all its
‘ Hardfhips, that all his faithful and loving Subjects,
‘ and Lovers of their Country, fhould with all
‘ poffible Speed put themfelves into Arms.

‘ Thefe are therefore, in his Majefty's Name and
‘ Authority, and by Virtue of the Power aforefaid,
‘ and by the King's fpecial Order to me thereunto,
‘ to require and impower you forthwith to raife

‘ your

' your fencible Men, with their beft Arms, and you
' are immediately to march them to join me and
' fome other of the King's Forces at the *Invor* of
' *Brae-mar*, on *Monday* next, in order to proceed
' on our March to attend the King's Standard,
' with his other Forces.

' The King intending that his Forces fhall be paid
' from the Time of their fetting out, he expects,
' as he pofitively orders, that they behave them-
' felves civilly, and commit no Plundering, nor
' other Diforders, upon the higheft Penalties and
' his Difpleafure, which is expected you'll fee ob-
' ferved.

' Now is the Time for all good Men to fhew
' their Zeal for his Majefty's Service, whofe Caufe
' is fo deeply concerned, and the Relief of our na-
' tive Country from Oppreffion and a foreign Yoke,
' too heavy for us and our Pofterity to bear ; and
' to endeavour the reftoring not only our rightful
' and native King, but alfo our Country to its an-
' cient, free, and independent Conftitution, under
' him, whofe Anceftors have reigned over us for fo
' many Generations.

' In fo honourable, good, and juft a Caufe, we
' cannot doubt of the Affiftance, Direction, and
' Bleffing of Almighty God, who has fo often re-
' fcued the Royal Family of *Stuart*, and our Coun-
' try from finking under Oppreffion.

' Your punctual Obfervance of thefe Orders is
' expected : For the doing of all which, this fhall
' be to you, and all you employ in the Execution
' of them, a fufficient Warrant.

To the Bailiff and
 the reft of the
 Gentlemen of
 the Lordfhip of
 Kildrummy.

Given at Brae-Mar, *the*
  9th of Sept. 1715.

MAR.

The

The Earl of MAR's LETTER *to his*
Bailiff of Kildrummy.

Invercauld, Sept. 9, *at Night,* 1715.

Jocke,

‘ YE was in the right not to come with the
‘ 100 Men ye sent up to Night, when I ex-
‘ pected four times the Number. It is a pretty
‘ Thing, when all the *Highlands* of *Scotland* are
‘ now rising upon their King and Country's Ac-
‘ count, as I have Accounts from them since they
‘ were with me, and the Gentlemen of our neigh-
‘ bouring *Lowlands* expecting us down to join them,
‘ that my Men should be only refractory. Is not
‘ this the Thing we are now about, which they
‘ have been wishing this Twenty-six Years? And
‘ now when it is come, and the King and Country's
‘ Cause at Stake, will they for ever sit still, and
‘ see all perish?
‘ I have us'd gentle Means too long, and so I
‘ shall be forc'd to put other Orders I have in Exe-
‘ cution. I have sent you enclosed, an Order for
‘ the Lordship of *Kildrummy*, which you are im-
‘ mediately to intimate to all my Vassals; if they
‘ give ready Obedience, it will make some Amends;
‘ and if not, ye may tell them from me, that it
‘ will not be in my Power to save them (were I
‘ willing) from being treated as Enemies, by those
‘ who are ready soon to join me; and they may
‘ depend on it, that I will be the first to propose
‘ and order their being so. Particularly, let my
‘ own Tenants in *Kildrummy* know, that if they
‘ come not forth with their best Arms, that I will
‘ send a Party immediately to burn what they shall
‘ miss taking from them: And they may believe
K 3   ‘ this

' this not only a Threat, but, by all that's sacred,
' I'll put it in Execution, let my Loss be what it
' will, that it may be Example to others. You
' are to tell the Gentlemen that I'll expect them in
' their best Accoutrements, on Horseback, and no
' Excuse to be accepted of. Go about this with all
' Diligence, and come yourself, and let me know
' your having done so. All this is not only as
' you will be answerable to me, but to your King
' and Country.

Your assured Friend

Sic Subscribitur.
To *John Forbes* of
Increrat, Bailiff
of *Kildrummy.*

and Servant,

M A R.

Upon the News of the Earl of *Mar's* being thus
in Arms, and of the Progress he made, Orders were
dispatched immediately to *Edinburgh,* to secure such
suspected Persons as were thought to be capable of
Mischief, whose Names are as follow:

The Marquis of *Huntley.*
The Earl of *Seaforth.*
The Earl of *Wintoun.*
The Earl of *Carnwath.*
The Earl of *Southesk.*
The Earl of *Nithsdale.*
The Earl of *Linlithgow.*
The Earl of *Mar.*
The Earl of *Hume.*
The Earl of *Wigtoun.*
The Earl of *Kinnoul.*
The Earl of *Panmure,*
The Earl of *Marischal.*
The Earl of *Broadalbin.*

The Lord Viscount of
Kenmure.
The Lord Viscount of
Stormount.
The Lord Viscount of
Kilsyth.
The Lord Viscount of
Kingston.
The Lord Viscount of
Strathallerton.
The Lord *Ogilvie.*
The Lord *Rollo.*
The Lord *Drummond.*
The Lord *Nairn.*

The

The Lord *Glenorgbay.*
Sir *James Campbell* of *Auchircbrech.*
Sir *Duncan Campbell* of *Locknell.*
Sir *Donald Mac-Donald.*
Sir *Patrick Murray* of *Auchtertyre.*
Sir *Hugh Paterson* of *Bannockburn.*
Sir *Alexander Ereskine,* Lord *Lyon.*
Sir *John Macklean.*
Lieutenant-General *George Hamilton.*
Master of *Stormount.*
Master of *Nairn.*
Master *Alexander Mackenzie* of *Frazerdale.*
James Sterling of *Keir.*
Robert Stuart of *Appin.*
John Campbell of *Actrabalder.*
William Murray, Younger, of *Auchtertyre.*
Alexander Robinson of *Strowan.*
Laird of *Mackinnan.*
William Drummond, Servant to Lord *Drummond.*
Mr. *Seaton* of *Touch.*
Lieutenant *Allen Cameron.*
Robert Roy, alias *Mac-Gregor.*
Mr. *Stewart* of *Ard.*
Master *Francis Stewart,* Brother to the Earl of
    Murray.
John Cameron of *Lochiell.*
Laird of *Clanronald.*
Laird of *Glenghairy.*
Laird of *Keppach.*
Mr. *John Fullerton* of *Greenball.*
Mackintosh, Younger, of *Borlam.*
James Malcolm.
Mr. *Harry Maule,* Brother to the Earl of *Panmure.*
Wackinshaw of *Barafield.*
Colin Campbell of *Glenderule.*
Graham of *Bucklivy.*
George Hume of *Whitfield.*
Master *John Drummond,* Brother to the Lord *Drum-*
    mond.   K 4   *Lyon.*

Lyon of *Auƈterhouſe.* Maſter *Balfour.*
Colonel *Balfour.* *Bothune* of *Balfour.*

At the ſame time Orders were ſent to Major-General *Wightman*, who was then Commander in Chief
in *Scotland*, and was upon the Spot, forthwith to
march with all the regular Troops that could be
ſpared, to form a Camp in the Park of *Stirling*, to
ſecure the important Paſs of *Stirling-Bridge* over
the *Forth*, and to quarter the Half-pay Officers in
ſuch a Manner all over the Country, as that they
might be in Readineſs to Encourage, Exerciſe, and
Command the Militia on any Emergence. Orders
were likewiſe given to all Officers in the Sea-Port
Towns, to have a watchful Eye over all Ships which
came into the ſaid Ports, or appear'd upon the
Coaſt, leaſt they ſhould land the *Pretender*, or any
others ſuſpeƈted Perſons, or bring the Rebels any
Supply of Arms or Ammunition. But notwithſtanding theſe Orders, and that all poſſible Care was
taken in the Caſe, there was a ſmall Ship came to
Arbroth, a little Port in the North of *Scotland*,
loaden with Arms and Ammunition, and which had
ſome Gentlemen on Board from *France*; which Ship
was there unloaded by the Highlanders. A few
Days after, another Ship arrived with ſeveral Officers, but no Stores of Arms, &c. The ſaid Officers
went direƈtly for *Perth* to the Earl of *Mar*, and
gave him an Account that the *Pretender* would be
ſoon in Perſon amongſt them; which News the
Earl of *Mar* cauſed to be immediately publiſh'd in
his Army, to encourage the Men. And now his
Forces being conſiderably increaſed, he reſolved to
croſs the *Forth*, if poſſible, and advance towards
Edinburgh. He deſign'd this Paſſage five or ſix
Miles above *Stirling*, and to make a ſwift March,
that he might not be prevented by the King's
Forces, who were yet but very weak. The Day
he

he appointed was the 18th of *October*; but upon
Intelligence receiv'd that his Plot was difcover'd,
and a Detachment order'd to wait upon his March,
he put it off; and tho' part of his Army was advanc'd fome Miles, he return'd back to *Perth*.

Some few Days before this, the Earl of *Mar*,
refolving to make ufe of the Advantages he had,
by poffeffing fo large an Extent of the Country,
thought of raifing fome Money, and to that End
iffued out the following Proclamation for an Affeff-
ment.

' PUrfuant and conform to an Order from the
' Right Honourable *John* Earl of *Mar*, Com-
' mander in Chief of his Majefty's Forces in *Scot-*
' *land*, dated at the Camp at *Perth* the 4th of *Octo-*
' *ber*, 1715. Thefe are commanding and requiring
' every Heretor, Fewer, or Woodfetter now at-
' tending the King's Standard, or that may be ex-
' cus'd, or their Factors and Doers in their Ab-
' fence, and likewife all Life - Renters; do im-
' mediately proportion and raife, among their Te-
' nants and Poffeffors of their refpective Eftates, and
' Life-Rent Lands, the Sum of Twenty Shillings
' Sterling on each Hundred Pounds of *Scots*, of
' valued Rent: And fuch Heretors who do not
' immediately, nor fhall, betwixt the 12th of *Octo-*
' *ber* Inftant, attend the King's Standard, if not
' excufed by the faid noble Earl, immediately pro-
' portion and raife out of their refpective Eftates,
' the Sum of Forty Shillings Sterling on each Hun-
' dred Pounds *Scots* of valued Rent; which feveral
' Proportions, according to their refpective Cafes
' aforefaid, are, by the faid Order, ordain'd to be
' paid by every Heretor, Fewer, Woodfetter, and
' Life-Renter, to —— Collector, againft the 12th
' Day of this Inftant *October*, at ——

Upon

Upon this the Duke of *Argyle*, to prevent as much as poſſible the Effect of it, made the following Counter-Order.

By John *Duke of* Argyle, *General and Commander in Chief of His Majeſty's Forces in* Scotland.

'WHereas I am certainly informed, That the
' Earl of *Mar*, and the other Rebels, have,
' in Proſecution of their Treaſonable Practices, ad-
' ventur'd to impoſe a Ceſs upon ſome Parts of the
' Shires of *Fife, Clackmanan, Kinroſs,* and *Perth*;
' and whereas the paying any Money to the Rebels,
' or complying with any of their Orders or De-
' mands, will infer High-Treaſon againſt ſuch as
' do the ſame, as being Aiders, Comforters, and
' Abettors of the Rebels: Therefore, and that all
' well-affected People may know and prevent their
' Danger in this Matter, I hereby, in His Ma-
' jeſty's Name and Authority, ſtrictly prohibit and
' diſcharge all His Majeſty's good Subjects, in the
' Countries above-mention'd, or any other-where
' within *Scotland*, to give or furniſh the Rebels with
' Money, Proviſions, or any other Aid or Aſſiſt-
' ance or Comfort whatſoever, directly or indi-
' rectly, under the higheſt Pains and Puniſhments
' of the Law. And this I appoint to be intimated
' at each Pariſh-Church-Door after divine Service,
' and before Diſſolution of the Congregation, the
' Sabbath immediately after this, or a Copy hereof
' comes to your Hand.

Given at Stirling *the* 25th
of October, 1715.

Sign'd

ARGYLE.

And

And another Order for Recruiting His Majesty's
Forces, as follows:

By John *Duke of* Argyle, *General and Commander
in Chief of His Majesty's Forces in* Scotland.

'WHEREAS our gracious Sovereign King
' GEORGE has been pleased, for the better
' suppressing the present Rebellion, to order and
' appoint two Companies to be added to each Re-
' giment of Foot now in His Majesty's Service in
' *Scotland*, and to appoint each Company to be aug-
' mented to the Number of Fifty private Centinels:
' And since it must be evident to all well-affected
' People, that the strengthening and augmenting
' the Regular Troops, is the most effectual way for
' suppressing the Rebellion, and that the same will
' bring no Charge nor Burthen upon the Country;
' and that the Harvest is over, whereby many Peo-
' ple that were that way employ'd, are now at Li-
' berty. And in regard the Officers of the several
' Regiments are so employ'd in His Majesty's Ser-
' vice, that they cannot conveniently attend the
' Recruiting in this Country: I hereby intreat and
' require all well-affected Noblemen, Gentlemen,
' Justices of the Peace, Magistrates, Ministers of
' the Gospel, or other well-affected Subjects, to
' contribute their best Endeavours to persuade and
' encourage all the able-bodied and well-affected
' Men, in their respective Parochins in Town and
' Country, within *Scotland*, to inlist themselves in
' the Regular Forces. And I, in his Majesty's
' Name, do promise, that the Endeavours of such
' as shall be useful in this Matter, shall be looked
' upon as good Service, and intitle them to His
' Majesty's Favour and Protection. And for the
' Encouragement of such as shall inlist themselves
volun-

' voluntarily in Compliance herewith, I, in His
' Majesty's Name, promise, that each Voluntier so
' inlisting and incorporating himself in any of His
' Majesty's Regiments of Foot now in *Scotland*,
' shall not only receive His Majesty's Bounty-Mo-
' ney of Forty Shillings Sterling in Hand, but
' shall, at the end of three Months, after the pre-
' sent Rebellion is suppress'd, draw and receive his
' Pass, discharging him from the Service, if he
' require the same; each Man who shall so desire
' to be discharged, always giving two Months Ad-
' vertisement before drawing his Discharge, to the
' commanding Officer of the Regiment for the
' Time, to the effect he may provide another Man
' in his room. And I appoint the Sheriffs and
' Stewards of the several Sheriffdoms and Steward-
' tries, and the Magistrates of Royal Boroughs,
' forthwith to dispatch Copies hereof to the Mini-
' sters of the several Parochins within their Juris-
' diction, as they shall be answerable at their Peril.
' And I appoint the same to be intimate at each
' Paroch-Church from the Pulpit, after divine Ser-
' vice, and before Dissolution of the Congregation,
' on the Sabbath immediately after this, or a Copy
' hereof comes to the respective Ministers Hands,
' and do recommend to the several Ministers,
' earnestly to exhort the People to their Duty in
' this Matter, for the Service of their King and
' Country.

' Given at the Camp at Stirling, the 27th
' of October, 1715.

                         Sign'd

                                 ARGYLE.

A few Days after, the Earl of *Mar* publish'd the
following Counter-Order to that Order.

By

By John *Earl of* Mar, *General and Commander in*
Chief of His Majesty's Forces in Scotland.

'WHereas by the Laws of God, the Right of
' Blood, and the ancient Constitution of
' these Kingdoms, our Sovereign Lord *James* the
' Eighth, by the Grace of God, of *Scotland*, *Eng-*
' *land*, *France*, and *Ireland*, King, Defender of the
' Faith, *&c.* has the only undoubted Title to the
' Crown of these Realms : And whereas his Ma-
' jesty's Restoration is the only way left to retrieve
' the unhappy Consequences of the *Union*, dif-
' burthen the People of the heavy Taxes and Mort-
' gages they now groan under, and to prevent our
' Posterity from being involved in endless Miseries:
' And whereas many of his Majesty's loyal Sub-
' jects of all Ranks have dutifully assembled them-
' selves to the Royal Standard, in order to restore
' our rightful Sovereign to his Crown, and these
' Kingdoms to their ancient and independent State.
' And I having seen an Order publish'd by the
' Commander in Chief of the pretended King's
' Forces in this Kingdom, setting forth, That the
' Forces under his Command were to be augmented,
' and inviting *all able-bodied Men to inlist themselves*
' *in* that Service, and requiring *all Noblemen, Gen-*
' *tlemen*, *Justices of the Peace, Magistrates, Mini-*
' *sters of the Gospel*, and others, *to contribute their*
' *best Endeavours to persuade and encourage Men*
' thereunto : These are therefore in His Majesty's
' Name, prohibiting and discharging all Noblemen,
' Gentlemen, Justices of the Peace, Magistrates,
' Ministers of the Gospel, and all other Subjects
' whatsoever, to publish, execute, or obey the said
' Order, and that under the highest Pain.
 ' And whereas I have promis'd, in His Maje-
' sty's Name, Protection to all Ministers who be-
' have

' have themfelves dutifully, and do not acknow-
' ledge the Elector of *Brunfwick* as King, by pray-
' ing for him as fuch in their Churches and Congre-
' gations, notwithstanding whereof several of them
' continue in that Abufe: For preventing whereof,
' and that they may not, by fo doing, involve and
' miflead innocent and ignorant People into Trai-
' terous and Seditious Practices: Thefe are there-
' fore exprefsly prohibiting all Minifters, as well in
' Churches as in Meeting-Houfes, to acknowledge
' the Elector of *Brunfwick* as King, and that upon
' their higheft Peril: And all Officers Civil and
' Military are hereby ordered to fhut up the
' Church-Doors, where the Minifters act in Con-
' tempt hereof, and to apprehend their Perfons;
' and bring them Prifoners to the King's Camp,
' wherever it fhall be for the Time. And I do by
' thefe Prefents promife Protection to all fuch
' Minifters as do behave themfelves dutifully to-
' wards his Majefty; and I appoint the Sheriffs
' and Stewards of the feveral Sheriffdoms and Stew-
' ardries, and the Magiftrates of Royal Boroughs,
' forthwith to difpatch Copies thereof to the Mini-
' fters of the feveral Paroches within their Jurif-
' dictions, as they fhall be anfwerable upon their
' Peril: And I alfo appoint the fame to be inti-
' mate at each Parifh-Church, by the Minifter,
' Precentor, or Reader, before divine Service, im-
' mediately after the Minifter enters the Pulpit,
' on the Sabbath next after a Copy hereof comes to
' their Hands.

Given at the Camp at Perth, *the* 1ft
of November, 1715.

Perth, Printed by Mr. *Robert*
Freebairn, 1715.

And

And thus for a while the two Generals fought with Pen, Ink, and Paper only: But we shall now come to several Actions of another Nature.

October the 20th, a certain Account was brought to *Edinburgh*, that a Body of the Western Highland Clans, consisting of 2300 Men commanded by General *Gordon*, came before *Inverrary* the chief Town in *Argyleshire*, and having that Night view'd the Place, march'd back to a Mill about half a Mile from the Town, and were soon after reinforced by 300 of the Earl of *Broadalbin's* Men. The next Day they view'd the Town a second time, and again return'd to their former Quarters. On the 22d they drew up a third time, and sent Detachments to cut Fascines, as if they designed to attack the Town: But finding that the Earl of *Ilay*, who commanded the Town, was ready to receive them, they thought fit once more to retreat to their Quarters, and on the 24th left the Place, and marched thro' *Glenaxchy* in their way to join the Earl of *Mar*.

The preserving the Town of *Inverrary* was a considerable Piece of Service; for had the Rebels been Masters of that important Pass, they might have pour'd in their Men, either towards *Glasgow*, or into the Shire of *Aire*, and must have been fought with, perhaps, to Disadvantage, as things then stood, or they would have joined the Rebels in the North of *England* at their pleasure.

The Earl of *Ilay*, who performed this, is Brother to the Duke of *Argyle*; he is a Gentleman of known Bravery, witness not only his indefatigable Care to settle the Western Highlands, and the Preservation of this Place, but his Conduct and Courage at the Battle of *Dumblain*, where he was wounded, add to the Greatness of his Soul, ready to undergo the greatest Hardships to serve his King, and to face

the

the greateſt Dangers that oppoſe his Country. I had the Honour to be educated under the ſame Tutor with him at the College of *Glaſgow*, but have gone wide in my Principles from thoſe equally infuſed into us.

· *October* the 23d, the Duke of *Argyle* had notice that a Party of the Rebels, conſiſting of 200 Foot and 100 Horſe, were marching by *Caſtle-Campbell* towards *Dumferling*. Upon this Intelligence, his Grace immediately ſent off a Detachment of Dragoons, under the Command of Colonel *Cathcart*, who came up with the Rebels the 24th, at five o' Clock in the Morning; and after having killed and wounded ſeveral of them, took ſeventeen Priſoners; amongſt them the following Gentlemen:

Mr. *Murray*, Brother to the Laird of *Aberkenny*.
Mr. *Hay*, Son to *Arboth*.
Mr. *Patrick Gordon*, *Abertour's* eldeſt Son.
Alexander Forbes, Son to *Buſlie*.
William Roberton, Brother to *Donſhills*.
Mr. *Kenloch*, a Phyſician.
Alexander Smith.
Mr. *Alexander Gordon*.
Francis Gordon of *Craig*.
Mr. *Hamilton* of *Gibſtown* in *Strabogie*: And,
George Gordon of the *Miln* of *Kincardine*.

The ſame Evening Colonel *Cathcart* returned to the Camp at *Stirling* with his Priſoners. A few Days after, a Detachment ſent by the Earl of *Hay* into *Lorn* to intercept about 400 of the Earl of *Broadalbin's* Men, who were in Motion to join the Rebels, being come up with, and having ſurrounded them, obliged them to ſeparate and return to their ſeveral Habitations.

By this time the Earl of *Mar* being joined by the Earl of *Seaforth*, Sir *Donald M'donald*, and others, with

with their refpective Clans to the Number of 8000
Men, were preparing to march from *Perth*, to join
General *Gordon* with the Weftern Clans at *Auchterar-*
der, in order to attempt the croffing the *Forth*,
which was indeed his main Defign. This was the
12th of *November*. Upon Intelligence of this March,
for the Rebels advanc'd from *Perth* with their whole
Army, the Duke of *Argyle* fent for a Train of
Field-Artillery from *Edinburgh*; and having receiv'd all the Reinforcements he expected from
Ireland, his Grace refolv'd not to fuffer them to
reach the Bank of *Forth*, but to fight them where-
ever he could come up with them. Accordingly
he pafs'd the *Forth* at *Stirling*-Bridge with his whole
Army, and advanced towards *Dumblain*.

This occafion'd a general Engagement, or Battle,
fought near *Dumblain*, at a Place called *Sheriff-Moor*,
on *Sunday, November* 13. And for the Reader's better Information, I fhall prefent him with an Account
of that Action, as it is related by both Parties; that
fo, feeing each Party claims the Victory, he may
judge whofe it was by the Conclufion. The Accounts are thus; the firft is that of Colonel *Harrifon*,
being fent Exprefs to His Majefty by the Duke of
Argyle, and who arrived at St. *James*'s *Saturday* the
19th. The fecond Account is that of Major-General *Wightman*. The third Account is the Earl of
Mar's Letter to Colonel *Balfour* Governor of *Perth*.
And the fourth Account is the Earl of *Mar*'s printed
one.

Colonel Harrifon's *Account of the* Victory.

THE Duke of *Argyle* being informed on the
12th, that the Rebels had come to *Auchte-*
rarder with their Baggage, Artillery, and a fufficient quantity of Bread for a March of many Days,
found he was obliged either to engage them on the
Grounds near *Dumblain*, or to decamp and wait

L   thefe

their coming to the Head of *Forth*. He chose the
first on many Accounts, and amongst others, that
the Grounds near *Dumblain* were much more advantageous for his Horse, than those at the Head of
the River; and besides this, by the Frost then beginning, the *Forth* might become passable in several
Places, which the small Number of his Troops did
not enable him to guard sufficiently. He likewise
received Advice, that the 12th at Night the Rebels
designed to encamp at *Dumblain*; upon which, judging it of Importance to prevent them by possessing
that Place, he marched the 12th in the Forenoon,
and encamped with his Left at *Dumblain*, and his
Right towards the *Sheriff-Moor*; the Enemy that
Night stopped within two Miles of *Dumblain*.
Next Morning his Grace being inform'd by his advanc'd Guard that the Rebels were Forming, he
rode to a rising Ground, where he viewed the Enemy distinctly, and found as they pointed their
March, they designed strait upon our Flank. The
Moor to our Right was the preceding Night unpassable, and guarded us from being flanked on that
side, but by the Frost was become passable. His
Grace therefore ordered his Troops to stretch to the
Right in the following Order; three Squadrons of
Dragoons upon Right and Left in the Front Line, and
six Battalions of Foot in the Center. The second Line
was compos'd of two Battalions in the Center, one
Squadron on the Right, and another on their Left,
and one Squadron of Dragoons behind each Wing
of Horse in the first Line. As the Right of our
Army came over-against the Left of the Rebels,
which they had put to a Morass, his Grace finding
they were not quite formed, gave Orders immediately to fall on, and charged both their Horse and
Foot. They received us very briskly; but after
some Resistance, were broke through, and were
pursued above two Miles by five Squadrons of Dragoons, the Squadron of Voluntiers, and five Battalions
lions

lions of Foot. When we came near the River *Allan*, by the vast Number of Rebels we drove before us, we concluded it an entire Rout, and resolved to pursue as long as we had Day-light. The pursuing to the River *Allan* had taken up a long time, by reason of the frequent Attempts they had made to Form in different Places, which obliged us as often to attack and break them. When they were in part passed, and others passing the *Allan*, Major-General *Wightman*, who commanded the five Battalions of Foot, sent to acquaint the Duke of *Argyle* that he could not discover what was become of our Troops on the Left, and that a considerable Body of the Rebels Horse and Foot stood behind us. Upon that his Grace halted, formed his Troops in Order, and marched towards the Hill on which the Rebels had posted themselves. Thereafter his Grace extended his Right towards *Dumblain*, to give his Left an Opportunity of joining him. There we continued until it was late, and not finding our Left come up, his Grace marched slowly towards the Ground on which he had formed in the Morning. So soon as it was dark, the Rebels, who continued undispersed on the Top of the Hill, moved to *Ardoch*. About an Hour after, our Troops which had been separated from the Duke of *Argyle*, joined his Grace. Our Dragoons on the Left, in the Beginning of the Action, charged some of their Horse on the Right, and carried off a Standard ; but at the same time the Rebels pressed so hard on our Battalions on the Left, that they were disorder'd, and oblig'd to fall in amongst the Horse. The Rebels by this means cut off the Communication betwixt our Left and the other Body ; and they being informed a Body of the Rebels were endeavouring to get to *Stirling*, the Troops of our Left retired beyond *Dumblain*, to possess themselves of the Passes leading there. We have as yet no certain Account of

the

the Numbers killed, but it's reckoned they may be about 800, amongst whom there are several Persons of Diftinction. The Quality of Prifoners is not yet fully known, only that the Vifcount of *Strathallan,* two Colonels, two Lieutenant-Colonels, one Major, nine Captains, befides Subalterns, are brought to *Stirling.* We have likewife carried off fourteen Colours and Standards, four Pieces of Cannon, Tombrells, with Ammunition, and all their Bread-Waggons. This Victory was not obtained without the Lofs of fome brave Men on our Side ; the Earl of *Forfar's* Wounds are fo many that his Life is defpair'd of. The Earl of *Ilay,* who came half an Hour before the Action, received two Wounds, the one in his Arm, and the other in his Side ; but the Bullet being cut out of his Side, it is hoped he is paft Danger. General *Evans* received a Cut in the Head. Colonel *Hawley* was fhot through the Body ; but there is hopes of his Recovery. Colonel *Lawrence* is taken. Colonel *Hammers,* and Captain *Armftrong, Aid de Camp* to the Duke of *Argyle,* are killed. The Courage of the King's Troops were never keener than on this Occafion ; who, though the Rebels were three times the Number, yet attacked and purfued them with all the Refolution imaginable. The Conduct and Bravery of the Generals and inferior Officers contributed much to this Succefs : But above all, the great Example of his Grace the Duke of *Argyle,* whofe Prefence not only gave Spirit to the Action, but gained Succefs as often as he led on. The Troop of Horfe Voluntiers, which confifted of Noblemen and Gentlemen of Diftinction, fhewed their Quality by the Gallantry of their Behaviour ; in a particular manner the Duke of *Roxburgh,* the Lords *Rothes, Haddingtoun, Lauderdale, Loudown, Belhaven,* and Sir *John Shaw.*

A LIST

A L I S T of the Officers and Soldiers killed, wounded, or missing, in the Battle of Sheriff-Moor, of the Troops under the Duke of Argyle.

Of Portmore's *Regiment* :

CAPTAIN *Roberson*, and a Quarter-Master wounded : Two Dragoons killed, and four wounded.

Of Evans's *Regiment* :

Captain *Farrer* his Thigh-bone broke : Colonel *Hawley* shot through the Shoulder : A Cornet, and a few private Men kill'd.

Of Lord Forfar's *Regiment* :

Himself shot in the Knee, and cut in the Head with 10 or 12 Strokes from their Broad-Swords after Quarter : Ensign *Branch*, and eight private Men kill'd.

Of Wightman's *Regiment* :

Ensign *Mark* wounded : Two Grenadiers, and two or three Men kill'd.

Of Shannon's *Regiment* :

Captain *Arnot* kill'd, and five or six Men kill'd and wounded. These, with a Squadron of *Stair*'s Dragoons, were the Troops that composed the Right, and beat the Rebels.

On the Left.

Of Morrison's *Regiment* :

Lieutenant-Colonel *Hamar*, two Captains, four Lieutenants, and three Ensigns missing, with a good many private Men.

Of

Of Montague's *Regiment :*

Lieutenant-Colonel *Laurence,* Captain *Umbell,* Captain *Bernard,* miffing ; and a good many private Men kill'd.

Of Clayton's *Regiment :*

Captain *Barlow* kill'd.

Of the Fuzileers.

Captain *Chieſly,* Lieutenant *Hay* and Lieutenant *Michelſon* miffing, and ſaid to be taken, and Captain *Urqhart* wounded.

Of Egerton's *Regiment :*

Captain *Danoer* wounded, and a few private Men kill'd.

A particular L I S T *of the Names of the Gentlemen Priſoners, brought to the Caſtle of* Stirling *the* 14th *of* November.

L ORD *Strathallan.*
    Barrowfield.
Logie Drummond.
Mr. *Murray* of *Auchtertyre.*
Mr. *Thomas Drummond,* Brother to the Viſcount of *Strathallan.*
Mr. *Drummond* of *Drumqubany.*
Captain *William Creighton.*
Mr. *John Roſs,* Son to the Archbiſhop of St. *Andrew's.*
Mr. *Nairn* of *Baldwale.*
Mr. *William Hay.*
John Gordon, Captain.
William Forbes, Lieutenant.
Archibald Fotbringbame, Lieutenant.

Alexander

Alexander Garrioch, Enſign.

Jn. Carnagie, Surgeon.

Nicol. Donalſon, Enſign.

Alex. Steuart of *Innerſlawie*, Foreſter to the Duke, of *Athol.*

Neil M'Glaſſon, Chamberlain to the Duke of *Athol.*

James Steuart, Lieutenant.

William Adamſon, Lieutenant.

John Robertſon, Lieutenant.

James Gordon, Surgeon.

David Gardin, Captain of *Panmure's* Regiment.

Kenneth Mackenzie, Nephew to Sir *Alexander Mackenzie* of *Coull.*

Charles Gardin of *Bittiſtern.*

John M'Lean, Adjutant to Colonel *Mackenzie's* Regiment.

Colin Mackenzie of *Kildin*, Captain of *Fairburn's* Regiment.

Mr. *John Rattray.*	Mr. *Donald M'pherſon.*
Peter Steuart.	*John Morgan.*
George Taylor.	*Donald Robertſon.*
Duncan M'intoſh,	*Robert Menzies.*
James Peddie.	*Will. Menzies,*
John Forbes.	*John Menzies,*
Alexander Steuart.	*Will. Menzies,*
Donald Mitchel.	*Will. Steuart.*
Francis Finlay.	*Alex. M'lachlan.*
James Lyon.	*Patrick Campbell.*
Auchterlony.	*Hugh M'raw.*
Lewis Cramond,	*Donald M'raw.*
William Steuart.	*Chriſtopher M'rae.*
George Mear.	*John Leſley.*
Heſter M'lean.	*James Edgar.*
Alexander Mill.	*James Mill.*
John M'intoſh,	*John Gordon.*
Robert M'intoſh.	*Donald M'murrie.*
Hugh Calder.	*Murdoch M'pherſon,*
James Innes.	*Alexander Cameron.*

Weem's Men

Mr. *Donald*

Donald M'nauchtie.
Ewan M'lachlan.
Ewan M'donald.
Donald Robertson.
James Keoch.
Thomas Robertson.
Alexander Morison.
Andrew Jamison.

Robert Miller.
Adam Grinsell.
Angus Steuart.
John Robertson.
John Cattinach.
John Richie, Merchant in Edinburgh.

Captain *Charles Chalmers*, late of the Foot Guards, one of the Earl of *Mar*'s Majors.

Major-General Wightman's *Account of the Battle.*

Stirling, Nov. 14, 1715, at 11 at Night.

LAST *Friday* I arriv'd from *Edinburgh*, where I had finish'd all the Works and Barricadoes that I had Orders to do for the Security of that Town ; and as soon as I came to his Grace the Duke of *Argyle*, he told me he was glad to see me, and that as he intended to make a March towards the Enemy the next Morning, he had sent an Express to *Edinburgh* for me. Accordingly on *Saturday* the 12th instant, our whole Army march'd over the Bridge of *Stirling* towards the Enemy, who lay at a Place call'd *Ardoch*, about seven Miles from this Place, and in the Evening our Army came within about three Miles of the Enemy's Camp. We lay all that Night on our Arms, and the next Morning being *Sunday*, by break of Day I went with his Grace where our advanc'd Guard was posted, and had a plain View of the Rebels Army, all drawn up in Line of Battel, which consisted of 9000 and 100 Men. They seem'd to make a Motion towards us : Upon which the Duke ordered me immediately back, to put our Men in Order; and soon after his Grace order'd them to march to the Top of a Hill against the Enemy : But before all, or not above
half

half our Army was form'd in Line of Battel, the Enemy attack'd us. The Right of their Line, which vaftly out-wing'd us, lay in a hollow Way, which was not perceived by us, nor poffible for us to know it, the Enemy having Poffeffion of the Brow of the Hill; but the Left of their Army was very plain to our View. The Moment we got to the Top of the Hill, not above half of our Men were come up, or could form; the Enemy, that were within little more than Piftol-fhot, began the Attack with all their Left upon our Right. I had the Command of the Foot: The Enemy were Highlanders, and, as it is their Cuftom, gave us Fire; and a great many came up to our Nofes Sword in Hand; but the Horfe on our Right, with the conftant Fire of the Plattoons of Foot, foon put the Left of their Army to the Rout, the Duke of *Argyle* purfuing, as he thought, the Main of their Army, which he drove before him above a Mile and a half over a River. As I march'd after him as faft as I could with a little above three Regiments of Foot, I heard great Firing on our Left, and fent my Aid-de-Camp to fee the occafion of it, and found that the Right of the Enemy's Army that lay in the hollow Way, and was fuperior to that Part of their Army which we had beaten, was fallen upon the Left of our Line with all the Fury imaginable; and as our Men were not form'd, they cut off juft the Half of our Foot, and our Squadrons on our Left. The Duke, who purfued the Enemy very faft, was not apprized of this; and as he had ordered me to march as faft as I could after him, I was oblig'd to flacken my March, and fend to his Grace to inform him of what had happen'd. I kept what Foot I had in perfect Order, not knowing but my Rear might foon be attack'd by the Enemy that had beat our Left, which prov'd to be the Flower of their Army. At laft, when the Duke had put to Flight that Part

of the Rebel-Army he was engag'd with, he came
back to me, and could not have imagin'd to fee fuch
an Army as was behind us, being three times our
Number; but as I had kept that Part of our Foot
which firft engaged in very good Order., his
Grace join'd me with five Squadrons of Dragoons,
and we put the beft Face on the Matter to the
Right about, and fo march'd to the Enemy, who
had defeated all the Left of our Army. If they had
had either Courage or Conduct they might have entirely deftroy'd my Body of Foot; but it pleafed
God to the contrary. I am apt to conjecture their
Spirits were not a little damp'd by having been
Witneffes fome Hours before of the firm Behaviour
of my Foot, and thought it hardly poffible to break
us. We march'd in a Line of Battel till we came
within half a Mile of the Enemy, and found them
ranged at the Top of a Hill on very advantageous
Ground, and above 4000 in Number. We pofted
ourfelves at the Bottom of the Hill, having the
Advantage of Ground, where their Horfe could
not well attack us, for we had the Convenience of
fome Earth-walls or Ditches about Breaft-high;
and as Evening grew on, we inclined with our
Right towards the Town of *Dumblain* in all the
Order that was poffible. The Enemy behav'd like
civil Gentlemen, and let us do what we pleafed;
fo that we paffed the Bridge of *Dumblain*, pofted
ourfelves very fecurely, and lay on our Arms all
Night. This Morning we went with a Body of
Dragoons to the Field of Battel, brought off the
wounded Men, and came to this Town in the Evening. General *Webb's* late Regiment, now *Morri-
fon's*, is one of the unfortunate Regiments that were
not form'd, and fuffer'd moft. Major *Hamar* is
kill'd, with young *Hillary*, and many other Officers. General *Evans* and I had the good Fortune
to be on the Right Wing with the Duke. General

Evans

Evans had his Horfe fhot dead under him, and efcaped very narrowly, as well as myfelf.

P. S. Our whole Army did not confift of above a Thoufand Dragoons, and two Thoufand five Hundred Foot; and but a little more than Half of them engaged. However I muft do the Enemy that Juftice to fay, *I never faw Regular Troops more exactly drawn up in Line of Battle, and that in a Moment; and their Officers behaved with all the Gallantry imaginable.* All I can fay is, *It will be of the laft Danger to the Government, if we have not Force to deftroy them foon.* The Lofs on both Sides I leave for another Time, when we have a more exact Account.

The Earl of Mar's *Letter to Colonel* Balfour, *Governor of* Perth.

Ardoch, Nov. 13. 1715.

‘ I Thought you would be anxious to know the
‘ Fate of this Day. We attack'd the Enemy
‘ on the End of the *Sheriff-Moor* at Twelve of the
‘ Clock this Day, on our Right and Centre; car-
‘ ried the Day entirely; purfued them down to a
‘ little Hill on the South of *Dumblain*; and there I
‘ got moft of our Horfe, and a pretty good Num-
‘ ber of our Foot, and brought them again into
‘ fome Order. We knew not then what was be-
‘ come of our Left, fo we return'd to the Field of
‘ Battle. We difcern'd a Body of the Enemy on
‘ the North of us, confifting moftly of the Grey
‘ Dragoons, and fome of the Black. We alfo dif-
‘ cover'd a Body of their Foot farther North upon
‘ the Field, where we were in the Morning; and
‘ Eaft of that, a Body, as we thought, of our own
‘ Foot, and I ftill believe it was fo. I form'd
‘ the Horfe and Foot with me in a Line on
‘ the

' the North Side of the Hill where we had engaged,
' and kept our Front towards the Enemy to the
' North of us, who feem'd at firft, as if they in-
' tended to march towards us ; but upon our form-
' ing, and marching towards them, they halted,
' and march'd back to *Dumblain*. Our Baggage
' and Train-Horfes had all run away in the begin-
' ning of the Action : But we got fome Horfes,
' and brought off moft of the Train to this Place,
' where we quarter to Night about *Ardoch*, whither
' we march'd in very good Order : And had our
' Left and Second Line behav'd as our Right,
' and the reft of the firft Line did, our Victory
' had been compleat : But another Day is coming
' for that, and I hope e'er long too.

' I fend you a Lift of the Officers Names who
' are Prifoners here, befides thofe who are dange-
' roufly wounded, and could not come along, whofe
' Words of Honour were taken. Two of thefe are
' the Earl of *Forfar*, who I'm afraid will die, and
' Captain *Urquhart* of *Buris-Yard*, who is very ill
' wounded. We have alfo a good Number of
' private Men Prifoners ; but the Number I do not
' exactly know.

' We have loft, to our Regret, the Earl of
' *Strathmore*, and the Captain of *Clan-Ranald*. Some
' are miffing ; but their Fate we are not fure of.

' The Earl of *Panmure*, *Drummond* of *Logie*,
' and Lieutenant-Colonel *Maclean*, are wounded.
' This is all that I have to fay now, but that I am,

Yours, &c.

M A R,

P. S. We have taken a great many of the Enemy's Arms.

Mon.

Montague's *Regiment* :
Lieutenant-Colonel *Albert Lawrence*,
Captain *John Edwards*.

Clayton's :
Captain *William Barlow*,
Lieutenant *Edward Gibson*,
Captain *Michael Moret*.

Lord Mark Ker's :
Captain *Walter Cheisly*.

Earl Orrery's :
Lieutenant *Thomas Mitchilson*, *Hay*, and *Richard Heneway*.

Brigadier Morrison's :
Ensign *Justin Holdman*, since dead ; *Glenkendy*, and a good Number of private Men and Arms.

The following Letter was written three Days after the Battle, by the Governor of Brunt-Island.

Nov. 16. 1715.

' THIS Morning we had the following Parti-
' culars by Letters from the Governor of
' *Perth*, and Mr. *Mark Wood*, Dean of *Guild* there,
' *viz.* That one Hundred and ten private Men
' were brought Prisoners to *Perth* Yesterday, with
' ten Officers. The Enemy lost on the Spot above
' eight Hundred Men ; and of ours, there is not above
' sixty private Men killed, but several of our Offi-
' cers are taken. We have got forty good Horses,
' and one Thousand five Hundred Stand of the
' Enemy's Arms. Upon Receipt of this News the
' Governor acquainted the Magistrates, whereupon
' they

' they went to Church, and thank'd God for the
' Victory.

An Account of the Engagement on the Sheriff-Moor
near Dumblain, Novem. 13. 1715. *betwixt the*
King's Army, commanded by the Earl of Mar, *and*
the Duke of B——k's *commanded by* Argyle.

THere being various and different Reports industriously spread abroad, to cover the Victory obtained by the King's Army over the Enemy;
the best way to set it in a clear Light, is to narrate
the true Matter of Fact, and leave it to the World
to judge impartially thereof.

Thursday, Nov. 10. The Earl of *Mar* review'd
the Army at *Auchterarder.*

Friday 11. Rested.

Saturday 12. The Earl of *Mar* order'd Lieutenant-General *Gordon,* and Brigadier *Ogilvie,* with
three Squadrons of the Marquis of *Huntley,* and
the Master of *Sinclair's* five Squadrons of Horse,
and all the Clans, to march and take Possession of
Dumblain, which was order'd to be done two Days
before, but was delay'd by some Interruptions; and
all the rest of the Army was order'd at the same time,
to parade upon the Moor of *Tullibardine* very early,
and to march after General *Gordon.* The Earl of
Mar went to *Drummond-Castle* to meet with my
Lord *Broadalbin,* and ordered General *Hamilton* to
march the Army. Upon the March, General
Hamilton had Intelligence of a Body of the Enemy's having taken Possession of *Dumblain,* which
Account he sent immediately to the Earl of *Mar.*
A little after, General *Hamilton* had another Express
from General *Gordon,* who was then about two Miles
to the Westward of *Ardoch,* that he had Intelligence
of a great Body of the Enemy's being in *Dumblain;*
upon which General *Hamilton* drew up the Army,

fo

ſo as the Ground at the *Roman* Camp near *Ardoch*
would allow. A very little after, the Earl of *Mar*
came up to the Army, and not hearing any more
from Lieutenant General *Gordon*, who was marched
on, judg'd it to be only ſome ſmall Party of the
Enemy to diſturb our March, ordered the Guards
to be poſted, and the Army to their Quarters, with
Orders to aſſemble upon the Parade, any time of
the Night or Day; upon the firing of three Cannon.
A little after the Army was diſmiſs'd, the Earl of
Mar had an Account from Leiutenant - General
Gordon, that he had certain Intelligence of the Duke
of *Argyle*'s being at *Dumblain* with his whole Army.
Upon which the General was order'd to halt, till
the Earl ſhould come up to him, and ordered the
three Guns to be fired ; upon which the Army
form'd immediately, and march'd up to Lieutenant-
General *Gordon* at *Kinbuck*, where the whole Army
lay under Arms, with Guards advanc'd from each
Squadron and Battalion till break of Day.

Sunday the 13th, The Earl of *Mar* gives Orders
for the whole Army to form on the Moor, to the
Left of the Road that leads to *Dumblain*, fronting
to *Dumblain* ; the General Perſons were ordered to
their Poſts. The *Stirling* Squadron with the King's
Standard, and two Squadrons of the Marquis of
Huntley's, form'd the Right of the firſt Line of
Horſe. All the Clans form'd the Right of the firſt
Line of Foot ; the *Perthſhire* and *Fifeſhire* Squadrons form'd the Left of the firſt Line of Horſe ;
the Earl *Marſhal*'s Squadron on the Right of the
ſecond Line, three Battalions of the Marquis of
Seaforth's Foot, two Battalions of my Lord *Huntley*'s,
the Earl of *Panmure*'s, the Marquis of *Tullibardine*'s,
the Battalions of *Drummond*, commanded by the Viſcount of *Strathallan* and *Logie Almond*, the Battalion
of *Strowan*, and the *Angus* Squadron of Horſe
form'd the ſecond Line. When the Army was
forming,

forming, we difcover'd fome fmall Number of the
Enemy on the Height of the Weft End of the
Sheriff-Muir, which looks into *Dumblain* ; from
which Place they had a full View of our Army.
The Earl of *Mar* call'd a Council of War, confifting of all the Noblemen, Gentlemen, General Officers, and Heads of the Clans, which was held in
the Front of the Horfe on the Left, where it was
voted to fight the Enemy, *Nemine Contradicente*.
Upon which, the Earl of *Mar* order'd the Earl
Marfhal, Major-General of the Horfe, with his
own Squadron, and Sir *Donald Mac-Donald*'s Battalion, to march up to the Height where we faw
the Enemy, and diflodge them, and fend an Account of their Motions and Difpofitions. No fooner
the Earl *Marfhal* begun his March, but the Enemy difappear'd, and the Earl of *Mar* order'd the
Army to march up after them. By the other Generals Orders, the Lines march'd off the Right, divided in the Center, and march'd up the Hill in
four Lines. After marching about a Quarter of a
Mile, the Earl of *Marifchal* fent back an Account
that they difcover'd the Enemy forming their Line
very near him, to the *South* of the Top of the Hill ;
upon which the Army, particularly the Horfe, was
order'd to march up very quickly, and form to the
Enemy ; but by the breaking of their Lines in
marching off, they fell in fome Confufion in the
forming, and fome of the fecond Line jumbled into
the firft, on or near the Left, and fome of the
Horfe form'd near the Center, which feems to have
been the Occafion that the Enemy's few Squadrons
on the Right were not routed as the reft.
The Earl of *Mar* plac'd himfelf at the Head of
the Clans, and finding the Enemy only forming their
Line; thought fit to attack them in that Pofture ;
he fent Colonel *William Clepham*, Adjutant-General
to the Marquis of *Drummond*, Lieutenant-General
of

of the Horfe on the Right, and to Lieutenant-General *Gordon* on the Right of the Right of the Foot,
and Major *David Erſkine,* one of his Aids-de-Camp,
to the Left, with Orders to march up and attack
immediately : And upon their Return, pulling off
his Hat, wav'd it with a Huzza, and advanc'd to
the Front of the Enemy's form'd Battalions ; upon
which, all the Line to the Right, being of the
Clans, led on by Sir *Donald Mac-Donald's* Brothers,
Glengary, Captain of Clan-*Ranald,* Sir *John Mac-
lean, Glenco Campbell* of *Glenlyon,* Colonel of *Broadalbin's,* and Brigadier *Ogilvy* of *Boyne,* with Colonel
Gordon of *Glenback,* at the Head of *Huntley's* Battalions, made a moſt furious Attack, ſo that in ſeven
or eight Minutes, we could neither perceive the Form
of a Squardon, or Battalion of the Enemy before us.
We drove the main Body and Left of the Enemy,
in this manner, for about half a Mile, killing and
taking Priſoners all that we could overtake. The
Earl of *Mar* endeavoured to ſtop our Foot, and
put them in ſome Order to follow the Enemy,
which we ſaw making off in ſome ſmall Bodies,
from a little Hill below, towards *Dumblain,* where
the Earl of *Mar* reſolved to follow them to compleat the Victory : When an Account was brought
him that our Left, and moſt of our ſecond Line
had given way, and the Enemy was purſuing them
down the back of the Hill, and had taken our Artillery ; immediately the Earl of *Mar* gave Orders
for the Horfe to wheel, and having put the Foot
in Order, as faſt as could be, march'd back with
them. When he was again near the Top of the
Hill, two Squadrons of the Enemy's Grey Dragoons
were perceived marching towards us. When they
came near the Top of the Hill, and ſaw us advancing in order to attack them, they made much
faſter down the Hill than they came up, and joined
at the Foot of the Hill to a ſmall Squadron or two

of the Black Dragoons, and a small Battalion of
Foot, which we judged had march'd about the West
End of the Hill, and join'd them. At first they
again seem'd to form on the Low Ground, and advanc'd towards us; but when they saw us marching
down the Hill upon them, they filed very speedily to
Dumblain. The Earl of *Mar* remain'd possess'd of the
Field of Battle, and our own Artillery, and stood
upon the Ground till Sun-set; and then, considering
that the Army had no Cover or Victuals the Night
before, and none to be had nearer than *Braco, Ardoch,* and Adjacents, whereby his Lordship expected the Left to rally, and the Battalions of the Lord
George Murray, Innernybe, Mac-Pherson, and *Mac-
Gregor,* to join him, resolved to draw off the Artillery, and march the Army to that Place, where
were some Provisions; there were two Carriages of
the Guns broke, which we left on the Road. But
these Battalions did not join us till the next Day
Afternoon, before which the Enemy was return'd
to *Stirling.*

· We took the Earl of *Forfar,* who was dangerously
wounded, Colonel *Lawrence,* and ten or twelve
Captains and Subalterns, and about 200 Serjeants
and private Men, and the Laird of *Glenkindy,* one
of the Voluntiers, four Colours, several Drums,
and about 14 or 1500 Stands of Arms. We com-
pute that there lay kill'd in the Field of Battle
about 7 or 800 of the Enemy; and this is certain,
that there lay dead upon the Field of Battle above
fifteen of the Enemy to one of ours: Besides the
Number of the Wounded must be very great.

The Prisoners taken by us were very civilly us'd,
and none of them stript. Some are allow'd to return to *Stirling* upon their Parole, and the Officers
have the Liberty of the Town of *Perth.* The few
Prisoners taken by the Enemy on our Left, were
most of them stript and wounded, after taken. The

Earl

Earl of *Panmure* being firſt of the Priſoners wounded after taken ; they having refus'd his Parole, he was left in a Village, and by the haſty Retreat of the Enemy, upon the Approach of our Army, was refcu'd by his Brother and his Servants, and carried off.

Monday 14. The Earl of *Mar* drew out the Army early in the Morning, on the ſame Field at *Ardoch* they were on the Day before. About Eleven o'Clock we perceived ſome Squadrons of the Enemy on the Top of the Hill, near the Field of Battle, which march'd over the Top of the Hill, and a little after we had an Account of their marching to *Stirling*. Upon which the Earl of *Mar* march'd back with his Army, who continued about *Auchterarder*.

Tueſday 15. Reſted.

Wedneſday 16. The Earl of *Mar* left General *Hamilton* with the Horſe, to Canton about *Duplin*, and Lieutenant-General *Gordon* with the Clans, and the reſt of the Foot about *Forgan* and Adjacents, and went into *Perth* himſelf to order Proviſions for the Army ; the want of which, was the Reaſon of his returning to *Perth*.

Thurſday 17. The Earl of *Mar* order'd General *Hamilton* to march with the Horſe, and ſome of the Foot to *Perth*, and Lieutenant-General *Gordon* with the Clans, to Canton about that Place.

After writing the former Narrative, we have Account from *Stirling*, that the Enemy loſt 1200 Men, and after Enquiry we can't find above 60 of our Men in all kill'd, among whom were the Earl of *Strathmore*, the Captain of Clan *Ranald*, both much lamented. *Auchterhouſe* is miſſing. Very few of our Men are wounded.

Perth, Printed by Mr. *Robert Freebairn*, 1715.

It

It was reported that one *Drummond* an Officer in *Argyle's* Army went to *Perth* under the Notion of a Deferter, and communicated his Mind to my Lord *Drummond*, who made him his *Aid-de-Camp*; and that at the Battle of *Dumblain* he was attending the Earl of *Mar* to receive his Orders. When the Earl of *Mar* thought that his right Wing was like to defeat *Argyle's* Left, he difpatch'd the faid Mr. *Drummond* to General *Hamilton* (who commanded the Left of the Earl of *Mar's* Army) with Orders to attack the Enemy brifkly, for he was like to have the beft on the Right; but that Mr. *Drummond*, inftead of delivering the faid Order, gave the direct contrary Orders to General *Hamilton*, and told him, That the Earl of *Mar* was worfted on the Right, and defired him to retire with all hafte with as good Order as poffible. Upon which General *Hamilton* gave Order to halt, which was obeyed; then the Right of the Duke of *Argyle's* Army approaching them, the moft part of them gave way without firing a Gun; and thofe that ftood, were for the moft part Gentlemen and Officers, who were feverely galled by the Duke of *Argyle* and his Right Wing; fo that many of them were killed on the Spot, and others taken Prifoners: And that Mr. *Drummond*, after he gave the aforefaid Orders to General *Hamilton*, deferted to the Duke of *Argyle's* Side. But this I do not affirm for a Truth.

There was another Thing very obfervable in that Day's Service, *viz.* That one *Robert Roy Mac-Grigor*, alias *Campbell*, a noted Gentleman in former Times for Bravery, Refolution, and Courage, was with his Men and Followers within a very little Diftance from the Earl of *Mar's* Army, and when he was defired by a Gentleman of his own to go and affift his Friends, he anfwer'd, *If, they could not do it without me, they fhould not do it with me:* That is, If they could not conquer their Enemies without

out

out him, he fhould not affift them in the doing
of it.

This Engagement being over, News was brought
that the Earl of *Sutherland* with Three or Four
Thoufand Men, of whom One Thoufand are his
own, Five Hundred of the *Rofs*'s, Five Hundred
of the *Frazer*'s, under the Command of the Lord
Lovet their Chief, Three Hundred *Mackay*'s, Three
Hundred *Forbes*'s, and Three Hundred *Monroe*'s,
march'd directly towards *Invernefs*, before which
Place they came the 10th of *November*, and fummoned the Governor Sir *John Mackenzie*, who,
with about Three Hundred of his Name, held it
for the Earl of *Seaforth*, and refufed to furrender,
retiring to the Caftle; out of which he retreated,
and upon the 12th they took Poffeffion of the Town
and Caftle. This Town was of no fmall Intereft
to the King's Forces; for it is commodioufly feated,
where formerly *Oliver Cromwell* built a ftrong Fort:
This Place can Mufter above Five Hundred ftout
Men upon any Occafion.

The Fact in general was true, tho' the Perfons were
wrong named in the Account, the E. of *Sutherland* not
being in the Action, or any of his Men. However, I
fay, the Town was taken, and the Lofs of this Important Place was no fmall Affliction to the Earl of
Mar and his Party, who, with his remaining Forces,
after his Difappointment at *Sheriff-Moor*, retired
to *Perth*, and the Duke of *Argyle* to *Stirling*, where
both continued quiet the remaining Part of *November*, and all the next Month; during which time
6000 *Dutch* Foot, lately landed from *Holland*, were
in feveral Detachments marching with the utmoft
Expedition, and by long Marches, to reinforce the
Duke of *Argyle*'s Army. Befides thefe Forces, the
General ordered a Set of General Officers to be fent
to him, for the directing the Troops, which indeed

were

were much wanted. Thefe were Lieutenant-General *Cadogan*, Generals *Whetham*, *Wightman*, *Evans*, *Stanwix*, and *Grant*. Major-General *Sabine* arrived there alfo from *Ireland*.

The 22d of this Month the *Pretender* landed within a few Miles of *Aberdeen*; from thence he marched to *Scoon**, two Miles from *Perth*, where he iffued out feveral Proclamations; one for a general Thankfgiving for his fafe Arrival, another for praying for him in the Churches, a third for the Currency of all Foreign Coins, a fourth for fummoning a Meeting of the Convention of States, a fifth for Arming all fenfible Men from Sixteen to Sixty, and ordering them to repair to his Royal Standard. He likewife fent this Declaration to be publifhed by all Minifters in their Parifh Churches, which thofe in the North of *Scotland* did accordingly.

His Majefty's moft Gracious Declaration.

James R.

JAmes the 8th, by the Grace of God, of *Scotland*, *England*, *France* and *Ireland*, King, Defender of the Faith; to all our loving Subjects of what Degree or Quality foever, Greeting.

As We are firmly refolved never to lofe an Opportunity of afferting our undoubted Title to the Imperial Crown of thefe Realms, and of endeavouring to get the Poffeffion of that Right which is devolved upon us by the Law of God and Man; fo We muft in Juftice to the Sentiments of our own Hearts declare, That nothing in the World can give us fo great Satisfaction, as to owe to the Endeavours of our loyal Subjects, both our own and

---

*. The Place where the Kings of *Scotland* are ufually Crown'd. Here the old Marble Chair, now in *Weftminfter*, ftood.

their

their Reftoration to that happy Settlement, which can alone deliver this Church and Nation from the Calamities which they at prefent lye under, and thofe future Miferies which may be the Confe-quences of the prefent Ufurpation ; during the Life of our dear Sifter, of glorious Memory, the Hap-pinefs which our People enjoy'd, foftned in fome degree the Hardfhip of our own Fate ; and we muft confefs, that when we reflected on the Good-nefs of her Nature, and her Inclination to Juftice, we could not but perfuade ourfelf, that fhe intended to eftablifh and perpetuate the Peace which fhe had given to thefe Kingdoms, by deftroying for ever all Competitions to the Succeffion of the Crown, and by fecuring to Us, at laft, the Enjoyment of that Inheritance, out of which we had been fo long kept ; which her Confcience muft inform her was our due, and which her Principles muft bend her to defire that we might obtain.

But fince the time it pleafed Almighty God to put a Period to her Life, and not to fuffer Us to throw our felf, as we then fully purpofed to have done upon our People, we have not been able to look upon the prefent Condition of our Kingdoms, or to confider their future Profpect, without all the Horror and Indignation which ought to fill the Breaft of every *Scotchman*.

We have beheld a Foreign Family, Aliens to our Country, diftant in Blood, and Strangers even to our Language, afcend the Throne.

We have feen the Reins of Government put into the Hands of a Faction ; and that Authority which was defigned for the Protection of all, exercifed by a few of the worft, to the Oppreffion of the beft and greateft Number of our Subjects. Our Sifter has not been left to reft in her Grave, her Name has been fcurriloufly abufed, her Glory, as far as in thefe People lay, infolently defaced, and her faith-

M 4   ful

ful Servants inhumanly perfecuted; a Parliament has been procured by the moſt unwarrantable Influences, and by the groſſeſt Corruptions, to ſerve the vileſt Ends; and they who ought to be the Guardians of the Liberties of the People, are become the Inſtances of Tyranny, whilſt the principal Powers engag'd in the late Wars, enjoy the Bleſſings of Peace, and are attentive to diſcharge their Debts and eaſe the People. *Great-Britain* in the midſt of Peace, feels all the load of War: New Debts are contraſted, new Armies are rais'd at Home, *Dutch* Forces are brought into theſe Kingdoms, and by taking Poſſeſſion of the Dutchy of *Bremen*, in violation of the Publick Faith, a Door is opened by the Uſurper, to let in an Inundation of Foreigners from Abroad, and to reduce theſe Nations to the ſtate of a Province to one of the moſt inconſiderable Provinces of the Empire.

There are ſome few of the many real Evils into which theſe Kingdoms have been betray'd, under pretence of being reſcued and ſecured from Dangers purely imaginary; and theſe are ſuch Conſequences of abandoning the old Conſtitution, as we perſuade ourſelves very many of thoſe who promoted the preſent unjuſt and illegal Settlement, never intended.

We obſerve, with the utmoſt Satisfaction, That the generality of our Subjeſts are awakened with a juſt Senſe of their Danger, and that they ſhew themſelves diſpos'd to take ſuch Meaſures as may effeſtually reſcue them from that Bondage, which has, by the Artifice of a few deſigning Men, and by the Concurrence of many unhappy Cauſes, been brought upon them.

We adore the Wiſdom of the Divine Providence, which has opened a Way to our Reſtoration, by the Succeſs of thoſe very Meaſures that were laid to diſappoint us for ever; and we moſt earneſtly conjure all our loving Subjeſts, not to ſuffer that Spirit to faint or die away, which has been so miraculously raised in all parts of the Kingdom; but to pursue, with all the vigour and hopes of Success, which so just and righteous a Cause ought to inspire, those Methods which the Finger of God seems to point out to them.

We are come to take our part in all Dangers and Difficulties to which any of our Subjects, from the greatest down to the meanest, may be exposed on this important Occasion; to relieve our Subjects of *Scotland* from the Hardships they groan under on account of the late unhappy Union; and to restore the Kingdom to its ancient, free and independent State.

We have before our Eyes the Example of our Royal Grandfather, who fell a Sacrifice to Rebellion; and of our Royal Uncle, who by a train of Miracles escaped the Rage of the barbarous and Blood-thirsty Rebels, and lived to exercise his Clemency towards those who had waged War against his Father and himself; who had driven him to seek shelter in Foreign Lands, and who had even set a Price upon his Head.

We see the same Instances of Cruelty renewed against us, by Men of the same Principles, without any other Reason than the Consciousness of their own Guilt, and the implacable Malice of their own Hearts; for in the account of such Men it is a Crime sufficient to be born their King: But God forbid, that we should tread in those Steps, or that the Cause of a lawful Prince, and an injured People, should be carried on like that of Usurpation and Tyranny, and owe its Support to Assassins. We shall Copy after the Patterns above-mention'd, and be ready with the former of our Royal Ancestors, to Seal the Cause of our Country, if such be the Will of Heaven, with our Blood; but we hope for better Things. We hope with the latter to see our

just

juft Rights, and thofe of the Church and People of *Scotland*, once more fettled in a free and independent *Scots* Parliament, on their Ancient Foundation ; to fuch a Parliament which We will immediately call, fhall we entirely refer both our and their Interefts, being fenfible that thefe Interefts, rightly underftood, are always the fame. Let the Civil as well as Religious Rights of all our Subjeƈts receive their Confirmation in fuch a Parliament ; let Confciences truly tender be indulged ; let Property of every kind be better than ever fecured ; let an Aƈt of general Grace and Amnefty extinguifh the Fears even of the moft Guilty, if poffible ; let the very Remembrance of all that has preceded this happy Moment, be utterly blotted out, that our Subjeƈts may be united to us, and to each other, in the ftriƈteft Bonds of Affeƈtion as well as Intereft.

And that nothing may be omitted which is in our Power to contribute to this defirable End, We do by thefe Prefents abfolutely and effeƈtually, for Us, our Heirs and Succeffors, pardon, remit, and difcharge all Crimes of High-Treafon, Mifprifion of Treafon, and all other Crimes and Offences whatfoever, done or committed againft Us, or Our Royal Father of Bleffed Memory, by any of Our Subjeƈts of what degree or quality foever ; who fhall at or after our Landing, and before they engage in any Aƈtion againft Us, or Our Forces, from that time lay hold on Mercy, and return to that Duty and Allegiance which they owe to Us their only Rightful and Lawful Sovereign.

By the joint Endeavours of Us and Our Parliaments, urged by thefe Motives, and direƈted by thefe Views, We may hope to fee the Peace and flourifhing Eftates of this Kingdom, in a fhort time, reftored : And We fhall be equally forward to concert with Our Parliament, fuch further Meafures as may be thought neceffary for leaving the fame to future Generations. And

And We hereby require all Sheriffs of Shires, Stewarts of Stewartries, or their Deputies, and Magiftrates of Burghs, to publifh this Our Declaration, immediately after it fhall come to their Hands, in the ufual Places and Manner, under the Pain of being proceeded againft for Failure thereof, and forfeiting the Benefit of Our General Pardon.

Given under Our Sign Manual, and Privy
Signet, at Our Court of *Commercy*, the 25th
Day of *October*, in the Fifteenth Year of Our
Reign.

He was here Addreffed by the Epifcopal Clergy in the Diocefe of *Aberdeen*, and from the Magiftrates of the faid City, which, with his Anfwers are as follow:

It is to be obferved, That only Two Prefbyterian Minifters in all Scotland complied to Pray for the Pretender, and were afterwards turn'd out by the General Affembly; and only Two Epifcopal Minifters Prayed for His Majefty King GEORGE.

To the King's moft Excellent Majefty.

The Humble Addrefs of the Epifcopal Clergy of the Diocefe of Aberdeen, *prefented to His Majefty by the Reverend Doctors* James *and* George Gardens, *Dr.* Burnet, *Mr.* Dunbreck, *Mr.* Blair, *and Mr.* Maitland, *at Fetteroffe, the 29th of* December, 1715. *Introduc'd by His Grace the Duke of* Mar, *and the Right Honourable the Earl Marfhal of* Scotland.

S I R,

WE Your Majefty's moft faithful and dutiful Subjects the Epifcopal Clergy of the Diocefe of *Aberdeen*, do, from our Hearts, render Thanks to Almighty God for your Majefty's fafe and
happy

happy Arrival into this your Ancient Kingdom of *Scotland*, where your Royal Presence was so much longed for, and so necessary to animate your Loyal Subjects, our noble and generous Patriots, to go on with that invincible Courage and Resolution which they have hitherto so successfully exerted, for the Recovery of the Rights of their King and Country, and to excite many others of your good Subjects to join them, who only wanted this great Encouragement.

We hope, and pray that God may open the Eyes of such of your Subjects, as malicious and self-designing Men have industriously blinded with Prejudices against your Majesty, as if the Recovery of your just Rights would ruin our Religion, Liberties, and Property, which by the overturning of these Rights have been highly encroached upon ; and we are persuaded, that your Majesty's Justice and Goodness will settle and secure those just Privileges, to the Conviction of your most malicious Enemies.

Almighty God has been pleased to train up your Majesty from your Infancy in the School of the Cross, in which the Divine Grace inspires the Mind with true Wisdom and Virtue, and guards it against those false Blandishments by which Prosperity corrupts the Heart: And as this School has sent forth the most illustrious Princes, as *Moses*, *Joseph*, and *David*; so we hope the same infinitely Wise and Good God designs to make your Majesty, not only a Blessing to your own Kingdoms, and a true Father of them, but also a great Instrument of the general Peace and Good of Mankind.

Your Princely Virtues are such, that, in the Esteem of the best Judges, you are worthy to wear a Crown, tho' you had not been born to it ; which makes us confident, that it will be your Majesty's Care to make your Subjects a happy People, and so to secure them in their Religion, Liberties, and

Property,

Property, as to leave no juſt Ground of Diſtruſt, and to unite us all in true Chriſtianity, according to the Goſpel of Jeſus Chriſt, and the Practice of the Primitive Chriſtians.

We adore the Goodneſs of God, in preſerving your Majeſty amidſt the many Dangers to which you have been expoſed, notwithſtanding the Helliſh Contrivances formed againſt you, for encouraging Aſſaſſins to Murder your ſacred Perſon ; a Practice abhorred by the very Heathens. May the ſame merciful Providence continue ſtill to protect your Majeſty, to proſper your Arms, to turn the Hearts of all the People towards you, to ſubdue thoſe who reſiſt your juſt Pretenſions, to eſtabliſh you on the Throne of your Anceſtors, to grant you a long and happy Reign, to bleſs you with a Royal Progeny, and at laſt with an Immortal Crown of Glory. And as it has been, ſtill is, and ſhall be our Care, to inſtil into the Minds of the People, true Principles of Loyalty to your Majeſty : So this is the earneſt Prayer of,

(May it pleaſe Your Majeſty)

Your Majeſty's moſt faithful,

Moſt dutiful, and

Moſt humble Subjects

And Servants.

To which Addreſs his (pretended) Majeſty was pleaſed to give the following Anſwer.

I Am very ſenſible of the Zeal and Loyalty you have expreſſed for me, and ſhall be glad to have Opportunities of giving you Marks of my Favour and Protection.

The

The Address of the Magistrates and Citizens of
Aberdeen *to the* Pretender.

To the King's most excellent Majesty.

WE your ever loyal and dutiful Subjects the
Magistrates, Town-Council, and other your
Majesty's loyal Subjects Citizens of *Aberdeen*, do
heartily congratulate your Arrival to this your native and hereditary Kingdom. Heaven very often
enhances our Blessings by Disappointments; and
your Majesty's safe Arrival, after such a Train of
Difficulties and so many Attempts, makes us not
doubt but that God is propitious to your just Cause.
As your Majesty's Arrival was seasonable, so it
was surprizing; we were happy, and we knew it
not; we had the Blessing we wish'd for, yet insen-
sible, till now, that your Majesty has been pleased
to let us know that we are the happiest, and, as so
we shall always endeavour to be, the most loyal
of,

May it please your Majesty, &c.

The Pretender's *Answer.*

I Am very sensible of the Duty and Zeal you express
for me in this *Address*; and you may assure your-
selves of my Protection.

In the mean time, to raise the Affections of the
People for the *Pretender*, the Earl of *Mar* issued
out a circular Letter in Praise of the *Pretender*.

Glames, Jan. 5, 1716.

I Met the King at *Fetteroffe* on *Tuesday* se'night,
where we staid till *Friday*, from thence we came
to *Briechin*, then to *Kinnard*, and yesterday here.
The King design'd to have gone to *Dundee* to Day,
but

but there is fuch a Fall of Snow, that he is forced
to put it off till To-morrow, if it be practicable
then; and from thence he defigns to go to *Scoon*.
There was no Hafte in his being there fooner, for
nothing can be done this Seafon, elfe he had not
been fo long by the way. People every where as
we have come along are exceffively fond to fee him;
and exprefs that Duty they ought, without any
Compliments to him; and to do him nothing but
Juftice, fet afide his being a Prince, he is really the
fineft Gentleman I ever knew! He has a very good
Prefence, and refembles King *Charles* a great deal.
His Prefence however is not the beft of him: He
has fine Parts, and difpatches all his Bufinefs himfelf
with the greateft Exactnefs. I never faw any Body
write fo finely. He is affable to a great degree,
without lofing that Majefty he ought to have, and
has the fweeteft Temper in the World. In a word,
he is every way fitted to make us a happy People,
were his Subjects worthy of him. To have him
peaceably fettled on his Throne, is what thefe Kingdoms do not deferve; but he deferves it fo much,
that I hope there's a good Fate attending him. I am
fure there is nothing wanting to make the reft of
his Subjects as fond of him as we are, but their
knowing him as we do; and it will be odd if his
Prefence among us, after his running fo many Hazards to compafs it, do not turn the Hearts even
of the moft Obftinate. It is not fit to tell all the
Particulars, but I affure you he has left nothing undone that well could be to gain every Body, and I
hope God will touch their Hearts.

I have reafon to hope we fhall very quickly fee
a new Face of Affairs abroad in the King's Favour,
which is all I dare commit to Paper.

M A R.

Likewife

Likewife the *Pretender* iffued out the following Order for burning the Country.

James R.

WHereas it is abfolutely neceffary for our Service and the Publick Safety that the Enemy fhould be as much incommoded as poffible, efpecially upon their March towards us, if they fhould attempt any thing againft us or our Forces; and being this can by no Means be better effected than by deftroying all the Corn and Forage which may ferve to fupport them on their March, and burning the Houfes and Villages which may be neceffary for quartering the Enemy, which neverthelefs it is our Meaning fhould only be done in cafe of abfolute Neceffity; concerning which we have given our full Inftructions to *James Graham* younger of *Braco*: Thefe are therefore ordering and requiring you, how foon this Order fhall be put into your Hands by the faid *James Graham*, forthwith, with the Garifon under your Command, to burn and deftroy the Village of *Auchterarder*, and all the Houfes, Corn, and Forage whatfoever within the faid Town, fo as they may be render'd entirely ufelefs to the Enemy. For doing whereof this fhall be to you, and all you employ in the Execution hereof, a fufficient Warrant.

Given at our Court at *Scoon* this 17th Day of *January*, in the fifteenth Year of our Reign, 1715-16.

By his Majefty's Command,

To *Colonel* Patrick Graham, *or the commanding Officer for the Time of our Garifon for* Tullibardin.

M A R.

According

According to this Order feveral Towns, as *Auch-terarder*, *Blackford*, *Dunning*, and *Muthell*, and other fmall Villages, were burnt to the Ground ; by which the poor Inhabitants, being only the old infirm Men, the Women and Children, the able-bodied being forced from their Homes, either into the Rebellion, or to feek Shelter, which made a moſt difmal and deplorable Sight, to behold thofe under thefe unhappy Circumſtances, expofed in the extremeſt Seafon of the Year, and in one of the coldeſt Winters that has been feen thefe many Ages, fo great a Load of Snow upon the Earth, that a fpeedy Difpatch or Death would have been more eligible to thefe poor naked Creatures than the unconceivable Pains that follow Cold, Hunger, and Nakednefs to the Old and Infirm ; befides the Tendernefs of the other Sex and fucking Infants. The Chevalier pretends to alleviate his Guilt in this, as the Earl of *Mar* hints in his Memorial, by the Rule of War, more to incommode his Enemies than injure his Friends ; who he pretends to relieve and redrefs, by leaving what Money he could fpare, to be diſtributed among the poor Sufferers by his Grace the Duke of *Argyle*.

During thefe Things the Government was not idle, the *Dutch* Troops began to arrive, and the General Officers above-named made the neceſſary Preparations at *Stirling*, to be in a Readinefs to march towards *Perth* to attack the *Pretender*'s Forces at all Hazards. At the fame time the agreeable News was publifh'd in the Army, that the Earl of *Seaforth* defign'd to return to his Duty and Loyalty to King GEORGE : Which, tho' it appear'd afterwards to be otherwife, yet at that Time it put no little Damp upon the Spirits of the Rebels. The chief Obſtacle that now retarded the King's Forces from marching, was not fo much owing to the Rigor of the Seafon, and the Fall of the Snow,

N   though

though that was extraordinary, as the want of Artillery, occasion'd by contrary Winds, which detain'd some Ships at the *Buoy* of the *Nore*, laden with a Train and Stores from the *Tower* of *London*. But his Grace the Duke of *Argyle* bethought himself of the Garison of *Berwick*, and sent thither 1500 Draught Horses and 500 Men, to bring from thence a small Train of Artillery consisting of ten Pieces of Cannon and four Mortars, with their Carriages of Ammunition, &c. which, together with fourteen Pieces of Cannon and two Mortars, the Duke had already with him, made a sufficient Train for his Expedition, at least for the first setting out. It is true, his Grace wanted a Company of Gunners and Engineers for the Service, which luckily were brought to him the 29th, by Colonel *Borgard*, who the Day before arrived in the *Frith* with the Men of War and Transports that had on Board the Artillery and Stores so long expected from *London*.

At the same time the Duke of *Argyle* order'd a great many Pioneers to be summon'd to attend the March of the Army, and about 2000 Waggons to be got ready, resolving to carry fourteen Days Provision for the whole Army, as also a proportionable Quantity of Forage for the Horses.

On the 21st of *January*, Colonel *Guest* was detach'd from *Stirling* with 200 Dragoons, to reconnoitre the Roads leading to *Perth*, in order to begin the March of the Army.

On *Tuesday* the 24th of *January*, the Duke of *Argyle* and General *Cadogan* went personally to view the Roads leading to *Perth*; which put the Rebels into such a Consternation, that some of their small Garisons abandoned their Posts in *Fife*, and retired behind the River *Ern*: But the Army was not yet march'd. Upon their Return to *Stirling*, the Duke of *Argyle* ordered a Detachment to take post at *Dumblain*, and another at *Down*.

January

January 29th, His Majesty's Army, under the Command of the Duke of *Argyle*, advancing from *Stirling* to *Dumblain*, and the same Morning a Detachment of Troops, with two Pieces of Cannon, approached the Castle of *Braco*, which was immediately abandoned by the Rebels.

January the 30th, a Detachment of 200 Dragoons and 400 Foot, with two Pieces of Cannon, march'd to *Tullibardine*, and dislodg'd the Rebels from thence, and took Post there, to cover the Country People that were employ'd in clearing the Roads from the Snow. The Army this Night advanc'd to *Ardoch* and *Auchterarder*, and lay all Night in the open Air in the Snow, the Country being destroy'd by the Rebels.

On *Tuesday* the last of *January* they past the River *Ern* without opposition, and advanced to *Tullibardine*, within eight Miles of *Perth*. About ten a Clock that Morning the Rebels abandon'd *Perth*, marching over the River *Tay* upon the Ice, and about Noon the *Pretender* and the Earl of *Mar* followed. The Duke of *Argyle* received notice of their Retreat about four in the Afternoon, whereupon he immediately order'd a Detachment of 400 Dragoons and 1000 Foot to march and take Possession of the Place, which they entred about Ten next Morning without Opposition. His Grace, with General *Cadogan*, and the Dragoons following the same Day, arrived there about one in the Morning; the rest of the Army marching slowly, by reason of the bad Weather and Ways, arrived in the Evening. They took some of the Rebels Prisoners here, who, being drunk, had stay'd behind the rest. The Place being thus possess'd, the Duke of *Argyle* with the utmost Diligence pursued the flying Enemy the next Day, being *February* the 2d, to *Errol*, with six Squadrons of Dragoons, three Battalions, and eight hundred detach'd Foot,

The

The next Day they proceeded to *Dundee*, where the reft of the Army came on the 4th. The Rebels retired from *Dundee* to *Montrofe*, keeping ftill two Days March before the King's Army; and his Grace fent on the 3d a Detachment towards *Aberbrotheck*, within eight Miles of *Montrofe*, and on the 4th in the Morning his Grace divided the Troops, and firft order'd Major General *Sabine* with three Battalions, 500 detached Foot, and fifty Dragoons to march to *Aberbrotheck*, there being two Roads to *Montrofe*, one by *Brechin*, the other by *Aberbrotheck*; and then detached the fame Day Colonel *Clayton* with 300 Foot and fifty Dragoons, to march by the way of *Brechin*, giving Orders, as well to Major General *Sabine*, as to Colonel *Clayton*, to fet the Country People to work to clear the Roads.

His Grace having divided the reft of his Army into two Bodies, for marching with the greater Expedition, proceeded on the 5th in the Morning with all the Cavalry by the upper Road towards *Brechin*, as did the Lieutenant-General *Cadogan* with the Infantry towards *Aberbrotheck*, the whole Army being to join the next Day near *Montrofe*.

An Account of the Pretender's *Conduct in this Flight, and his getting off, you'll find as follows:*

ON the 15th of *February*, about Noon, in his March to *Aberbrotheck*, General *Cadogan* receiv'd Intelligence, That the Day before, about Four in the Afternoon, the *Pretender* receiv'd Advice at *Montrofe*, that Part of the King's Army was advancing towards *Aberbrotheck*; whereupon he ordered the Clans which had remained with him after his Flight from *Perth*, to be ready to March about Eight at Night towards *Aberdeen*, where he affur'd them a confiderable Force would foon come from *France*.

France. At the Hour appointed for their March, the *Pretender* ordered his Horses to be brought before the Door of the House in which he lodged, and the Guard which usually attended him to Mount, as if he design'd to go on with the Clans to *Aberdeen:* But at the same time he flipped privately out on Foot, accompanied only by one of his Domesticks, went to the Earl of *Mar*'s Lodgings, and from thence by a By-way to the Water-side, where a Boat waited, and carried him and the Earl of *Mar* on Board a *French* Ship of about 90 Tons, called the *Maria Teresa* of St. *Malo.* About a quarter of an Hour after, two other Boats carried the Earl of *Melfort* and the Lord *Drummond*, with Lieutenant-General *Sheldon*, and ten other Gentlemen, on Board the same Ship, and then they hoisted Sail and put to Sea. The Earls of *Marischal* and *Southesk*, the Lord *Tinmouth*, Son to the Duke of *Berwick*, General *Gordon*, with many other Gentlemen and Officers of Distinction, were left behind to shift for themselves: Upon which the Clans for the most part dispersed, and ran to the Mountains, and about a Thousand of them who continued in a Body, march'd towards *Aberdeen.*

Upon the Receipt of this Intelligence, General *Cadogan* hasten'd his March towards *Montrose*, where he arrived the same Afternoon ; the same Night the Duke of *Argyle* came to *Brechin*, within five Miles of *Montrose* with all the Dragoons ; Lieutenant-General *Vanderbeck* with the Foot lay at *Aberbrotheck* ; on the 6th they all continued their March to *Aberdeen*. The same Day General *Gordon*, who took upon him the Command of the Remains of the Rebel Forces, produced to them a Letter from the Chevalier, in which he acquainted his Friends, That the Disappointments he had met with, especially from abroad, had obliged him to leave that Country.

That

That he had thanked them for their Services, and
advised them to advise with General *Gordon*, and
consult their own Security, either by keeping together in a Body, or separating. On the 7th of *February* in the Morning, the Van of the Rebels
marched from *Aberdeen*, as did their Rear about
Two in the Afternoon; their main Body lay at
Meldrum, but near 200 of their Chiefs, with *Irish*,
and other Officers, who came lately from *France*,
went towards *Peterhead*, in order to embark there.
The Duke of *Argyle* followed the Rebels very closely, for on the 8th of *February* his Grace arrived at
Aberdeen, with a Detachment of 50 Dragoons and
400 Foot, and the rest of the King's Forces being
come the same Day into the Neighbourhood, his
Grace detached Major General *Evans*, with 200
Dragoons, and 400 Foot, to intercept the Horse of
the Rebels, if finding they could not get off at *Peterhead*; but they got to *Fraserburgh*, a March before him, and were gone to *Bamf*; whereupon he
detached after them Colonel *Campbel* of *Finab*, with
40 Dragoons and 400 Foot; at *Fraserburgh* the
Chevalier's Physician surrender'd.

February 13. His Grace had Intelligence from
Colonel *Grant*, That he had taken Possession of
Castle *Gordon*, and that General *Gordon* and the main
Body of the Rebels were gone past that Place, and
marched up *Strath-Spey* and *Strath-Don*, which made
him believe they were returning home to separate:
But the Day before he sent this Account to his
Grace, they rendezvouz'd at *Badenock*, to the Num-
ber of 400 Horse, and 500 Foot; after which, the
Horse, for the Convenience of Forage, marched to
Lochabar, and the Foot to the Mountains, with a
Design to wait till such time as they heard from the
Pretender, according to his Promise when he left
them: However 120 Gentlemen on Horseback,
among whom were the Lord *Duffus*, Sir *George
Sinclair*,

Sinclair, General *Eclyn*, Colonel *Hay*, Sir *David Threpland*, and others, took towards *Burgh* in *Murray*, where they embark'd in ten open Boats for *Caithnefs*. General *Eclyn*, that ever brave and bold Man, to prevent his Horfe being of fervice to the Enemy, fhot him through the Head, and a great many followed his Example. They landed at *Dunbeth*, and thence paffed in two Boats, fixty of them into the *Orkneys*, where a Ship of Twenty Guns, belonging to the Chevalier, was ready to take them on Board; the other to the Ifland of *Arfkerry*, where they feized a *Scotch* Ship to carry them away, defigning for *France*, but the Wind proving contrary they failed towards *Gottenburgh*. About this time, two Boats full of thefe unfortunate Gentlemen, were caft away going to the *Weftern* Ifles, twenty one being in one Boat, and twenty-fix in another.

Major-General *Wightman* had near taken the Marquis of *Huntley*, at the Houfe of *Tannachy Tullocks*: This Marquis, now Duke of *Gordon*, is accounted one of the moft inconftant Men of his Age, having in this very Rebellion acted fo much the Trimmer, that whenever Opportunity ferved, he fided with the rifing Party: Thus when he heard nothing of the Chevalier's Landing, he was inclinable to furrender to Mercy, and made fuch Advances as any Man of Honour would have fix'd to; but the *Pretender* Landing, and his Affairs, by his Prefence feeming to put on a better Face, he deferted his Speculations, and returned to the old Caufe. When Fortune put a fecond Frown upon the Caufe, he was inclinable again to fubmit; but Jealoufy made him miftruft the leaft Hopes of abufed Clemency; yet the Goodnefs of His Majefty has extended itfelf in fuch a Latitude to him, that he enjoys his Life, and all; which thinking People hope he will not abufe again.

Befides

Besides those above-mention'd that endeavoured to make their Escapes, the Earls of *Marischal*, *Linlithgow*, and *Southesk*, the Marquis of *Tullibardine*, Viscount *Kilsyth*, Lord *Tinmouth*, and others, found means to shift from place to place, till an Opportunity offer'd in their Behalf, to shew them a way after their old Master.

A great many more of the Rebels submitted, others fled to the *Western* Isles: A good Number getting together in the Isle of *Skye*, others under the Command of Brigadier *Campbell* in *South-West*, formed a Body, as if they resolved to oppose the King's Forces ; but upon the Approach of the Grenadiers to attack them, they immediately run away : But the Brigadier, an old experienc'd Soldier, not used to turn his back, stood upon his Guard till the commanding Officer advanc'd, delivered his Sword, and became Prisoner ;, this Gentleman was brought to *Carlisle*, stood his Trial, pleaded Not Guilty, but found means to make his Escape. Thus I have given an Account of the Rebellion in its blazing Origin, and its Dawning and Setting ; but I must desire my Reader to read the * Journal written by the Earl of *Mar* at *Paris*, and there you will find such Reasons as he gives for his Master's Retreat, and it's hop'd it will be the last with him. You will find an Account of the Strength of the Highland Clans added, which will never again be at the *Pretender*'s Service ; since they were ready to fight, and he unwilling to lead them or head them, unless to the Sea-shore.

* Vide A P P E N D I X.

A LIST

A LIST of the most confiderable Chiefs in
Scotland, *and the Number of Men they can
raife, with an Account of their Difpofition
for or againft the Government.*

THE Duke of *Hamilton* can raife 1000 Men,
all, with their Chief, difpos'd well for the
Government.

The Dutchefs of *Buccleugh* 1000 Men, all, with
their Chief, for the Government.

The Duke of *Gordon* 3000 Men, with their Chief,
who is Neutral ; but moft of them with his Son the
Marquis of *Huntley*, who is againft the Government,
and in the Rebellion.

The Duke of *Argyle* 4000 Men, moft of them
with their Chief, for the Government. This great
Duke defcended from one of the moft ancient Fami-
lies in *North-Britain*, had the Honour to Command
His Majefty's Forces in *Scotland* during the late
Rebellion ; which he difcharged with the greateft
Care, under the greateft Difadvantage, being une-
qual in Number and Strength to his Enemies ; yet
his wife Conduct has made it appear that he is a great
Mafter in the Art of War : For his Behaviour and
Conduct, whilft a Commander in *Spain* and elfe-
where, though ftill unequally in Force and other
Proportions, he ftill deferved the juft Glory of a
Conqueror ; however he may ftand in Court Fa-
vour, nothing will oblige him to revolt from his
Loyalty.

The Duke of *Douglafs* 500 Men, all, with their
Chief, for the Government.

The Duke of *Athol* 6000 Men, few with their
Chief, who is for the Government ; and moft of
them with his Son the Marquis of *Tullibardine*, who
is againft it, and in the Rebellion.

The

The Duke of *Montrose* 2000 Men, few with their Chief, who is for the Government; but moſt againſt it.

The Duke of *Roxburgh* 500 Men, all, with their Chief, for the Government. This Noble Duke, whoſe Father was drowned at Sea, when coming from *London* with the Duke of *York*, had his generous Education from a careful Parent, which he improv'd to the general Satisfaction of all Men: He is a Nobleman of good Senſe, with the Advantage of ſo much Reading and Learning, and other neceſſary Accompliſhments, with the agreeable Looks of good Humour, that by all that are ſo happy as to be acquainted with him, he gains their Affection and Applauſe: His Courage and noble Soul, animated in the Defence of his Invaded Country's Liberty and Religion, is a laſting Standard of his Sincerity, to have both eſtabliſh'd upon the true Ground-work of the Proteſtant Succeſſion: Witneſs his good and gallant Behaviour at the Battle of *Sheriff-Moor*, where he acted the part of an undaunted Hero: His Sovereign's Confidence in his Fidelity, fixes him in a Poſt of Credit beyond the common Compliment given to Courtiers.

The Marquis of *Annandale* 500 Men, all, with their Chief, for the Government.

The Earl of *Errol* 500 Men, few with their Chief, who is Neutral; but moſt of them againſt the Government.

The Earl *Mariſchall* 500 Men, moſt, with their Chief, againſt the Government, and in the Rebellion.

The Earl of *Sutherland* 1000 Men, moſt, with their Chief, for the Government. This Noble Lord, who had the Honour to Command His Majeſty's Forces in the *North*, was the only Inſtrument of keeping that Country in Obedience to His Majeſty: He had gained Promiſes both from *Seaforth*

and

and *Huntley* to submit, which was no small Hinderance to *Mar's* Proceedings, though neither of these Lords performed their Engagements. Had the Arms designed him from *Edinburgh*-Castle arrived safe to him, he would have given a better Account of the Rebels, than it was possible for him to do, being destitute of all Warlike Provisions; yet his Care and Vigilance, and the daily Advantages he gained, notwithstanding his pressing Difficulties, make his Courage, Care, and Zeal for his King, and Preservation of his Country, beyond Dispute.

I must take notice, that though I give the Glory of taking *Invernefs* to another, it is only as a Subaltern acting according to the Command of a superior Officer; which when duly executed, is not to be passed over in Silence.

The Earl of *Mar* 1000 Men, most, with their Chief, against the Government, and in the Rebellion.

The Earl of *Rothes* 500 Men, all, with their Chief, for the Government.

The Earl of *Mortoun* 300 Men, all, with their Chief, for the Government.

The Earl of *Glencairn* 300 Men, most, with their Chief, for the Government.

The Earl of *Eglingtoun* 300 Men, most, with their Chief, for the Government.

The Earl of *Caffils* 500 Men, all, with their Chief, for the Government.

The Earl of *Cathnefs* 300 Men, few, with their Chief, who is Neutral; but most of them against the Government.

The Earl of *Murray* 500 Men, few, with their Chief, who was lately against the Government, and is now for it; but most against it.

The Earl of *Nithfdale* 300 Men, with their Chief, against the Government, and in the Rebellion.

The

The Earl of *Wintoun* 300 Men, moft, with their Chief, againft the Government, and in the Rebellion.

The Earl of *Linlithglow* 300 Men, moft, with their Chief, againft the Government, and in the Rebellion.

The Earl of *Hume* 500 Men. He was confin'd in the Caftle of *Edinburgh*; but moft of his Men, with his Brother, againft the Government, and in the Rebellion.

The Earl of *Perth* 1500 Men, moft, with their Chief, who lives Abroad, with his Son the Lord *Drummond*, againft the Government, and in the Rebellion.

The Earl of *Wigtoun* 300 Men, moft, with their Chief, againft the Government.

The Earl of *Strathmore* 300 Men, in the Rebellion.

The Earl of *Lauderdale* 300 Men, all, with their Chief, for the Government.

The Earl of *Seaforth* 3000 Men, moft, with their Chief, againft the Government, and in the Rebellion.

The Countefs of *Dumfries* 200 Men, for the Government.

The Earl of *Southefk* 300 Men, moft, with their Chief, againft the Government, and in the Rebellion.

The Earl of *Weems* 300 Men, all, with their Chief, for the Government.

The Earl of *Airly* 500 Men, few, with their Chief, who is Neutral; but moft, with his Son the Lord *Ogilvie*, againft the Government, and in the Rebellion.

The Earl of *Carnwath* 300 Men, moft, with their Chief, againft the Government, and in the Rebellion.

The Earl of *Penmure* 500 Men, moft, with their Chief, againft the Government, and in the Rebellion.

The

The Earl of *Kilmarnock* 300 Men, all, with their Chief, for the Government.

The Earl of *Dondonald* 300 Men, all, with their Chief, for the Government.

The Earl of *Broadalbine* 2000 Men, moſt, with their. Chief, againſt the Government, and in the Rebellion.

The Viſcount of *Stormount* 300 Men, all, with their Chief, againſt the Government.

The Viſcount *Kenmure* 300 Men, moſt, with their Chief, againſt the Government, and in the Rebellion.

The Lord *Forbes* 500 Men, moſt, with their Chief, for the Government.

The Lady *Lovat* 800 Men, moſt, with their Chief, againſt the Government, and in the Rebellion.

The Lord *Roſs* 500 Men, all, with their Chief, for the Government.

The Lord *Rae* 500 Men, all, with their Chief, for the Government.

The Lord *Nairn* 1000 Men, moſt, with their Chief, againſt the Government, and in the Rebellion.

Here follow the C L A N S.

SIR *Donald Mac-Donald* 1000 Men, all, with their Chief, againſt the Government, and in the Rebellion.

The Laird of *Glengary* 500 Men, all, with their Chief, againſt the Government, and in the Rebellion. This Gentleman was inferior to none for Bravery.

The Captain of *Clanranald* 1000 Men, all, with their Chief, againſt the Government, and in the Rebellion. This Clan did act the part of Men that are reſolute and brave, under the Command of their Chief; who, for his good Parts, and genteel

Accompliſh-

Accomplishments, was look'd upon as the moft gallant and generous young Gentleman among the Clans; mantaining a fplendid Equipage; keeping a juft Deference to People of all Sorts; void of Pride or Ill-humour: He performed the part of one that knew the part of a compleat Soldier; but a fatal Bullet from the King's Forces, through the Body, difabled him, but did not daunt him; fo finding a Neceffity of yielding to the Fate of his Wound, he withdrew, and told he could do no more; only his Well-wifhes attended his King and Country. He was lamented by both Parties that knew him.

The Laird of *Keppoch* 300 Men, all, with their Chief, againft the Government, and in the Rebellion. Colonel *M'Donald*, commonly call'd Laird of *Keppoch*, brought 300 Men into the Rebellion with him; he has no Eftate or Fortune properly his own, being Tenant at Will to the Laird of *M'intofh*, of the Farms called *Keppoch*, *Glenroy*, and *Glenfpean*, called *Brac-lochaber*; fo that thefe 300 Men, living upon *Mackintofh*'s Eftate, are properly at his Command, whenever his Occafion requires him to raife his Dependants or Vaffals; tho' in the late Rebellion, *Keppoch*, out of Emulation to *Mackintofh*, and to raife his own Character, and to make a Figure, he formed thefe Men into a diftinct Battalion, under his own Denomination and Command; fo that the Reader is defired to take Notice, That this was not juft in him, according to Cuftom in *Scotland*, to withdraw himfelf from his Mafter, being in the fame Intereft with him; yet *Mackintofh*'s good Nature pardon'd this in him, as alfo in the *M'Pherfons*, &c. *Keppoch*'s Character is fuch in his Country, that he is efteemed a Man of great Subtilty and Cunning, as hereditary in him from his Predeceffors, who have been conftantly in Fewds among themfelves, fhedding
ding

ding each others Blood in the moſt bàrbarous Manner ever heard of. His Pretenſions to ſerve the Family of *Stewart* have been very great ; but yet he
never made that known by any one ſingle Aᷣ of
Bravery : For when Occaſion required him to ſhew
his Courage, and to aᷣ his Part, as at *Gilley-cranky,
Cromdale,* and *Sheriff-Moor,* he ſtill ſhewed his
Face, but never drew his Sword, for his People are
expert at nothing more than Stealing and publick
Robberies ; for at *Perth* they made a good Hand in
this way of Buſineſs among the Country People,
and others of their own Party.

The Laird of *Mac-Intoſh* 1000 Men, all with
their Chief againſt the Government, and in the
Rebellion. Moſt of this Clan were in *England,* and
others were poſted off *Inverneſs.*

The Laird of *Mac-Gregor* 500 Men, moſt with
their Chief againſt the Government, and in the
Rebellion. This Clan did nothing worth mention-
ing at *Sheriff-Moor.*

The Laird of *Strowen Robertſon* 500 Men, all
with their Chief againſt the Government, and in the
Rebellion.

The Laird of *Mac-Pherſon* 500 Men, all with
their Chief againſt the Government, and in the
Rebellion. This Clan is part of the *Mackintoſh's*
Family.

Sir *Evan Cameron* 1000 Men, moſt, with their
Chief, againſt the Government, and in the Rebellion. This Knight is ſo old and infirm, that he
could not lead his Vaſſals to the Field, but were
commanded by his Son, who returning home after
the Battle of *Dumblain,* ſeemingly concealed the
Aᷣion from the old Gentleman ; but he having
ſome Intelligence thereof, enquired narrowly for a
juſt Account ; he found by that, that his Vaſſals
did not behave according to their former Bravery,
which made him anſwer thus : Son, I can call to
mind

mind since the *Camerons* were not so numerous as
they are at this Day, but I find by your Account, that the older they grow the more Cowardice; for in *Oliver's* Days, your Grandfather with
his Men could fight double their Number, as I
right well remember; for it is reported, that when
Oliver had built a Fort, to curb the Highlanders at
Inverlochy, that the *Camerons* did annoy them
strangely, beating and pursuing them whenever they
came out into the Country, to the very Walls of
their Garison. And it is recorded of this Sir *Evan*
Cameron of *Locheal*, that following his Enemy too
far, one of *Oliver's* Men vanquish'd him, being
then young, and having thrown him upon the
Ground, refused to grant him Quarter, and endeavouring to draw his Bajonet to stab his Captive,
the vanquish'd found an odd way to deliver himself;
for with a fierce Spring he raised his Body, till he
caught hold of his Conqueror by the Throat with
his Teeth, and pulled it out; so that the other immediately died, and young *Locheal* return'd home.
He is a Gentleman, tho' old, of a sound Judgment, and yet very healthful and strong in Constitution.

Sir *John Mac-Lean* 1000 Men, most with their
Chief against the Government, and in the Rebellion.

The Laird of *Grant* 1000 Men, all with their
Chief for the Government. This Clan belongs to
a very loyal Gentleman, who himself is very gallant
and brave; but his Followers at *Sheriff-Moor* did
not act the part of Fighting, so well as that Family
has done upon other Occasions.

The Laird of *Appin* 300 Men, all with their
Chief against the Government, and in the Rebellion. These Men did not behave so well as was
expected.

The

The Laird of *Mac-Leod* 1000 Men, moſt with their Chief, who is a Minor and Neutral.

The Laird of *Mac-Kenning* 200 Men, all with their Chief againſt the Government, and in the Rebellion.

The Laird of *Glenco* 100 Men, all with their Chief againſt the Government, and in the Rebellion.

The Laird of *Glenmoriſton* 100 Men, all with their Chief againſt the Government, and in the Rebellion.

Mac-Neil of *Barra* 120 Men.

Chriſolme of *Straglaſs* 100 Men, with their Chief, in the Rebellion.

Note, *That all the Chiefs in* Scotland, *are Chiefs of Clans, properly ſo ſpeaking, whether Noblemen or Gentlemen; but commonly the laſt only are call'd the Clans, and particularly thoſe of them who live in the North and Weſt Highlands and Iſles.*

APPEN-

APPENDIX.

The Earl of Mar's *Journal, Printed at* Paris, *(as referr'd to Page* 190.)

S I R,

YOU feem furpris'd at the fudden Change our Affairs here have taken, from what you expected by the Accounts you had from fome of our Friends at *Edinburgh,* before our leaving *Perth* ; and even after we were gone from thence : I will therefore, for your Satisfaction, give you a true Account of that whole Matter.

It is plain enough, that it was our Bufinefs to reprefent our Affairs then to the Publick, to be in fuch a Pofture as might moft encourage our Friends every where, and difcourage our Enemies, and ftop them from marching againft us until we were in a better Condition to receive them ; which we had reafon to expect foon to be, by our Friends joining us, as they daily promis'd to do, and until we fhould receive the Money, Arms, and Ammunition we were every Day expecting, as we had been for a long Time.

But that Time being now over, I may freely own to you, and it's fit you fhould know, that a

Month

Month before the *Chevalier* landed, the Refolution was taken of abandoning *Perth*, as foon as the Enemy fhould march againft it : And tho' this Refolution was known to a good Number in our Army, yet the Secret was fo well kept, that it never came to the Publick ; fo that the Enemy believing that we would ftand our Ground, thought themfelves obliged to delay their March for a long time, until they had made great Preparations of Artillery, &c. as if they had been going to befiege a fortified Town : But in reality, our Condition was then fuch, as obliged us to take that Refolution, having neither a fufficient Number of Men, Ammunition, nor Arms.

Upon the *Chevalier*'s Arrival, we expected that our Friends·would then have certainly joined us ; both thofe who had formerly been with us and were gone Home, and thofe who before had given, the *Chevalier* not being come, as the only Reafon of their not joining the Army ; and alfo that thofe, to whom the reducing of *Invernefs*, the Lord *Sutherland*, and thofe with him was committed, would have vigoroufly performed that Service, and then have joined us; and we had no reafon to doubt, but Money, Ammunition, and Arms would immediately be fent after the *Chevalier*.

But, to our great Misfortune, we were difappointed in all thofe our Hopes, though never fo well grounded in Appearance.

The Rigor of the Seafon, and the great Fall of the Snow on the Hills, kept in fome Meafure the reft of the Highlanders from joining us. Moft of thofe who before had excufed themfelves upon the *Chevalier*'s not being come, kept ftill at home, now that he was come, waiting perhaps to fee how his Affairs were like to fucceed. Thofe employed for reducing of *Invernefs*, were fo far from acting with Vigor, that they made, what they called it, a

Ceffation

Ceffation of Arms with the Enemy. Some Gold was fent to us in *Lingo*'s ; but the Ship in which it came was Stranded, and the Gold loft. Several Ships came with Officers, but neither Arms nor Ammunition in any of them : So that our Condition after the *Chevalier*'s Arrival, was no ways better'd, except by the new Life his Prefence gave to the fmall Number we at that time had got together : Even in that weak Condition, the *Chevalier* would gladly have maintained *Perth*, or ventur'd a Battle ; but when the Enemy with all their great Preparations, and an Army of above 8000 effective regular Troops were actually in march, and advanced near to the Place, it was found impracticable to defend the Town, and unadvifeable to enter into a Battle with a fmall Number of Men that were in it, for a great many Reafons too long to be here mentioned. But in fhort, we had not above 4000 both Horfe and Foot ; and of thefe, for want of Arms, and for other Reafons, not above 2500 to be rely'd upon as good fighting Men. The Town is little better than an open Village at any Time ; and at this, the River on one fide, and a kind of Foffe or Ditch on the other, were frozen up ; fo that it was eafy to be entred on all Quarters. The long continued Froft had kept the Mills from going ; fo that there was not above two Days Provifions in the Town. The Enemy being then in Poffeffion of the moft part of *Fife*, where the Coal-pits are, there were no Coals to be got ; and Wood being fcarce in the Country, there happen'd to be almoft no Fuel at all. Befides this, the Highlanders are not ufed to defend Towns ; nor had they wherewithal to defend this.

On the other hand, to have gone out to fight the Enemy, when there was no advantageous Poft or Pafs to be defended, had been expofing our Men to vifible Deftruction, the Enemy being provided with

every

every thing, and thrice our Number of fighting Men, might have surrounded us on all Sides, and prevented all Possibility of Retreat. All this put us into an absolute Necessity of leaving *Perth*, and retiring Northwards, which we did in good Order, and came in two Days to *Montrose* and *Briechin*. Neither of these Places are tenable, tho' we had been provided, as we were not, with a sufficient Number of Men, Ammunition, and Provisions. But *Montrose* being a good Harbour, where we expected our Succours from abroad, we were unwilling to quit it, so long as we could remain safe in it. We thought indeed, that the Enemy would have made a Halt at *Perth*, and not have marched so quickly after us, as we soon found they did, they being within a few Miles of us before we had certain Intelligence of it, tho' great Pains had been taken to be informed of their Motions. The Earl of *Panmure*, not being recovered of the severe Wounds he had received at the Battle of *Sheriff-Moor*, was not in a Condition to march along with the Army, which otherwise he would have done ; upon which the *Chevalier* advis'd him, as he pass'd *Dundee*, to endeavour to get off in the first Ship he could find ; and by Accident finding a little Bark at *Arboth*, went off in it for *France*.

Before this Time, several People had very seriously represented to the *Chevalier*, the deplorable Circumstances in which his Affairs now were on all Sides; that being over-power'd in *Scotland*, no Appearance of any Rising in *England*, nor any News of the Succours he expected from abroad ; he had no Course at present to take, that was consistent with what he owed to his People in general, to those who had taken Arms for him in particular, and to himself upon their Account, but by retiring beyond Sea, to preserve himself for a better Occasion

fion of afferting his own Right, and reftoring them
to their ancient Liberties.

It was indeed hard to bring him to think of this;
but thofe about him found it now high time to prefs
the Matter more than ever, the Enemy being within
three Miles upon their March towards us. They
therefore again reprefented to him the Impoffibility
of making a Stand any where, till they fhould come
to the moft inacceffible Places of the Mountains,
where in that Seafon of the Year, there being fo
much Snow on the Ground, there could be no
Subfiftance for any Body of Men together, and
where no Succour could come to them : That when
his fmall Army was divided in leffer Bodies, they
could not avoid being cut off by the Enemies
Troops, who would then be Mafter of all the Low
Countries, and efpecially by the Garifons they had
in *Inverlochy* and *Invernefs*, which they would reinforce : That as long as they knew he was in the
Kingdom, they would purfue him, even with the
Hazard of their whole Army, his Perfon being the
chief Object of their Purfuit, as his Deftruction
was the only thing that could fecure their U——n ;
whereas, if he were gone off, they would not purfue with that Eagernefs, nor would they find their
Account in haraffing their Army in the Snow and
exceffive Cold of the Mountains, to purfue the
fcatter'd Remains of the Loyal Party, who might
fculk in the Hills, till Providence fhould open a
Way for their Relief, or that they could obtain
Terms from the Government. That his Perfon
being with them, would defeat even thefe faint
Hopes ; and that in fhort, whilft he was in the
Kingdom, they could never expect any Terms or
Capitulation, but by abandoning him, or giving
him up ; which rather than ever confent to, they
would be all to the laft Man cut in Pieces.

Tho'

Tho' the *Chevalier* was ftill extremely unwilling to leave his Loyal People, who had facrific'd their All with fo much Zeal and Alacrity for his Service; yet when he confider'd, that as Things then ftood, his Prefence, far from being a Help and Support to them, would rather be an Occafion of haftening their Ruin, he was fenfibly touched to find himfelf, for their Sakes, under a Neceffity of leaving them; there was no anfwering their Reafons, nor any Time to be loft, the Danger increafing every Moment. He therefore at laft told them, that he was forry to find himfelf obliged to confent to what they defired of him; and I dare fay, no Confent he ever gave, was fo uneafy to him as this was.

In the mean time, frefh Alarms coming of the Enemy's approaching, Orders were given for the Army's marching towards *Aberdeen*, and the Refolution was taken for his going off in the Evening. It happen'd very providentially, that there was juft ready in the Harbour a fmall Ship, that had been defigned to carry a Gentleman he was then to have fent to a Foreign Court. This Ship was now pitch'd upon to tranfport him; fhe was but a fmall one, and could carry but a few Paffengers; and therefore to avoid Confufion, he himfelf thought fit to name thofe who fhould attend him. The Earl of *Mar* who was the firft nam'd, made Difficulty, and begg'd he might be left behind; but the *Chevalier* being pofitive for his going, and telling him, that in a great meafure there were the fame Reafons for his going as for his own; that his Friends would more eafily get Terms without him than with him; and that as Things now ftood, he could be no longer of any ufe to them in that Country, he fubmitted.

The *Chevalier* likewife ordered the Marquis of *Drummond* to go along with him: This Lord was then lame by a Fall from his Horfe, and not in a

Condi-

Condition to follow the Army, and was one of the four with the Earl of *Mar*, Lord *Tullibardine*, and Lord *Lithgow*, againſt whom there was then a Bill of Attainder paſſing. The *Chevalier* would have willingly carried with him the other two Lords ; but it happen'd that they were both then at a Diſtance ; Lord *Tullibardine* at *Briechin* with a part of the Foot, and Lord *Lithgow* at *Bervie* with the Horſe. Lord *Mariſchal*, Gentleman of his Bed-Chamber, was alſo ordered to go, though he ſeem'd very deſirous to ſtay and ſhare in the Fate of his Countrymen. Lieutenant-General *Sheldon*, Vice-Chamberlain, had the ſame Orders ; as had alſo Colonel *Clephan* who had left the Enemy. Lord *Edward Drummond*, who was alſo Gentleman of his Bed-Chamber, happen'd to be with Lord *Tinmouth* at five Miles diſtance, and ſo could not go with the *Chevalier*, as he intended they both ſhould ; but he wrote to them to follow in a ſmall Ship that was then in the Harbour ; but the Maſter of this Ship was frighten'd, and went away without carrying any Body.

The *Chevalier* then order'd a Commiſſion to be drawn for Lieutenant-General *Gordon* to Command in Chief, with all neceſſary Powers inſerted ; and particularly one, to Treat and Capitulate with the Enemy : He left alſo the ſaid General the Reaſons of his leaving this Kingdom, and all the Money that was in the Paymaſter's Hands, or that he had himſelf, (ſave a ſmall Sum for defraying his own and Company's Charges) and left Orders for a Sum of Money (if there ſhould be any left after paying the Army) to be given to the poor People who ſuffer'd by the Burning of *Auchterarder*, and ſome Villages about it, which had been thought neceſſary to be done, to prevent the Enemy's March, tho' very much againſt his Inclination ; which made him delay from time to time, until the Enemy was actually

on

on their March ; and the *Chevalier* left a Letter with General *Gordon* for my Lord *Argyle*, to be deliver'd when the said Money should be given, desiring that it should be diftributed accordingly.

About Nine o'Clock the *Chevalier* went on Board the Ship, which was about a Mile at Sea ; Lord *Marifchal* and Colonel *Clephan* came some time after to the Shore, but by an Accident found no Boat, and so could not go off ; tho' as the Boat-men, who carried the *Chevalier*, affure us, he ftay'd for them till near Eleven o'Clock, but could ftay no longer, becaufe of the nine Men of War that were cruifing thereabouts ; and it was great good Luck that the Ship, having ftay'd fo long, got out of their Reach before it was Day-light.

As foon as the *Chevalier* parted, we marched, and we are now a good way advanced towards the *Highlands*, for there was no Stand could be made at *Aberdeen* ; nor could we think of going to *Inver-nefs*, that being ftill in the Enemy's Hands. Some went to *Peterhead*, and thought to have got off in a Ship they found there ; but we hear they were foon forc'd back'd by a Man of War ; fo it's like they may join us again, if they are not intercepted by the Enemy.

I muft here add one Thing, which however in-credible it may appear, is, to our Coft, but too true ; and that is, That from the Time the Earl of *Mar* fet up the *Chevalier's* Standard to this Day, we never received from Abroad the leaft Supply of Arms and Ammunition of any Kind : Tho' it was notorious in itfelf, and well known, both to Friends and Enemies, that this was what from the Beginning we mainly wanted ; and as fuch, it was infifted up-on by the Earl of *Mar*, in all the Letters he writ, and by all the Meffengers he fent to the other Side. Several Ships came with Officers, and fome fmall Sums of Money ; after the Battle of *Sheriff-Moor* ; and

three

three or four Ships more came after the *Chevalier's*
Arrival; but even when he was with us in Perfon,
no Powder was fent, nor a Sword nor Mufquet:
So that when we march'd from *Perth*, we had not
300 Weight of Powder for the whole Army; nor
fhould we have wanted Men, had we had Arms to
put in their Hands. How the main Point came to
be fo entirely neglected by thofe who had the
Managment of the *Chevalier's* Affairs in their Hands
on the other Side, is yet a Myftery to us; and it
furprizes the more, that thofe who came lately over
affure us, that both Arms and Ammunition might
have been gotten from private Hands, without
having the Obligation to any Foreign Prince. So
whether this unaccountable Omiffion proceeded from
mere Negligence, want of Money, or from a Jealoufy in fome, who were, perhaps, unwilling that
we fhould be the Inftruments of this great Work,
and that it fhould fucceed in our Hands, or for
fome other By-reafons, is what Time may difcover.

Thus I have given you true Matter of Fact,
and a fincere Account of our unfortunate Condition.
Whatever may now be our Fate, we have ftill one
folid Ground of Comfort, that the *Chevalier* hath
(as we hope) got fafe out of the Reach of his E-
nemies; for in the Safety of his Perfon is all our
Hopes of Relief; and we look on him as the Inftrument referved by God, (and he now feems the
only one in the ordinary Courfe of Providence)
to refcue thefe Nations in due Time from their
Oppreffion, and the lawlefs Dominion of *E——*.

Now if we look back a little, and confider our
Affairs from the Beginning of this laft Attempt,
I believe it will be found that no Nation in our
Circumftances, and fo deftitute of all kind of Suc-
cour from Abroad, ever made fo brave a Struggle
for reftoring their Prince and Country to their juft
Rights.

Rights. And when it comes to be known to the World, (as some time or other it may) what Encouragements there were at Home and Abroad, reasonably to make us expect and hope for Success in this great, good, and necessary Work; it will appear no chimerical, rash, or ill-grounded Undertaking; and it's not proving Successful, plainly appears, by what has been already said, and what follows, is not owing to the *Chevalier*, or his faithful Friends on this Side.

When the Earl of *Mar*, by the *Chevalier's* Command, came down to *Scotland*, he found the People there more forward to take Arms, than his Instructions allowed him to consent to; and it was not without Difficulty that we could allay their first Heat. But the *Chevalier* not going into *England*, nor the Duke of *Berwick* coming to *Scotland*, as was generally expected, abated very much of that Forwardness; so that when the Government summon'd those they suspected to appear and give Bail for their good Behaviour, many of them seem'd inclin'd to comply. The Earl of *Mar*, in Pursuance of his Instructions, found it then high time for preventing this Step, to appear openly; and it was not without Difficulty that he could persuade some to join with him, they apprehending great Uncertainty of Success in the Affair, by no Account being come of the *Chevalier*, or the Duke of *Berwick's* Arrival, nor of Money, Arms, Ammunition, or Officers, tho' others were all along very forward. Upon the Resolution of taking Arms, he sent a Gentleman to give the *Chevalier* an Account of it.

It was near a Month after the Earl of *Mar* set up the Standard before he could produce a Commission; and it is no small Proof of the Peoples Zeal for their Country, that so great a Number followed his Advice and obey'd his Orders before he could produce one. It must tho' be own'd, and it is the less to be

wonder'd

wonder'd at, that his Authority being thus precarious, some were not so punctual in joining him,
and others perform'd not so effectually the Service
they were sent upon ; which had they done, not only
Scotland, but even Part of *England*, had been reduced to the *Chevalier*'s Obedience before the Government had been in a Condition to make head against
us. But as it was, most of those who had promised,
and some who had not, join'd the *Chevalier*'s Standard at *Perth* about the End of *October* ; at which
Time the Earl of *Mar* sent two Gentlemen to give
the *Chevalier* an Account of the Condition they were
in, of what they had, and what they wanted, and
to hasten his own, the Duke of *Ormond*'s, and the
Duke of *Berwick*'s Coming into *Britain*.

About this Time there was a Rising of some Noblemen and Gentlemen in the South of *Scotland*,
who marching over the Borders, were join'd by some
in the North of *England* ; and they all together
marching back into *Scotland*, the Earl of *Mar* sent
over the *Firth* of *Forth* 1500 Foot to join them.
This occasion'd the Duke of *Argyle*'s leaving *Stirling*,
and going with a Part of his Army to *Edinburgh*.
Now, had the *Scots* and *English* Horse, who were
then in the South of *Scotland*, come and join'd the
1500 Foot, as was expected ; had the Highland
Clans perform'd as they promised the Service they
were sent upon in *Argyleshire*, and march'd towards
Glasgow as the Earl of *Mar* march'd towards *Stirling*, he had then given a good Account of the Government's Army, the Troops from *Ireland* not having yet join'd them, nor could they have join'd
them afterwards. But all this failing by some cross
Accidents, Lord *Argyle* returned with that Part of
his Army to *Stirling* ; and the Earl of *Mar* could
not, with the Men he then had, advance farther
than *Dumblain* ; and for want of Provisions there,
was soon after oblig'd to return to *Perth*.

But

But immediately after we had got Provisions, and that the Clans and my Lord *Seaforth* had join'd us, we marched again towards the Enemy; and notwithstanding the many Difficulties the Earl of *Mar* had upon that Occasion with some of our own People, he gave the Enemy Battel; and, as you saw in our printed Account of it, had not our Left Wing given way, which was occasion'd by Mistake of Orders and Scarcity of experienc'd Officers, that being compofed of as good Men, and march'd as chearfully up to the Field of Battel as the other, our Victory had been compleat; and as it was, the Enemy, who was advanced on this side the River, was forced to retire back to *Stirling*.

Amongst many good Qualities, the Highlanders have one unlucky Custom, not easy to be reform'd; which is, that generally after an Action they return Home. Accordingly a great many went off after the late Battel of *Sheriff-Moor*; so that the Earl of *Mar* not being in a Condition to pursue the Advantage he had by it, was forc'd to return to *Perth*, waiting there, not without Impatience, both for the Return of the Highlanders, and for Money, Arms and Ammunition, he had so often ask'd, and still expected from Abroad. But the Highlanders hearing nothing of the *Chevalier*, or the Duke of *Berwick*'s Coming, nor of the Supplies, did not return to the Army, as they had promised. And the Gentlemen of the Army, who had been long from Home, living still at their own Charge, which they could not well longer support, went also mostly Home, some without Leave, and others after a Leave, which the Earl of *Mar* saw well enough would be to no purpose to refuse. Some indeed never thought of quitting the Army, and others return'd soon to it; but our Number was never again near so great as it had been before the Battel. About this Time we had the News of the fatal

Affair

Affair at *Preston*, which was no small Difcouragement to the Army; fo that fome who had been caballing privately before, began then to fpeak openly of capitulating with the Enemy, and found others more eafy to join with them.

We had at the fame Time another Piece of bad News; which was, That *Simon Frazer* of *Beauford* (by fome call'd Lord *Lovat*) had join'd Lord *Sutherland*; and that they, with the Help of fome other difaffected People thereabouts, had retaken *Invernefs*. Upon this News, moft of the Name of *Frazer*, who had join'd the *Chevalier*'s Army with *Frazerdale*, went now away, and join'd *Beauford*, or Lord *Lovat*, their Chief.

This oblig'd the Earl of *Mar* to fend Lord *Seaforth* North to get his Men together, who had moftly return'd Home after the Battel, and in Conjunction with the *Chevalier*'s Friends in that Country, to endeavour to recover *Invernefs*.

In the mean time, thofe who were for capitulating with the Enemy, preffed the Earl of *Mar* fo hard to confent to it, that to prevent fome Peoples making private feparate Treaties, which he found they were about, he was at laft forc'd to comply fo far with them, as to fend a Meffage from the whole Army to my Lord *Argyle*, to know *if he had Power to treat with them?* That Lord return'd with great Civility this Anfwer: *That he had no fufficient Power to treat with them in a Body, but that he would write to Court upon the Subject.* To which it was reply'd; *That when he fhould let them know he had fufficient Power, they then would make their Propofitions.* By which the Affair was put off at that time; and we were fince informed, that the Lord *Argyle* never received thofe Powers; and that even his former Power, which he fent up to be enlarged, were never returned to him.

Much

Much about this time, the Marquis of *Huntley* having, for fome time, prefs'd his going home with his Horfe, the Earl of *Mar* confented to it, and gave him a Commiffion, in Conjunction with my Lord *Seaforth*, for reducing of *Invernefs*, and thofe who oppos'd the *Chevalier's* Intereft in that Country, which we then hop'd would be foon done.

After this, fome, though but few, were difcovered to have private Dealings with the Enemy; and fome others went home, and never returned to the Army; but a good Number of the Noblemen and Gentlemen, and all the Heads of the Clans, ftill remained with the Army at *Perth*.

We had, about this time, the long-wifh'd for News of the *Chevalier's* being Landed; and that put an End, for the prefent, to any farther talking of Capitulations.

I have now given you a true, and, I hope, fatisfactory Account of the Condition we have been in, ever fince our firft taking Arms; of the bad Condition in which the *Chevalier* found us at his Arrival; and of the Reafons that oblig'd him at laft to leave us.

There remains yet to anfwer one Queftion, which you may naturally afk, as moft People do, on this Subject; and that is, Why the *Chevalier* delayed his Coming fo long?

To anfwer this Queftion to your Satisfaction, I muft tell you, That I have what I fhall here relate, from Perfons of unqueftionable Veracity, who were then upon the Place, Eye and Ear Witneffes of what pafs'd; and fo you may fafely rely upon it.

You have certainly heard, what was generally faid of the *Chevalier's* Sifter's Inclinations towards him, whilft fhe was in Poffeffion of his Throne. But whatever there was of Truth in that, what I am well affured of is, that he was at laft fo little fatisfied with what was faid to him from thence, that he

was

was fully refolved, whilft fhe was yet alive, to have gone into *Scotland*; and, in order to that, had already prepared a Declaration, or Manifefto, to have been there publifhed upon his Arrival. How he was hinder'd from putting this Defign in Execution by fome real Friends, that were themfelves impos'd upon, and by other pretended Friends, who were at the Bottom real Enemies, is a Myftery which Time may difcover.

Upon the firft News of his Sifter's Death, he immediately took Poft, refolved to endeavour, at any Rate, to get into fome Part of his Dominions; but was ftopp'd by thofe who had Power to do it effectually. Being then forc'd back to *Lorain*, he made and publifhed his Proteftation, which it's likely you have feen, and which, I can affure you, was drawn entirely by himfelf.

From that Time, as before, he had nothing in his Thoughts, but how and when he could affert his own Right, and deliver his People. He faw little Ground to hope for Succour from any foreign Prince, and had only the Affections of his People, and the Advice of his Friends on this Side of the Water, to rely upon. Their Intereft feemed now more than ever linked to his; and they being upon the Place, and confequently beft able to judge of the fitteft time for his coming to them, it muft be allow'd, that it has been no ways prudent nor advifeable in him, to act contrary to their Opinion: And yet it is moft certain, that it was only by following their Advice, contrary to his own Judgment and Inclination, that fo much time was loft. Some of them in *England* infifted upon having a certain Number of Regular Troops to make Head at firft, without which, they faid, nothing was to be attempted; and though he fent them Word over and over, That, after all the Endeavours he could ufe, he found it abfolutely impoffible to obtain any Troops;

P   yet

yet they infifted for feveral Months in this Opinion,

yet they infifted for feveral Months in this Opinion, and by that Means the moft favourable Time he ever had, was loft. Other Friends there pretended, that the Difpofitions of the People would ftill grow more favourable towards him; and that there was no Danger, but Advantage, by delaying.

Thus, though he had feveral times fixed a Day for his Departure, he was ftill forced to delay, that he might not act contrary to the Advice of his Friends; and at another time, becaufe he found that his Enemies had difcover'd his Defign, and taken infallible Meafures to intercept him. But as foon as his Friends began to fee, and own the Mi-ftakes they had been in, he, without any regard to the many Dangers he had to go through, fet out from *Commercy* the 28th of *October*, and went *incognito* through a great Part of *France*, to the Coaft of *Britany*; and to avoid falling into the Hands of Many, who were plac'd upon the common Road to intercept him, he was obliged to crofs the Country through Bye-ways, with only three People with him. His Defign was to go to *England*, if things appeared favourable there; or, if they did not, to go to *Scotland*.

When he arrived at St. *Malo's*, he found the Duke of *Ormond* returned from the Coaft of *England*, to which he had gone fome Days before, in hopes to have found Friends ready to join him; but that having failed, by fome Accidents of Difco-veries, he was forced to return. Upon this he refolved to go into *Scotland*; and it not being thought fafe for him to go through the *Britifh* Chan-nel, he had been advis'd to go round *Ireland*; and, by a Meffage from his Friends in *Scotland*, it was propos'd to him to Land at *Dunftaffnage*, which was at that time in their Poffeffion; but foon after the Enemy came to be Mafters of it, by the Clans not performing what they were charg'd with in *Argyle-fhire*, *shire*, as is aformentioned. His Friends immediately inform'd him of this Change, by a second Message; and this confirm'd Him in the Resolution he had himself before taken, of changing all his Measures, and, in place of taking that long, tedious Way, which was indeed the safest, to take a much shorter, though a more dangerous Way for being intercepted by the Enemies Ships; he sent therefore immediately to prepare a small Ship privately for him at *Dunkirk*; which was accordingly done, though not without Difficulty.

He was now a second time oblig'd to traverse a great Part of *France*, and that on Horseback, in the very coldest time of this hard and severe Winter; exposed to greater Danger than in the *South*, from the greater Number of those who lay in wait for him on all the great Roads, which obliged him to travel by unfrequented Routs, where there was Accommodation bad enough; and yet all this time, in that terrible Cold, he never had the least Ailment or Indisposition.

It was about the Middle of *December* (our Stile) before he could reach *Dunkirk*; he was there inform'd, that there was a Man of War then lying in that very Road; and that there were a great many more cruizing on the Coast of *France*, *England*, and *Scotland*, all of them in wait for him; but he, without any regard to these Dangers, went immediately on Board this small Ship with only three Servants, and, conducted by good Providence, arrived safe at *Peterhead*, where he Landed the 22d of *December* (old Style).

Having, I hope, now fully satisfied your Curiosity, I have only to add, That though it hath pleased God to permit, that this Attempt, though never so just, had not the wish'd-for Success; we have still reaped by it one great Advantage, which is, That we have seen with our own Eyes, and per-

sonally

totally known our lawful S-------n; and, to our unfpeakable Satisfaction, difcover'd in him all the great and good Qualities that are neceffary for making a People every-way happy.

The time may, and I hope will yet come, when God, in his Mercy, will open the Eyes, and turn the Hearts of thefe Nations to a Senfe of their Duty, and not permit fo accomplifh'd a Perfon to be always unfortunate: But however it fhall pleafe Providence to difpofe of him, this I can affure you, and you may rely upon it, that as his Right is indefeafible, he is firmly refolved, by the Help of Almighty God, to affert it, whenever he finds a fit Opportunity, and never to depart from it, but with his Life.

The Lord *MAR*'s Letter to ------

SIR,

THE inclofed Relation having come to my Hands fince I came to this Country; and having, upon Perufal, found it very exact in Matters of Fact; I thought you would be glad to fee it, which makes me fend it to you; and, if you think fit, you may fhew it to your Friends where you are.

I am,

SIR,

Your moft humble Servant,

Sic fub. MAR.

I could

I could not conveniently infert the following Particulars in the former Part of this Hiftory ; but to
be more particular in relating the feveral Confpira-
cies of His Majefty's fecret Enemies, I fhall here
give my Reader a diftinct Account of an early concerted Defign to furprize *Briftol*, a City ftrong,
populous, ftored with all manner of Provifions ;
being the fecond City in *Great-Britain*, famous for
Trade and Riches.

Upon Information, that the Difaffected had laid
a Defign to furprize the Place, and make it a Magazine of Arms, the Earl of *Berkley*, Lord-Lieute-
nant and Governor of that City and County, repair'd thither with all Speed towards the End of
September 1715, and with unwearied Application
and Diligence, took all the neceffary Meafures and
Precautions for the Security of that important Town.
Several Perfons, under Pretence of being Members
of the Royal Society, carried on Treafonable Defigns, were fecured, amongft them, one Mr. *Hart*
a Merchant, who was charged for having gathered
great Quantities of Warlike Stores for the Ufe of the
Difaffected. Befides part of *Lumley*'s Regiment of
Horfe, and two Battalions of *Stanwix* and *Pocock*,
who were already in *Briftol*, Colonel *Chudleigh*'s
Regiment of Foot was ordered to March thither;
which they did about the Beginning of *October* ; at
the fame time the Lord *Windfor*'s Regiment of
Horfe, and *Rich*'s Dragoons, under the Command
of Major-General *Wade* marched to *Bath*, which
Place was both the Rendezvous, and one of the
Arfenals of the Confpirators, who having recovered
their firft Alarm, and returned to *Bath*, were fecured, with about 200 Horfes. Upon ftrict Search,
the King's Officers found and feized Eleven Chefts
of Fire-Arms, a Hogfhead full of Bafket-hilted
Swords, and another of Cartouches, and three

Pieces

Pieces of Cannon, one Mortar, and Molds to Caſt Cannon, which had been hid in the Ground.

Mr. Secretary *Stanhope* having written a Letter to the Magiſtrates of *Bath*, ſignifying the Occaſion of Major-General *Wade's* marching thither with the two Regiments above-mentioned; they thought fit to return an Anſwer, with an Aſſurance of their Loyalty, and the Apprehenſions they were under from the vaſt Concourſe of Nonjurors and Papiſts that flock'd thither: But their Fear ceaſed upon Major-General *Wade's* coming.

The Deſigns of the Diſaffected upon the Important City of *Briſtol* being defeated, they laid a Project to ſeize on the Port and Town of *Plimouth*; but the ſame was happily prevented, by the timely ſecuring of ſeveral ſuſpected Perſons. I have heard Mr. *Buxton* ſay, that he had been taking a View of this Port, and *Portſmouth*; and had counted how many Cannon were mounted in each. Part of the common People in *Cornwal* were at this time ripe for Rebellion, ſome of them having got together, had the Inſolence to proclaim the *Pretender* at *St. Columbe.*

The Tory Party, tho' diſappointed in their firſt Attempt to ſurprize *Briſtol*, yet their Zeal for the Cauſe animated them for to undertake another Deſign upon that City. Being informed about the middle of *January* 1715—16, That the late Duke of *Ormond* intended to Land in the *Weſt*, and put himſelf at the Head of a Body of Diſcontents, who, upon Pretence of repairing to *Briſtol* Fair deſigned to make themſelves Maſters of that famous City; the Government thought fit to reinforce that Gariſon with Colonel *Pocock's* Regiment of Foot, and ſome other regular Forces. Major General *Wade*, who Commanded in thoſe Parts, repaired thither, to give the neceſſary Directions; and at the ſame time, the Loyal Citizens formed two voluntary Troops of Horſe

Horſe to ſuppreſs Mobs, which were grown Inſo-
lent: Nor were theſe Precautions altogether needleſs:
For the Night between the 14th and 15th of _Ja-
nuary_, a Waggon laden with Goods for _Briſtol_ Fair,
being by accident ſet on Fire at _Hounſlow_, there was
diſcovered in it a great Quantity of Fire-Arms and
Ammunition lying under the Goods; upon which
the ſame were ſeized by a Trooper of the Duke of
Argyle's Royal Regiment of Guards; ſo this ſecond Deſign miſcarried, Fate ſtill purſuing all their
Projects.

Beſides all theſe Schemes ſo artfully laid, prevíous
to theſe a mortifying Accident befel them; an Order was Sign'd by the Secretary of State, for to ſeize
Sir _William Windham_, ſuſpected to be concerned in
forming a Party of his Intereſt to riſe in favour of
the _Pretender_: This happened _September_ 21, 1715.
The Meſſenger and Captain _Huſk_ of the Foot
Guards, were diſpatch'd to apprehend him at his
Seat, called _Orchard Windham_ in _Somerſetſhire_, who
got thither between Four and Five in the Morning;
the Door being opened to them, they appeared to
be in haſte to ſee Sir _William_, but the Porter told
them he was in Bed, and could not yet be ſpoke
with. The Colonel told him, he came Expreſs,
and the Perſon with him had a Packet of Letters of
ſuch Conſequence, his Maſter muſt be immediately
told of it. This convinc'd the Man, and Sir _William_
preſently leaped out of Bed, and came in his Gown
to the Colonel, who told him he was his Priſoner;
the Meſſenger at the mean time ſhewing his Scutcheon,
the Badge of his Office, Sir _William_ told them, that
he readily ſubmitted; but he deſired no Noiſe might
be made to frighten his Lady who was with Child.
They then entred a Chamber, where the Colonel
ſeeing Sir _William's_ Coat and Waiſtcoat lie, told
him, he had Orders to ſeize all his Papers, and
that he muſt take leave to ſearch his Pockets, where-

in

in he found a Bundle of Papers, which he fecured.
Sir *William* would have diverted him, by offering
him very frankly the Keys of his Efcrutore; but
the Colonel happened to fecure the main Chance
above, (finding nothing in the Efcrutore.) Sir *William*'s Countenance alter'd when the Colonel took the
Bundle out of his Waiftcoat Pocket. Sir *William*
then defired the Colonel, that he would ftay till Seven o'Clock, and he would order his own Coach
and Six Horfes to be got ready, which would carry them all; telling the Colonel, he would only go
and put on his Cloaths, and take leave of his Lady,
and then he would wait on him. The Colonel,
who had particular Orders to ufe him with Decorum,
readily complied with the Requeft, looking on it
as his Parole to return; but he foon found himfelf
miftaken; for tho' the Colonel had caufed Two
Doors of Sir *William*'s Bed-Chamber to be fecured,
yet there being a Third, he made his Efcape thro' it.
The Colonel having directed the Meffenger to ftay
at *Orchard-Windham* till farther Orders, returned
with all Speed to *London*, to acquaint the Government with what had happened; whereupon the King
in Council thought fit to publifh a Proclamation,
with a Reward of a Thoufand Pounds for Apprehending him.

Sir *William* being purfued with this Proclamation
and feveral Meffengers, he thought a Clergyman's
Habit the beft Difguife, fo order'd a Letter to be
fent to a Gentleman in *Surry*, to defire Refuge in
his Houfe; the Gentleman being abroad, his Lady
open'd it, and fearing the Confequence of Harbour-
ing one in his Circumftances, fhe fent the Letter to
a Nobleman of her Acquaintance, who failed not
immediately to acquaint the Government. Sir
William, rightly judging that he was clofely purfued, thought it Prudence to make Neceffity a Virtue, and furrender himfelf to the Government; in
order

order to that, having croffed the *Thames* near *Thiftle-worth*, he went firft to *Sion Houfe* belonging to the Duke of *Somerfet*, his Father-in-Law, and coming from thence to *London*, on Monday Night, *October* the 3d, he put himfelf into the Hands of the Earl of *Hertford* (his Brother-in-Law) Captain of one of the Troops of Life-Guards ; who gave Notice thereof to Mr. Secretary *Stanhope*, who fent one of his Clerks, with a Meffenger, to take Sir *William Windham* into Cuftody : Three Days after, he was Examin'd at the Council-Board, where he denied he knew any thing of a Plot, or the intended Rebellion ; yet an Order was fign'd for his Commitment to the *Tower*. Whether this Gentleman was privy to any fuch Defigns, I fhall not pretend to determine, but this I can affirm, that it was a feeling cold Blow to all the Party, efpecially to the *Northumberland* Rebels who found themfelves very much leffened by this Gentleman's Confinement ; and I believe this occafion'd another Knight to play the Sculker with the *Northumberland* Gentlemen, notwithftanding his folemn Engagements : But his Conduct in all the Parts of his Life reveal him of being incapable of ferving any Side to Advantage or Credit, for his own is funk with all fincere honeft Men. If my old Friend Mr. *Forfter* had fqueaked, as was not without good Reafon fufpected, it's believed this Gentleman would have gone out of the World without his Head.

D E R W E N T-

DERWENTWATER's *Pedigree*.

THIS Family of *Radcliff* or *Radclive*, is of
good Antiquity, flourish'd at *Kefwick* in the
County of *Cumberland* for many Generations: It
cannot be made appear, that they were the fame
with the *Ratcliffe* or *Radchiffe* in *Lancafhire*, from
whom defcended the Family of the Earls of *Suffex*;
yet it is prefumed they are a Branch thereof; for we
find one Sir *Thomas Radcliff*, who lived in the time
of *Henry* V. by *Margaret* his Wife, Daughter to
Sir *Thomas Parr* of *Kendal*, had Iffue, Sir *Richard
Radcliff*, and a younger Son, *John*, who married
the Heir-General of the ancient Family of *Derwentwater* in *Cumberland*, where they had long flourifhed,
by whom he had Iffue *John Radcliff*, who had that
Poffeffion.

John, laft named, had Iffue Three Sons, *John
Radcliff* of *Derwentwater*, Sir *Edward*, and Sir
Richard Ratcliff, Knight of the Garter in the Reign
of *Hen.* VII.

John, the elder Son, is probably the fame who
was Sheriff of *Cumberland* feveral times, during the
Reign of *Hen.* VIII. (as many of his Anceftors had
been before) of whom at that Time there were feveral Defcents; but the Iffue Male failing, the Eftate
of *Derwentwater* came to the Defcendants of Sir
Edward Radcliff, Knight, younger Brother of *John*,
in the Perfon of Sir *Edward Radcliff*, Bart. Son of
Sir *Francis Radcliff* of *Cartington*, which Sir *Edward* fettled at *Derwentwater*, and was created Baronet, vi. *Jac.* I. *Anno* 1619. He married *Elizabeth*,
fole Daughter and Heir of *Thomas Barton*, Efq;
and had Iffue Sir *Francis Radcliff*, his Son and Heir,
and feveral Daughters.

Sir

Sir *Francis Radcliff*, Son and Heir of Sir *Edward*, was created Earl *Derwentwater*, Vifcount *Radcliff* and *Langley* in *Com. Cumberland*, and Baron *Radcliff* of *Tyndale*, by Patent dated the 7th of *March* 1687—8. 4 *Jac*. 2. and died *Anno* 1696—7. and was buried at *Dilston*. His Wife was *Catharine*, Daughter and Heir to Sir *William Fenwick* of *Meldon*, Com. *Northumberland* (by his fitft Wife *Margaret*, Daughter and Heir of Sir *Arthur Grey*, Kt. fixth Son of Sir *Ralph Grey*, of the Houfe of *Wenk*) and Relift of —— *Lawfon* of *Barough*, in *Com. Ebor*. by whom he had Iffue Five Sons, and Four Daughters ; *Francis* his Succeffor, *Edward* died unmarried, *Thomas*, a Lieutenant-Colonel to ——, *William* and *Arthur* ; *Anne*, married to Sir *Philip Conftable* of *Flamborough*, in *Com. Ebor*. Bart. *Catharine*, *Elizabeth*, and *Mary*.

Edward his Son and Succeffor, married in the Lifetime of his Father, *Mary Tudor*, Natural Daughter of King *Charles* the 2d, by Mrs. *Mary Davis*; he died whilft his Father lived, and left Iffue *James*, late Earl of *Derwentwater*, Executed on *Tower-Hill* for High-Treafon againft King *George* I. Feb. 24, 1715—6. His fecond Son died in *London* fome Years ago ; *Charles* the third Son, being taken in the Rebellion, was found Guilty, made his Efcape out of *Newgate*. Befides the Three Sons, he left a Daughter, *Mary Tudor Radcliff*, a very fine Lady, late returned from Abroad.

The late *James* Earl of *Derwentwater* married the Daughter of Sir *John Webb*, Bart. who has Iffue, a Son and a Daughter.

His Arms,

Argent, a Bend Ingrail'd Sable.

Lord

Lord WIDDRINGTON.

THIS Family has flourished with great Eminence for many Ages in *Northumberland*, and were ftiled Lords of *Widdrington*, fo early as the Reign of *Hen*. 1.

Sir *Gerrard* was Knight for the County, 10 *Ed*. 3. and *Roger* his Brother, from the 25 of *Ed*. 3. to the 35 of the fame Reign.

Sir *John de Widdrington*, Son of *Roger*, was Knight of the faid County, 5 and 8 of *Hen*. 4. and Sheriff of *Northumberland*, 11 of *Hen*. 4. and 4 *Hen*. 6.

Roger Son of Sir *John* had the fame Office, the 14, 21, and 28 of *Hen*. 6.

Sir *Ralph Widdrington*, Grandfon of *Roger*, was made a Banneret in *Scotland* by the Duke of *Gloucefter*, 22 of *Edw*. 4.

A Defcendant from whom was Sir *Henry Widdrington* of *Widdrington*, Knighted at the Creation of *Henry* Prince of *Wales*, 19 of *Hen*. 7. He had Iffue by his Wife *Margery*, Daughter of Sir *Henry Piercy*, Knt. Sir *John* and Four Daughters.

Sir *John* married to his firft Wife *Agnes*, Daughter to Sir *James Metcalfe*, Knt. and had Iffue Sir *Henry*, who died without Iffue, 7 *Eliz*.

Edward *Widdrington* fecond Son, who was of *Swinbourne*, and became Heir to his Brother; and a Daughter *Dorothy*, who was married to Sir *Roger Fenwick*, Knt. and fecondly to ———— *Conftable* Efq; The fecond Wife of Sir *John*, was *Anne*, Daughter of Sir *Edward Gower* of *Stetnam*, in the County of *York*, by whom he had Iffue, *Robert Widdrington* and feveral others.

Edward *Widdrington*, Brother and Heir to Sir *Henry Widdrington*, married *Urfula*, Daughter of Sir *Reginald Carnaby* Knt. and had Iffue Sir *Henry Widdring-*

Widdrington, *Ralph* fecond Son, and *Roger* third Son of *Cartington*, Father of *Edward Widdrington*, created a Baronet of *Scotland*, and after of *England*, 16 *Car*. 1. *Anno* 1642. The Daughters of *Edward Widdrington* of *Widdrington* were: three, *Agnes*, *Dorothy*, and *Catherine*.

Sir. *Henry Widdrington* Son and Heir, was Sheriff of *Northumberland* 21 of *Eliz.* and died 13 *Jac*. 1. *Anno* 1575, and by his Wife *Mary*, Daughter of Sir *Henry Curwen* Knt. he had Sir *William Widdrington* Knt. and three Daughters.

Which Sir *William Widdrington* was created a Baronet, *ib*. *Car*. 1. *Anno* 1643, and highly diftinguifhed himfelf by his fignal Services to his King in the time of the grand Rebellion, by raifing a confiderable Power for his Majefty's Service, and had his fhare in feveral Exploits: He continued in Arms, and active in his Majefty's Service till all was loft, and then fhared in the general Ruin with all the King's Friends. He afterwards attended King *Charles* II. beyond Sea, and in his Voyage to *Scotland*; and had a principal Command in the Army under the Earl of *Derby*, which was employed to open a Paffage for the King's March towards *Worcefter*; but being met and encounter'd near *Wigan* in *Lancafhire*, by a much more numerous Force under *Lilburne*, after a very valiant Refiftance was there killed, of whom the Lord *Clarendon* gives a fine Character. He had Iffue *William* his Succeffor, *Henry* and *Ephraim*, who both died young; *Edward*, Captain of Horfe, killed at the Battle of the *Boyne*. He had Iffue by his fecond Wife, Sir *Edward Horfley Widdrington*, and *Ralph*, who loft his Eyes in the *Dutch* Wars; *Anthony* who died unmarried, and *Roger* who was killed at the Siege of *Maeftricht*; alfo two Daughters.

To

To whom fucceeded *William* his Son and Heir, who took to Wife *Elizabeth*, Daughter and Heir to Sir *Perigrine Bertie* of *Eveden*, *Com. Lincoln.* a younger Son to *Robert* Earl of *Lindfey*, by whom he had Iffue, *William* his Son and Heir, *Henry*, *Roger*, and *Edward*, which laft died unmarried; alfo fix Daughters, *Mary* a Nun, *Elizabeth* a Nun, *Anne* married to Mr. *Clavering* of *Calalee*; *Jane* unmarried, *Dorothy* a Nun, *Catherine* married to Sir *Ed. Southcote.*

William his eldeft Son fucceeded him, and married *Alathea*, Daughter and Heir of Lord Vifcount *Fairfax*, of the Kindgom of *Ireland*, by whom he had Iffue *William*, *Charles* and *Peregrine*; alfo three Daughters, *Appolonia* who took a Religious Habit; *Elizabeth* married to *Marmaduke*, Son and Heir to *Marmaduke* Lord *Langdale*; and *Mary*, married to Mr. *Townly* of *Townly.*

William, who was in the *Tower* for High-Treafon, and now received the Benefit of the Act of Grace, married *Jane*, only Daughter and Heir to Sir *Thomas Tempeft* of *Stella*, Baronet, in the Bifhoprick of *Durham*, and hath Iffue *Henry*, Born 1702. *Alathea.*

Arms,

Quarterly Argent, Gules a Bend Sable.

Mr. Gafcoigne's LETTER *to a Friend, a little before his Execution.*

Dear SIR,

I Cannot leave the World without some Tokens of Gratitude for the many and undeserved Favours which I have received from you; therefore I send this by the Hands of the Reverend Father, with my Prayers to the Divine Being, That he will shower down such Blessings upon you, in his good time, as may return the many good Offices you have done me Seven-fold. What you have done for my Body under a crazy state, and the Wants that are generally attendant upon Prisoners divested of all Necessaries of Life, require more Acknowledgments than I am capable of paying; but the Care you have taken in providing for the Welfare of my poor and immortal Soul, by sending this holy Man to assist me with his Prayers and Advice, is beyond Expression. 'Tis to this Act of Compassion that I owe the Recovery of myself from a State of Perdition, than which, nothing could have been more ruinous and miserable: To this, that I am rescued out of the Jaws of Eternal Death, and can say with the blessed Apostle, O Death, where is thy Sting! O Grave, where is thy Victory! Nor can I leave the World without due Acts of Acknowledgment for so endearing, so invaluable a Favour.

Be pleased then, to accept this last Testimony of Gratitude which is not in Words to express, and to believe I am ready to pass through the Vale of Death with all Chearfulness, being well assured of Eternal Bliss and Salvation, through the Merits of Christ Jesus our common Saviour, and the Intercession of the Blessed Virgin, and of Saints and Angels, with him that sitteth upon the Throne, and will at the last Day judge the World in Righteousness.

I have

I have nothing more than to defire your and all good Catholicks Prayers, and to take care that the Paper inclofed in this, a Copy of which I intend, God willing, to give the Sheriff at the Place of Execution, may be made Publick as I have written it ; and afk leave to fubfcribe, Dear Sir,

Your Dying Friend,

and moft Humble Servant,

R. Gafcoigne.

A LETTER *to the* Author.

S I R,

I Have *feen the Character which you have given the brave Earl of* Strathmore ; *you have done him nothing but Juftice. I beg you will be fo kind as to give this Letter a Place in your next Edition, which may ftill add to preferve the Memory of that never to be forgotten Hero : He is defcended from one of the beft and ancienteft Families in* Scotland, *being Chief of the Name of* Lyon ; *he was a Youth of very promifing Qualifications, of unfhaken Courage, and ftedfaft Zeal to the* Pretender ; *being brought up in thofe Principles that infufed fuch into him, that made him adhere to the Companions of his Fate. He raifed a Regiment out of his own Dependants and Followers, who were fent over the* Forth *with* Mac-Intofh ; *but he and his Lieutenant Colonel* Walkinfhaw *of* Barrowfield, *were forced back in their defign of croffing the* Forth *into the Ifle of* May, *where he made the Greatnefs of his Soul vifible, by the refolute and obftinate Defence which he made on that Ifland againft his* Majefty's

Majefty's Ships, by intrenching himfelf and thofe with him, and made this memorable Speech to his Followers: Gentlemen, We are embarked in a Caufe which fhould be dear to every *Scotfman,* who ftudy to have themfelves freed from *Englifh* Bondage, into which the Enemies of our Country have betrayed us : I hope you will exert yourfelves upon this Occafion ; I fhall make my Sincerity vifible, by expofing my Perfon where the greateft Danger offers itfelf, thinking it my Glory to die in this Caufe. *All the Gentlemen and Common Men gave their Parole of Honour to ftand by him to the laft Drop of Blood; but they faved their Honour and Blood by finding a Way to get into Fife. If this noble Lord had been inftructed in the Principles of the Eftablifhed Government, he would have been the greateft Glory of his Age: But yet it muft be allowed, that Men are not to be buried in Oblivion, that have Generofity and Greatnefs of Mind to defend the Caufe which they efpoufe.*

I am Yours,

July 15, 1717.

W—m D—fs.

Q   The

The Lord LOVATT's *Account of the taking of* Inverness; *with other Advantages obtain'd over the Rebels in the North of* Scotland.

ON the 15th of *September*, the Laird of *Mackintosh* convened his Men at *Farr*, as was given out, to review them; but in the Evening he marched strait to *Inverness*, where he came by Sunrising with Colours displayed; and after he had made himself Master of what Arms and Ammunition he could find, and some little Money that belonged to the Publick, proceeded to proclaim the *Pretender* King, under the Name of *James* the VIIIth of *Scotland*, and IIId of *England*. At this time *Jean Gordon*, Lady *Culloden*, found it absolutely necessary, for the Safety of a great many of the King's Friends and their Goods, to shut up the House of *Culloden*; where she had taken in great Store of Provision. Her Husband, then Member of Parliament, tho' at *London*, had some very good Arms in his House, and ordered One Hundred Men to be taken in, knowing that the Rebels could not omit to Garison it, being a very strong House, and so near *Inverness*, that it hinder'd any to go or come from it on that side of the Water of *Ness*; which M' *Intosh* finding, sent a Message to the Lady to give up the House; but she refusing it, he went himself, and spoke to the Lady over a Window, but to no purpose. She understood that there was no Means but the Rebels would use to have that House, which might be so troublesome to *Inverness*, that now there was a Garison of Four Hundred Men settled, of the Name of *M'Kenzie* of *Coull*. Upon the 20th of *September*, M' *Intosh* march'd with six Hundred Men, the first of all the Clans, towards the Earl of *Mar*, who then had set

up

up the publick Standard of Rebellion. The want of Cannon was the only Thing that grieved the Lady *Culloden*; but being informed that there was a Merchant Ship lying in the Harbour of *Invernefs*, which had fix Guns on Board, and a Number of Ball for them ; fhe detached a Party of Fifty Men, under Silence of the Night by Boats, who had the fix Pieces of Cannon before it was Day mounted upon the Houfe to the great Surprize of the *Jacobites* in the Town, who look'd upon that Cannon as their Security.

While this loyal Lady was fortifying her Houfe, fhe had the good Luck of being affifted by the Arrival of Mr. *Duncan Forbes*, her Brother-in-law, who from that Time diftinguifhed himfelf both by his Wit and Refolution; that if Things were acted by the Rebels according to the Hardinefs expected from them, it might be improper to have fuch a Governor and Governefs in one Houfe, and fome other Places not fo well ferved.

The Earl of *Seaforth*, who was nominated Lieutenant-General, and Commander in chief of the Northern Counties to his Majefty K. *James* VIII. (for fo was the Defignation then) was not idle, gathered his Men from the *Lewes*, and all his Inland Country, to the Place of *Braban*, where Sir *Donald M'donald* of *Slate* with 600 Men, and the Laird of *M'kinnon* with 150, join'd him. *Alexander M'kenzie* of *Frazerdale*, who affumed a Command of the Name of *Frazer* by his Lady, had forced together 400 of that Name, which, with the 100 Men that *Chifolme* (who is Vaffal to that Family) had, made up 500 under *Frazerdale*'s Command, which lay at and about *Caftledouny*, five Miles from *Braban*, and fix from *Invernefs* : But the *Frazers* of *Struy*, *Foyer*, *Culduthell*, &c. kept the reft of that Name on Foot for the Government, having Affurance that the Lord

Q 2   *Lovat*,

Lovat, their natural Chief, was at *London*, firm for the Proteftant Succeffion, and daily expected. This procured them not only the Ridicule, but the Objects of the Rebels Threats. *Frazerdale* finding his Party few to what he expected, refolv'd (if it was poffible) to bring thofe Gentlemen into their Party; and fo wrote to *Struy* and *Foyer*, that he wanted much to meet with them, in order to fatisfy them with the Juftice and Reafonablenefs of what they were to rife for; and that he hoped either he fhould fatisfy them, or that they would him.

The Gentlemen upon his Letter refolv'd to truft him, and fhew him freely that they would continue firm to the Proteftant Succeffion as by Law eftablifh'd: And having come with 150 Men near his Houfe of *Caftledouny*, they were told he was at *Braban* with my Lord *Seaforth*, from whom they immediately receiv'd a Meffage by one *Donald M'urchifon*, Factor to the Lord *Seaforth*; that he underftood they had got in Arms, and that, anfwerable to his Power as Lieutenant-General and Commander in chief of thofe Counties, he demanded them to join him, and have themfelves lifted to ferve his Majefty K. *James* VIII. To which they return'd Anfwer, That they were Proteftants of the Low-Church, and that they would let his Lordfhip know fo much whenever he pleafed. But in the mean time that his Meffage was deliver'd them, he detach'd 600 Men, commanded by *M'kenzie* of *Frazerdale*, *Aplecrofs*, and *Fairburn*, with an Order to take them dead or alive; but by good Luck it was one of the moft boifterous Nights that could be; and when they came to the Place, they found that they had been apprized of their Coming, and had got themfelves in a Pofture of Defence; which obliged them to return, half ftarv'd with Cold and Hunger.

Here

Here was feen the Honour and Conduct of the one who was a Proteftant Commander, whofe Letter brought thofe Gentlemen there, and the other a Popifh General, who would not give his own Honour the fair Play of ftaying for the Return of his Meffage, but fent his Party to cut off thofe Gentlemen, who look'd upon themfelves fafe during their Treating. The Earl of *Sutherland*, who was fent down from Court to command in the North of *Scotland*, had got of the *Mackays*, *Roffes*, *Monroes*, and his own Men, 1800 together at a Place in *Rofs* called *Alnes*, and thought proper to divert *Seaforth* from joining *Mar*; that the King's other Friends in the North, who were in Readinefs to join him, if they could come together, they would have been able to give the Earl of *Seaforth*, or *Huntley*, or both, Battel: But *Seaforth* finding himfelf 4000 ftrong, and *Sutherland* but 1800, thought it was fit to take the Advantage, and fo march'd directly towards *Alnes*, where *Sutherland* lay; who found, that by retiring to *Sutherland*, *Seaforth* would be for fome Time diverted, and he would fave his Men from fighting fo unequally. *Seaforth* coming to *Alnes*, which is the *Monroes* Country, allowed his Men to commit all the Barbarity that could be expected from *Turks*, deftroy'd all the Corn and Cattle in the Country, took of every thing that was ufeful within as well as without Doors; lodg'd their Men in the Churches, where they kill'd Cattle, and did every thing difrefpectful to Places of Worfhip; and treated the Minifters, of all the People, the worft; took fome Gentlemen Prifoners; and now believed, that fince *Sutherland* retired, all the Caufe was gain'd there.

Next Care was to come to *Invernefs*, and fettle a ftronger Garifon in it; reduce the pitiful Whighoufe Garifons, as they called *Culloden* and *Killra-*

vock

vock Houses, and force all the silly People who stood out along with them.

Being come to *Inverness*, General *Seaforth* called a Council of War, where were present the Lord *Duffus*, Sir *Donald M'Donald*, *Frazerdale*, *M'Kinnon*, the *Chisolmes*, and several other Officers, besides Sir *John M' Kenzie* of *Coul* the Governor, where it was resolved that *Culloden* House must be reduced at any Rate ; and so commanded Mr. *George M' Kenzie* of *Grumziord* to go with a Trumpet along with him, and summon the House formally to surrender. Coming to the Place, *Grumziord* ordered the Trumpet to Sound, and called to Mr. *Duncan* who kept the House : Mr. *Forbes* not only told him, but shewed him, that the House was not in their Reverence, and so Defiance was returned for Answer. But in a second Council of War, the Lord *Duffus* was sent in order to reduce Mr. *Forbes* by Reason, or otherwise to assure him of the hardest Treatment if the House was taken. But my Lord returned without Success ; and so a Disposition was made for the Siege, and the Party for the Attack order'd ; but finding that the House was strong, and the Governor and Garison obstinate and brave, after twelve Days Deliberation, marched forward toward their Grand Camp at *Perth*. From *Inverness* they marched to *Strath-Spey*, the Laird of *Grant*'s Country, where they found the *Grants* all in Arms, in order to secure their Country from harm; they only asked some Baggage Horses to the next Country, and Quarter'd their Men civilly, and returned the Horses home next Day ; and so they joined the Earl of *Mar* at *Perth*, where they continued till the decisive Stroke of *Dumblain*, from whence they returned in a Hundred Parties, to the Satisfaction of many who were very careful of disarming them in their Retreat. But the four Hundred
dred

dred *Frazers* that Mr. *M' Kenzie* had brought there
four Days before to *Dumblain*, hearing that the
Lord *Lovat* was come home, deserted that Cause,
and came home full armed with their Affection to
their Natural Chief, and their Love to the Protestant Interest; for which that Name distinguished
themselves since the Reformation, was plainly seen
in their Services thereafter, till the Rebellion was
extinguished. On the 5th of *November*, the Lord
Lovat, with Mr. *Forbes* of *Culloden*, arrived at *Culloden's* House, from whence my Lord wrote to the
Gentlemen of his Name that stood for the Government, to come and receive him: *Rofs* of *Killravock*,
and *Forbes* of *Culloden*, conducted him with three
Hundred Men by *Invernefs*, near the Bounds of his
own Country; he was informed, that *M' Donald*
of *Keppoch* was marching with three Hundred Men
to reinforce Sir *John M' Kenzie* of *Coull* at *Invernefs.*
My Lord had concerted with Captain *George Grant*,
who then commanded that Name in Absence of his
Brother *Rofs* of *Killravock*, and *Forbes* of *Culloden*,
that he should go through all his Countries and get
all his Men together, and that then they would in-
vest *Invernefs.* But finding now that *Kepoch* was on
his March, resolved to intercept *Kepoch* in his Road,
and so resolved to cross the River *Nefs*; but just as
he was ready to cross, he gets an Account, that
what were not marched to *Perth* of the *M' Intoshes*,
were in Arms ready to go into *Invernefs* and
strengthen that Garison. Upon which, having con-
sulted the Gentlemen that were with him, resolved
to disperse those *M' Intoshes*, and so came directly
on his Way to the Place where he heard they lay;
and on his Way found two or three of their chief
Gentlemen, which bound themselves for the peaceable Behaviour of such as were at home, and that
they would give up their Arms, and give in any

thing

thing they could afford in *Invernefs*, when they were Mafters of it. His Lordfhip having on the 7th of *November* croffed the Water, refolved to throw himfelf in directly betwixt *Kepoch* and Sir *John*, who hearing of his coming, refolved to fally out, and that *Kepoch* on one fide, and he on the other, would attack him. But *Kepoch* finding himfelf not fafe to go forward, returned home by the Country of *Urquharts*, belonging to the Laird of *Grant*, where he did feveral Barbarities, and carried off three or four Gentlemen Prifoners, in hopes they would relieve themfelves by a Booty, which they not yielding to, he difmiffed in two or three Days. Upon News of *Kepoch*'s fudden retiring, my Lord *Lovat* marches ftrait to the Town of *Invernefs*, and in his way found fome Cows that belonged to the Garifon, kept by a Guard, which he took, and chafed in one other Party to the Town. Having fettled his Men within a Mile of the Town, ordered a Party to the fide of the *Firth*, to ftop any Boats coming with any Succours of Men or Provifions to the Garifon ; and now he began to think that it was not reafonable to be idle a Minute, and fo acquaints *Rofs* of *Killravock*, and *Forbes* of *Culloden*, who had the Town Blockaded on the Eaft-fide of *Nefs*, that it was proper to attempt the Town, fince the *Grants* were eight Hundered on their March. Mr. *Duncan Forbes*, a Man that was moft active in thefe Affairs, hardly giving himfelf Reft, was order'd to go and concert fome things with my Lord *Lovat*, and *Arthur Rofs*, Brother to the Laird of *Killravock* ; a young Gentleman that had been Captive in *Turkey* for many Years before, and but juft come home, was order'd to cover Mr. *Forbes*'s paffing the River with a Party : He finding the Rebels Guard relieving their Centinels by the River-fide, purfued them fo clofe to the heart of the Town, that entering

tering

tering the *Talbooth* Door, where the Governor had lodged himfelf with his Main Guard, he was by the Centinel within fhot through the Body, and thereafter he difcharged two Piftols he had under his Safh, among the Guard, and had they not crufhed his Sword-Hand in forcing the Door clofe, he might have lived fome longer time than he did, which was but about ten Hours.

At the Alarm of this Shooting, the whole Garifon got to Arms, firing fo from all Quarters, that the fix or feven Men that came up with Mr. *Rofs,* had very good luck to efcape. The Death of this gallant Gentleman fo vex'd my Lord his Brother, and all his other Friends, that they fwore Revenge of his Blood, and accordingly fummoned the Town to fend out their Garifon and Governor, or if they did not, they would burn the Town, and put them all to the Sword. The Governor expecting no great Favour from Eaft or Weft-fide, was in a Surprize. My Lord ordered all the Men to be ready, which the Governor finding, on *Saturday* the tenth of *November* got together all the Boats he could find, and with high Water made off with all imaginable Confufion, to the Joy and Grief of the fundry Parties within. *Rofs* of *Kilravock,* and *Colloden's* Men lay at and about *Colloden,* the eight Hundred *Grants* to the Weftward of them two Miles ; and the Lord *Lovat* who had got of his Name five Hundred together on the North and Weft-fide of the Town, marched all in, having prepared Bullets for their Men. They now found it convenient to let the Earl of *Sutherland* know they had the Town : And his Lordfhip receiving my Lord *Lovat's* Letter, returned him a very kind Letter, wherein he was glad his Lordfhip, by his Conduct and Diligence, was fufficiently entitled to the King's Favour, and that none would more truly reprefent it than he.

At

At this time the Earl had got together his Men, and the others that were with him in *Rofs*, and was to march forward to join that confiderable Body that were then together at *Inverness*: His Lordfhip being thirty fix Miles from *Inverness*, marched his Men, being a confiderable Number, to the Weftern Divifion of *Rofs*, where they encamped; and his Lordfhip, with the Lord *Rae*, *Monro* of *Fouls*, and feveral other Gentlemen, came into *Invernefs* on *Tuefday* the 13th of *November*; which Day we had the joyful News of his Grace the Duke of *Argyle's* Victory at *Dumblain*, which was obferved with great Solemnity of Joy; and two Days thereafter, having left Colonel *Robert Monro* of *Fouls*, Governor of *Invernefs* there, with a fuitable Party, the Earl of *Sutherland* with his Men, and the Lord *Lovat* with a part of his Men, went to the Place of *Braban*, and obliged all the refponfible Men of the *M'Kenzie's* that were not with my Lord *Seaforth* at *Perth*, to fecure their peaceable Behaviour, and return the Arms taken from the *Monro's* by my Lord *Seaforth* before, and releafe the Prifoners, and that they would not affift my Lord *Seaforth* directly or indirectly; and that they would anfwer to his Lordfhip of *Sutherland* any Sum of Money he required for the ufe of the Government, upon a due Advertifement; and that the Lord of *Seaforth's* Houfe of *Braban* would be made a Garifon for his Majefty King *George*.

Things being put in this order in that Country, the *Monroe's* being left at *Invernefs*, the Earl of *Sutherland* marched with his Men; the *Frazer's*, the *M'Kay's*, the *Rofs's*, *Killravock's* Men, *Culloden's*, and Sir *Archibald Campbell* Tutor of *Calder*, with a Party of two Hundred to *Murray*, to bring that Country's Difaffection to good Order, and divert my Lord *Huntley* from croffing the River *Spey*,

who

who made the Rocks in that Country refound his Refolutions, having got, as he gave out, new Or- ders, and a Detachment fent with General *Eclin* to him from *Perth:* But they were not long in that Country, when things were put in that Condition, that the Earl of *Sutherland* came back to *Invernefs*, and left the Lord *Lovat*, *Killravock*, Sir *Archibald Campbell*, &c. behind, to act as he directed them, and as Matters required. The *Murray Jacks* being put in pretty good Order, the King's Authority own'd over all the Country, it was thought proper to fend *Hugh Frazier* of *Foyer* to *Stirling*, to let the Duke of *Argyle* know how Matters ftood, and re- ceive his Grace's Command. The whole Country betwixt *Fort-William* and *Aberdeen* being in the Re- bels Hands, except *Murray* and *Strath Spey*, he was obliged to go all over the Country under the Silience of Night, in the deepeft Storm that was feen of a long time : Having given Sir *Robert Pollock*, Governor of *Fort-William*, the News of their Country, he went forward for *Dunftafnage*, and from thence to *Inverary*, where he gave the Earl of *Boot*, who then commanded there, Sir *Dun- can Campbell* of *Lochnell*, and Colonel *Alexander Campbell* of *Faunab*, account of their Country; and went forward to *Glafgow*, where he found the whole Town rejoicing at the good Account of Affairs from the North; and having got the Magiftrates Pafs, went forward for *Stirling*, where he arrived the 17th of *December*, and was introduced to his Grace the Duke of *Argyle* by Brigadier General *Grant*, Lieutenant of the County of *Invernefs*. His Grace was mighty well pleafed that Matters went fo well there, and took particular Pleafure and Care to examine every leading Man's Zeal and Conduct; in which Examination he took up near two Hours, and the next Day made his Orders

ready,

ready, and order'd him aboard a Ship belonging to the Town of *Forres*, that lay ready at *Borou-ftounnes* to fail ; but being informed that there was a great many Barks cruifing on the Coaft of *Fife* and *Angus*, belonging to the Rebels, and had taken fome People and Arms that were bound North, ordered him to fteer his Courfe home through the. Mountains, as he came there, which he did ; tho' he was fo clofe purfued by the Rebels, that he was forced to take fhelter in the Garifon of *Fort-William* for feveral Days. The Governor and Lieutenant-Governor, Men very active, and of fpecial Intelligence, having got particular Notice, that all the Fords and Paffes were fo guarded for him that he could not efcape, kept him with all imaginary Care and Civility, till by a Country Man he was conducted privately through the Hills, and arrived fafe at *Invernefs*. At this time Mr. *Alexander Gordon* of *Ardoch*, and Lieutenant *Donald M' Neil*, were fent down to the Earl of *Sutherland* with Arms and fome Money, which was very much wanting: And had not Mr. *Forbes* of *Culloden*, who had an Intereft in the Town of *Invernefs*, taken up a confiderable Sum, the Men had been very much in want.

During this time the Earl of *Seaforth* was not idle, having got his Men that fcatter'd at *Dumblain* together near *Brahan*. My Lord *Huntley*, on the other hand, made the World believe he was with all Fury to attack the Earl of *Sutherland* and thofe with him : *Seaforth* and his Friends thought that with boafting *Sutherland* would retire a fecond time, but found it otherwife. The Earl of *Sutherland* hearing that the Highlanders that run home from *Dumblain* were to be at a Head, and join *Seaforth*, marched with his own Men, my Lord *Rae's* Men, the *Monroes*, and the *Roffes*, of each but Parties,

made

made up 800 ; 200 of the *Grants, Culloden,* and the *Frazers,* making up the reft of 800, lay at *Bewley* near *Lovat,* within four Miles of *Seaforth's* Camp, whofe Boafting furpaffed Rehearfal. The Earl, my Lord *Lovat,* and the other Gentlemen, being moved by their Menaces, refolve to give them Battle. *Fouls,* who in all thefe Tranfactions was forward and diligent, with a People of good Principle and Refolution, wanted nothing more than one good Stroke to avenge their bad Ufage before by them ; to be fure *Culloden's* Men wanted not good Will ; and if the *Frazer's* had not Reafon by their former Attempt upon them, any Man may judge. The People being all found well refolv'd and chearful, were put in order for the Diverfion ; which when my Lord *Seaforth* faw, he thought convenient to Capitulate, own the King's Authority, difperfe his Men, and propofe the Mediation of thefe Government Friends for his Pardon.

Upon his Submiffion, and after the King was gracioufly pleafed to fend down Orders, That upon giving up his Arms, and coming into *Invernefs,* he might expect his Pardon : Yet upon the *Pretender's* Arrival at *Perth,* and my Lord *Huntley's* Suggeftions to him, that now was the Time for them to appear for their King and Country, and that what Honour they loft at *Dumblain* might yet be regain'd : But while he this infinuated to my Lord *Seaforth,* he privately found that my Lord *Seaforth* had, by being an early Suiter for the King's Pardon, by promifing to lay down his Arms, and owning the King's Authority, claimed in a great Meafure to an Affurance of his Life and Fortune, which he thought proper for himfelf to purchafe at the Rate of difappointing *Seaforth,* with Hopes of ftanding by the Good Old Caufe, till *Seaforth,* with that vain Hopes, loft the King's Favour that was

promifed

promifed him : Which *Huntley* embraced, by taking
the very firft Opportunity of deferting the *Pretender's* Caufe, and furrendering himfelf upon Terms
made with him of Safety to his Life and Fortune.
This founded fo fweet·with him, that he flept fo
fecure, as never to dream of any Prefervation for a
great many good Gentlemen that made choice to
ftand by him, and ferve under him ; tho' many
other Worthy Nobles would Die or Banifh, rather
than not fhew their Perfonal Bravery, and all other
Friendly Offices to their Adherents.

Tho' the King's Order was fent down for taking
the *Mac Kenzie's* Arms and *Seaforth's,* having the
Liberty of the Town of *Invernefs,* the Hopes of
the Pretender's Caufe taking Life again, made him
defer coming in from Day to Day, till it was
found out again that he defigned to rife yet a-new :
While in thefe middle of the Hopes, the main Chance
was blafted, the Duke of *Argyle* marched from *Stirling* towards *Perth* ; the Pretender not only abandon'd *Perth,* but the whole Caufe, left fome of his
Worthieft Friends untaken leave of, and the reft all
at the Mercy of the Enemy ; but they had to deal
with Chriftians, true Proteftants, and faithful Subjects to the beft of Proteftant Kings. After the
Pretender left the Country by Sea, his Grace the
Duke of *Argyle,* at the Head of Ten Thoufand
gallant Troops, came to *Aberdeen,* and from thence
ordered Brigadier General *Grant,* with a Detachment to *Invernefs,* and fent Detachments to the feveral proper Places in thofe Countries ; and then
fent Major-General *Wightman* to *Invernefs,* who went
carefully through the Countries of *Weft* and *Eaft
Rofs,* and upon Information took in the Earl of
Cromarty, and fome other *Mac Kenzies* Prifoners,
and ordered, that upon giving in their Arms, fuch
as were not Attainted might live peaceably and improve the Country.

His

His Grace having now put an End to the Gene-ral Rebellion, went up to Court, leaving Lieutenant-General *Cadogan* to Command, who with Four Thoufand Horfe and Foot marched by *Perth* to *Blair* of *Athol*, and from thence to *Ruthven* in *Badenoch*, where one *Mac Donald* of *Gallovie*, and fome *Mac Pherfons*, Vaffals to my Lord *Huntly*, contemning the Order given for furnifhing the Neceffaries for the Army, and giving up their Arms, had their Lands burnt, and all their Cattle taken in. From *Ruthven* of *Badenoch*, he marched the Troops to *Borlum* near *Invernefs*, the Seat of Brigadier *Mackintofh*, appointed a Party to *Seaforth's* Country to take in all their Arms, and order'd the Garifons in all their confiderable Houfes to be continued as General *Wightman* placed them, and commanded Mr. *George Monro* of *Culcairn*, and Lieutenant *Donald Mac Neil*, with a Party through all the *Highlands* and Ifles, to bring in all the Arms, and apprehend any Attainted Rebel they could find, which they did accordingly. From *Borlum* he went to *Fort-William*, and viewed that Place ; ordered the Garifon of *Glengary* Caftle, and appointed Brigadier *Pettit*, and fome others with him, to furvey fome Ground at the Head of *Lochnefs* for a Fort, which was done ; and all Things being in good Quiet, his Excellency went to Court, leaving the Command upon Lieutenant-General *Sabine*.

So much from one who was Eye-witnefs to what is here faid.

F I N I S.

CPSIA information can be obtained at www.ICGtesting.com
Printed in the USA
BVOW011205100412

287319BV00009B/92/P